American Sculpture of the Sixties

Los Angeles County Museum of Art

April 28–June 25, 1967

Philadelphia Museum of Art

September 15–October 29

Exhibition selected and Book-Catalog

edited by Maurice Tuchman

Sponsored by the Contemporary Art Council

4

Lenders to the Exhibition

The Abrams Family Collection, New York

Arlo Acton, San Francisco

Dr. and Mrs. Nathan Alpers, Los Angeles

Irving Beck, New York

Mr. and Mrs. Donald Factor, Beverly Hills

Mrs. Digby Gallas, Los Angeles

Victor Ganz, New York

W. R. Geis, III, Stinson Beach, California

Mrs. Sally Hellyer, San Francisco

Mr. and Mrs. Melvin Hirsh, Beverly Hills

Conrad Janis, New York

Edwin Janss, Jr., Los Angeles

Charles S. Jules, New York

The Kleiner Foundation, Beverly Hills

Mr. and Mrs. Harold Ladas, New York

Mr. and Mrs. John McCracken, Los Angeles

Mr. and Mrs. Robert B. Mayer, Winnetka, Illinois

Harold Persico Paris, Oakland

Alan Power, London

George Rickey, New York

Mr. and Mrs. Robert A. Rowan, Pasadena

Mr. and Mrs. Eugene M. Schwartz, New York

Estate of David Smith

Michael Todd, New York

Mr. and Mrs. Max Wasserman, Chestnut Hill, Massachusetts

William T. Wiley, Mill Valley, California

California State College at Long Beach

The Art Museum, University of New Mexico, Albuquerque

Pasadena Art Museum

San Francisco Museum of Art

Walker Art Center, Minneapolis

Bianchini Gallery, New York

Grace Borgenicht Gallery, New York

Leo Castelli Gallery, New York

Cordier & Ekstrom, Inc., New York

Dilexi Gallery, San Francisco

Dwan Gallery, Los Angeles and New York

Egan Gallery, New York

Robert Elkon Gallery, New York

Andre Emmerich Gallery, New York

Ferus-Pace Gallery, Los Angeles

Fischbach Gallery, New York

Allan Frumkin Gallery, New York

Martha Jackson Gallery, New York

Sidney Janis Gallery, New York

Felix Landau Gallery, Los Angeles

Landau-Alan Gallery, New York

Royal Marks Gallery, New York

Marlborough-Gerson Gallery, New York

Rolf Nelson Gallery, Los Angeles

Pace Gallery, New York

Herbert Palmer Gallery, Los Angeles

Park Place Gallery, New York

Betty Parsons Gallery, New York

Perls Galleries, New York

Poindexter Gallery, New York

Stephen Radich Gallery, New York

Esther-Robles Gallery, Los Angeles

Allan Stone Gallery, New York

David Stuart Galleries, Los Angeles

Nicholas Wilder Gallery, Los Angeles

Howard Wise Gallery, New York

Acknowledgments

Many devoted individuals contributed to the organization of the exhibition and the preparation of the book-catalog. Mrs. Betty Asher, Assistant to the Curator of Modern Art, was deeply involved in many diverse aspects of the preparation of the project. Virginia Ernst, Curatorial Aid, researched the biographies and bibliographies. Lucy R. Lippard acted as adviser in the development of this material. (I want to note here my gratitude to Katherine C. Kline of the Jewish Museum for allowing us to consult her unpublished bibliography of contemporary sculpture.) Mrs. Jane Livingston prepared the selection of artists' statements, and also assisted in the formulation of the bibliography. Ed Cornachio, Head, Photography Department, John Gebhart and Robert Kays, Photographers, took 54 of the photographs in this book-catalog and deserve special thanks for their efforts.

I also want to thank the ten distinguished critics who have contributed essays to this publication: Lawrence Alloway, Wayne V. Andersen, Dore Ashton, John Coplans, Clement Greenberg, Max Kozloff, Lucy R. Lippard, James Monte, Barbara Rose and Irving Sandler.

Philip Leider helped edit some of the essays in this publication and he, along with William C. Seitz graciously offered useful advice. Bruce Glaser, Lucy R. Lippard and James Monte assisted me generously in setting up studio visits over the past two years.

For special assistance my gratitude is extended to Charles Cowles; George Rickey; Paul Bianchini and Dorothy Herzka, Bianchini Gallery; Borgenicht Gallery; James Newman, Dilexi Gallery; Virginia Dwan and John Weber, Dwan Gallery; Mrs. Marilyn Fischbach and Donald Droll, Fischbach Gallery; Allan Frumkin Gallery; Felix Landau Gallery; Charles Alan, Landau-Alan Gallery; Royal Marks Gallery; Arnold Glimcher and Fred Mueller, Pace Gallery; Betty Parsons Gallery; Poindexter Gallery; Nicholas Wilder Gallery; Herbert Palmer Gallery; Esther and Robert Robles, Esther-Robles Gallery.

I am also grateful to the Contemporary Art Council for their encouragement and support of my research on this project.

Finally I want to thank Henry T. Hopkins, Curator of Exhibitions and Publications, for his advice and for his assistance in the installation of the exhibition.

M. T.

Contents: American Sculpture of the Sixties

9

Introduction

American Sculpture of the Sixties is an anthology of the most ambitious and interesting sculpture that has developed in the present decade. Since the exhibition is basically a survey, no theme is specifically declared, although implicit in its conception is the belief that our decade has witnessed the quite unanticipated emergence of a genuinely independent American sculpture. Common to virtually all the sculptors here is a fresh grappling with formal and thematic ideas and a receptivity to the possibilities opened by new materials and processes.

Although eighty artists are shown, many well-known sculptors of the Sixties have been omitted; I did so to throw the sharpest possible emphasis on that fertile body of work which has been concerned with new forms. Many of the artists omitted from this survey have made important contributions to sculpture earlier in their development, as the catalog essays by Wayne Andersen and Irving Sandler point out. Nevertheless, only those artists of the older (i.e., David Smith) generation who have either maintained their level of achievement (sometimes, as in the case of Cornell, without having to evolve new styles) or who have posited a new manner are represented. Most of the artists in the exhibition are younger, and are represented by proportionately fewer works than, for example, Smith or Cornell (an exception is Oldenburg, whose fecundity called for additional objects). English sculptor Anthony Caro is included in this exhibition of American work because of the high quality of the work he made in this country and the influence he exerted on new American sculpture.

The conventional manner in which an exhibition of this nature is presented is to exhibit one work by each artist. *American Sculpture of the Sixties*, however, is designed to present each artist in a manner that will most clearly demonstrate his particular sculptural concerns. For some, this could best be accomplished by commissioning works specifically for this exhibition (Andre, McCracken). For others, for whom large scale constituted a central concern (Von Schlegell, di Suvero, Snelson), the Museum's resources were employed to accommodate the largest works. For still others, proper presentation required the installation of an entire suite of works, and this, too, was unhesitatingly done. No piece in this exhibition is presented as a mere "example": the entire presentation is designed to stress the individual quality of each work in the show.

Ordinary sculptural expectations are violated with such regularity in this exhibition that there is some point in noting the anti-traditional characteristics of most of these 166 works. Almost none of the sculpture is modelled; instead, much of it appears to have been struck off in one blow, sometimes fabricated by industrial means for the artist from a drawing. Elements of nuance and light and shade modulation seem irrelevant here beside the concern for a grand and authoritative presence (Morris, Judd, Bladen). An air of gravity and stillness is engendered by the use of repeated modular units, so often encountered in the exhibition (Smithson, Andre, Gerowitz, Truitt). Bright colors are commonly encountered—more frequently than in any large body of sculpture for five centuries, and it is employed far more diversely now than it was in medieval work. Color can appear arbitrary or changeable (this needn't be detrimental) or necessary and exactly right (as with Price). It can subsume or transcend the forms (McCracken), contradict or disguise them (Hudson), or articulate them (Caro). Color can be neutral, not perceived as a hue, yet, because of its singular identification with a material or surface, be important and affecting: witness Tony Smith's *Die*, which, although it is grey, is reproduced in color in this publication because of the tension that occurs when this great grey shape encounters nature.

Besides the characteristics of new sculpture described in the following essays one other feature should be noted: the compelling surface quality of this work. It is sometimes sensuous (McCracken), sometimes deadpan (Morris, Judd), sometimes scabrous (Nauman), but almost never expectable, casual, easy to ignore. The surface of most sculpture of the Sixties exemplifies the message of the forms. It is rarely *put on* the forms, or so it seems, but is singularly wedded to the sculpture. Robert Smithson's description of Judd's work holds for many artists of different persuasions: "An uncanny materiality inherent in the surface engulfs the basic structure. Both surface and structure exist simultaneously in a suspended condition. What is outside vanishes to meet the inside, while what is inside vanishes to meet the outside."

Sculpture here comes at you from all directions—from the ceiling (Rickey, Grosvenor), the wall (Judd, Smithson, Snelson), or it may snake around a corner (Todd). When it rests on the ground it doesn't really rest (contrast Henry Moore's many reclining figures) but still comes at you; it never reposes on a pedestal—indeed much new sculpture explicitly denies the role of a base or plinth (Morris, Hamrol) and it can achieve this, startlingly, by even looking like a plinth (Andre). (Price, like Brancusi, weds the stand and pedestal to the work by precise finishing and place adjustments: the stand is not a resting place but a part of the work.) New sculpture may threaten to fall (Bladen). Certain sculptures can be turned upside down (McCracken, Bell) with no loss of effectiveness. By violating the tradition of having an object sit on a base, all these works unsettle our common perceptions of things in relation to the ground and consequently of all things outside of us in relation to us.

In line with this attempt to question the nature of spatial relationships in our environment, certain contemporary sculptors (all except for Kiesler were cued by the extraordinary dimensions of New York School painting) have moved into space deliberately to imply a transformation of a room (Weinrib, Sugarman, Doyle), sometimes by using light to break down structural spaces (Flavin). Other artists have made self-sufficient environments, which enclose the viewer, pressing a certain system upon him (Kienholz, Paris, Oldenburg's *Bedroom*). Sometimes these environments need the presence of the viewer to fully exist (Samaras' all mirror *Room*). There is sculpture here which cannot be transported, since it is made for a particular location and only has full meaning within it (Andre, McCracken).

Scale is of foremost concern to sculptors now—and the extraordinary sensitivity to it reveals how limited older sculpture was in this regard. Even Constructivist sculptures, probably (with Brancusi) the most salient point of origin for the new sculpture, now look unhappily like maquettes rather than full-fledged constructions. Scale in the past was too often arbitrary, or obviously influenced by restricting conditions of process. Much older sculpture now seems rather primitive in its simplistic connection between the largeness and importance of subject. Oldenburg's giantism refers to this. One cannot imagine Price's objects, the smallest in the exhibition, greatly magnified; or the enormous sculptures of Kienholz, di Suvero, Grosvenor or Bladen reduced to table size. (The models for large work by an artist like Snelson are merely winning and attractive while the large works are compelling and intellectually provocative.) Yet versions of a single image by Rodin and later sculptors exist in a variety of sizes. It should be pointed out that certain contemporary sculptors make their work for modular amplification in many different sizes (DeLap and McCracken are perhaps the best examples) but their calculations have to do with the meaning of the work itself (the work is in part *about* scale), and there is built-in control over the different degrees of enlargement.

We were all taught in school that sculpture is something you have to walk around—but when we went to museums we found that objects were usually up against the wall—and that it didn't really seem to make much difference anyway. Sculpture was supposed to be in-the-round, but only recently has a great deal of it become so. Again, Brancusi pointed the way, and today artists press the point home, constantly denying the viewer the boring security of a frontal viewpoint. More recently the influence of artists like Judd, Morris and Bladen has been to fill sculpture out—to put volume in

sculpture, where it always was supposed to be. You *have* to walk around a Morris, at least once, and thereafter no one view of it is satisfying enough; you have to walk in, through and around the ample volumes of the Bladen and the Gerowitz in this exhibition. You have to walk into a Kienholz—or you may be deliberately stopped from entering, as in *The State Hospital*. An artist like LeWitt or Bell will make all sides and views of his work exactly the same—again stressing centrality not frontality. If a sculpture today is to be frontal then it projects frontality with a direct and hardly precedented affirmativeness— as for example, in the flat painted steel shapes of Ellsworth Kelly.

Much of the best sculpture today is completely non-objective, not "semi-abstract," not anthropomorphic or reminiscent of viscera. Sculptors have become dissatisfied with the manner in which non-representational constructions uncomfortably call to mind human gestures. At the same time the recent period has witnessed a more direct confrontation with the possibilities of representation than has been the case since, perhaps, the early Giacometti. Largely absent in the present decade is the equivocation characteristic of some of the abstract expressionist sculptors, an equivocation resultant from the desire to be abstract and still maintain figurative evocation.

Many artists of this decade are explicitly concerned with the presentation of Man, and say so clearly. Toward this end, artists like Nakian and Trova utilize traditional methods and materials, and employ symbols—myths old and new—as well. Marisol sheds traditional symbolism for emblems of chic that approximate the portrayed sensibilities. Rodin was censured for allegedly casting from life: today this process is central to the work of Kienholz and Segal; realism formerly spurned becomes macabre or haunting. Real props fill out the works. Conner makes savagely mutilated life-size free-standing figure assemblages, primarily from cloths and fabrics; so does Paul Harris in his sewn and stuffed personages, although his effigies are as poignant as they are terrifying. There is as little precedent for these cloth sculptures as there is for the soft vinyl-encased toilets of Oldenburg. In all of these artists' work the "representational" element—the potency of the image—is so charged as to blind our cognizance of the forms. Originality of content seemingly overpowers "style." In a period marked by the contributions of abstraction, objects and the figure have been re-introduced into sculpture with directness and conviction.

Though "content," where it exists, must be original, all of the hieratic values which had been traditionally ascribed to subject matter have been discarded. Oldenburg's sculpture is usually soft; that fact in itself challenges an ancient attribute of sculpture, that a three-dimensional construction, being real, must be redolent of eternity, of timelessness and stasis. Nauman and certain other San Francisco artists also present sculpture which incorporates change and is patently vulnerable ("I'm trying to make a less important thing to look at") as in a different way do artists like Morris ("The object itself has not become less important. It has merely become less *self*-important . . ").

The essays written for this book-catalog describe most of the interesting problems which are raised in the diversity of contemporary sculpture: serial repetition of simple forms, ideas of single-gestalt imagery, the effect upon sculpture of new materials and processes, the role of color and connections between painting and sculpture. Varying evaluations are made about the merit of new work. The evolution of the contemporary period is outlined, and seminal forces are marked. The reader will note certain disparities here—for example, the opposing views about the influence of David Smith upon the younger generation. The reader should also observe that most of the essays, having been written by New York writers, reflect, naturally enough, the predominance of knowledge in New York *about* New York. Certain polarities which are proffered, for example, about American art, insufficiently take into account important work made outside of New York, particularly in San Francisco and Los Angeles. Another discussion of a new medium omits many artists who work with this medium in the West. These omissions are also noteworthy insofar as they point up regional differences which still exist—in spite of all the claims made for instant, national and world-wide communication. Kienholz or Price probably could not have developed in New York as they have in Los Angeles; it is doubtful that Hudson or Nauman would be working elsewhere as they have been in San Francisco; an artist like Carl Andre would be an anomaly—even now—in San Francisco. San Francisco, for better and worse, insists on the past (Wiley: "Everybody I know has a real nostalgia about something which happened a long time ago"); Los Angeles, alone of all metropolitan cities without a past, gears for the future; New York—again, for better and worse—fuses both.

MAURICE TUCHMAN

Contents: Critical Essays

13

Serial Forms

Lawrence Alloway

The technique of sculpture lends itself to serial production, as the proliferation of casts by, say, Arp, Lipchitz and Moore makes clear. However, serial, in the context of this exhibition, means a great deal more than meeting a market bigger than the supply of unique works of art. Construction as a technique, the use of standard iron or wood elements, is one application. Unlike Russian Constructivism, which validated the declared use of additive structure, but retained ideals of visual differentiation, recent American sculpture has proposed an aesthetic radically unlike garrulously inventive Constructivism.

Bars, slats, boxes, are used in ways that oppose previous expectations of sculpture. Basically the medium has been regarded as the extension of uniquely invented form into three dimensions. Thus the sculptors have felt obliged to invent all-round entertainment for the prowling viewer and this is as true of David Smith as it is of Gabo and earlier sculptors. The use of standard units, in disciplined open arrays, shifts the emphasis away from incident, so that the work becomes a form visibly and continuously structured up and out from the basic unit. Modular-based sculptures, such as LeWitt's or forms in tension, like Snelson's, have this kind of structure, in which the unit remains distinct within the aggregate. It should be pointed out, perhaps, that serial imagery in sculpture has nothing to do with a Purist-type homage to industrial production. The line on the wall or the procession on the floor of Judd's boxes have no more semantic cargo than they do formal nuance. They are firm examples of quantitatively rigorous structure.

Serial, then, can be used to refer to the internal parts of a work when they are seen in uninterrupted succession. This is stated almost as principle by Hamrol, whose sculptures consist of jointed identical bars, combinable in various permutations. Instead of creating a rigid structure, he maintains control by anticipating, and limiting, future movement of the parts; however the bars may be shifted they are still within Hamrol's system. One of the chief factors is the sameness of the units. Other artists who do not keep to repetitive identical forms in single works can be considered as serial in another respect. This is when one form is common to a series of distinct but related works; the cross-references are more numerous than those which usually exist in an artist's work of, say, a particular period, because of the reiterated image. (The idea was derived from the work of painters like Noland and Feeley, who preserve a continuous image through long runs of work; my application of it here to sculpture is due to the suggestion of Maurice Tuchman.)

Such image series are not the same as a theme and variations (with a clear major statement accompanied by subsequent elaboration, often becoming frivolous) but, on the contrary, are a succession of moves, all of equal value. Repetition of the non-thematic image or structure in time seems to replace the assumption that a high degree of unpredictable formal play is necessary for every work. In sculpture the luminescent cubes of Bell or the plank sculptures of McCracken are examples of a form perpetuated over a series of works, not because the forms have some Platonic virtue or authority, but because they are adequate to the artists' purposes. This being so, why should artists feel obliged to diversify their works simply in order to prove their cause of invention?

McCracken's sculptures, incidentally, each one a smoothly painted fiberglass plank that leans on the wall, could be said to be a witty solution of the problem of space-occupancy in plinth-less sculpture, that is if one regards works of art as answers to questions posed by historical process. It is true that I am making assumptions about history as I write. The two senses of serial, as internal repetition and as successive whole images, are being used to characterize aspects of the artists' work in the exhibition in opposition to some other kinds of sculpture. Thus I am referring to common stylistic features that touch a Coast-to-Coast scatter of artists. My observations are statistical rather than categorical. McCracken, it seems to me, is making a sharp gesture at the center of this trend in current sculpture. The characteristics of legible and unaccented structure with less elaboration and contrast are shared even by those artists who preserve unique parts and views, such as Smith and Gerowitz.

The usages described as serial are part of the present tendency of sculptors, or some of them, towards highly legible forms and systems. Legibility of image and consistency of development are stated as rigorous aesthetic principle. Clearly, a many-angled, many-sided closed sculpture is no less visible than a simple, regular solid, but it is less legible, in the sense that it is less easily grasped conceptually as a complete form. There is now, often, a suspension of the planar and volumetric transitions within the work, or at least a reduction of the sense of transitional flow which characterizes earlier 20th century sculpture. When a form is known, it can always be seen fairly clearly, no matter how it is viewed (e.g. Morris). Smith's polygons, for example, although not self-explanatory from any one view are not, as a rule, dramatically surprising from the other side.

To classify this kind of sculpture as minimal is perhaps off the mark, because there exists no agreed-upon point of formal and image complexity which is Enough. Because there is no consensus on what is Enough, or

Looking Back from the Sixties

Wayne V. Andersen

Too Much, one cannot accurately characterize these structures as minimal (except as a handy slang label referring to what a number of artists have in common). It is a weakness of "minimal" as a critical term that it assumes, or rather memorializes, a point in time when such work was less than expected. In fact, it must be remembered that forms of this kind sustain variables and complexities, too. LeWitt's lucid right-angles grids, beyond a certain size, take on a labyrinthine potential in our act of perception, if not in our grasp of the governing system. In viewing Smithson's solid stepped forms one hesitates (at least, I do) between sequence and progression, between the steps on each unit and the relation between the units as they change size along the row. The idea of boredom and monotony as the aesthetic experience induced by such works seems to postulate an absolute level of visual animation or entertainment. In fact, the combinatory steps of Andre, with the regular sections making a giant cube in this exhibition, is not boring to me, but a new Calder is. The recognition of frequent events is as appropriate to aesthetics as the shock of surprise, which is what the literature of 20th century art has dwelt on so much.

To use repeatable forms as a constituent of one work or as a series, in preference to intricate unique forms, is not a recourse by artists to reduced elements. Nothing is simple. For one thing, our continuing contact as spectators with such work replaces blankness and the sense of zero with recognition of purpose. Without wishing to revive an expressionistic notion of art as the personal property of authorship, I want to stress that none of this legible and consistent sculpture is really impersonal. The individuality of the artist is recorded by the population of formal elements in his work and their distributional patterns (even when other people help to fabricate the work).

In 1949, Clement Greenberg, in explaining why the number of promising young sculptors in this country was proportionally so much larger than that of young painters, singled out David Smith, Theodore Roszak, David Hare, Herbert Ferber, Seymour Lipton, Richard Lippold, Peter Grippe, Burgoyne Diller, Adeline Kent, Ibram Lassaw, and Isamu Noguchi as having the potential to contribute sculpture that was ambitious, serious, and original. In 1956, expressing disappointment about the trend of world sculpture since the Forties, Greenberg cancelled out all the Americans except Smith, and suggested that, among the Europeans, Marcks and Wotruba were the most convincing—the rest had succumbed to artiness and fanciful improvisation. Now, ten years later, the present exhibition shows a selection of works from the Sixties, by sculptors who started working in one of the last four decades; of those Greenberg hailed in 1949 only David Smith and Noguchi are represented; the three other exhibitors representing Smith's generation, Kohn, Nakian, and Nevelson, moved into modernist styles only in the early fifties. Greenberg's criticism has thus turned out to be a prediction. I cite Greenberg to point to the timing of his remarks, for the year 1949 was within a pivotal period for a number of sculptors, and 1956 was a critical date for both modern art and modern criticism. By 1949 Noguchi, de Rivera, Roszak, Grippe, and Hare had achieved their most influential, and in some cases, best works. Lassaw, Ferber, and Lipton, though all mature sculptors, entered the Fifties with important changes in style, caused in part by their having begun welding; even Smith's sculpture changed somewhat from 1949 to 1951 in a direction that was to increase the viability of his form. In the first half of the Fifties, a dozen more good modernist sculptors had come on stage, as had the second wave of Abstract Expressionist painters; but whereas painting sustained a relatively stable character, the new sculpture surged forth in multiple and inter-mixed styles, proving that Abstract-Expressionism was a fairly well defined style of painting, but lacked a clear counterpart in sculpture. Sculptors had access to a wider range of materials and methods, and were drawing on a more checkered tradition than that from which painting had emerged during the previous decade. By 1956 sculpture in this country seemed to have gotten out of genetic control, whereas Abstract Expressionist painting seemed poised on a peak of its own achievement. Depending on the observer's point of view, sculpture, in relation to painting, was either healthy and fertile for new and multiformed ideas, or it was merely frothing divertissements that showed neither direction nor quality. Greenberg took the negative view; he even found Smith's achievement hard to formulate, finding him a headlong and reckless sculptor who showed everything he made, worked in diverse styles, and had an "aggressive originality."

I suggest that the principal cause underlying the different ways sculpture and painting in this country emerged from the Forties was that there occurred groupings of modernist painters, but not of sculptors; groupings of the latter have begun only in recent years. Before the second World War, there was a handful of important sculptors—Calder, de Rivera, Smith, Roszak, Noguchi, Lassaw, and Grippe, in order of appearance; stylistic links among them are hard to find, and they never associated. Yet they all were moving ahead with remarkably inventive freshness. By the end of the Fifties, with the addition of Hare and Lippold, each was a major sculptor, but there was no group, nor had any of the other important starters in the Forties followed one of the earlier sculptors' leads. The effort some critics have made to link these sculptors by the use of direct-metal techniques have been foolish and futile, for even in the early Fifties, when most of them were welding, they were doing it in different ways, proving that technique and style were not the same.

I believe that the rise of modernist sculpture in this country has been more a matter of successive inventions built upon a variety of influences than of a unified stylistic development. By 1956, in New York, Chicago, Los Angeles, and the San Francisco Bay area, the course of sculpture appeared to be out of control, yet each center evidenced fairly coherent directions in painting. Largely, this had resulted because Abstract Expressionism was a powerful force in painting, relatively clear-cut in ideas, and everywhere available. Its easy proliferation was also greatly aided by the art criticism of the Fifties, which helped to unify the style by naming it, by explaining its aims and technical process, and by ignoring those who didn't fit. Harold Rosenberg's article on "action painting" was in some ways as important a factor as De Kooning's painterly style, and Clement Greenberg's and Thomas Hess' sensitive explanations of the genesis and direction of the style helped it to sustain a unified flow across the country.

Some sculpture did fit into the formula of Abstract Expressionism: Smith and partly Lassaw, especially after 1950, may be compared with Pollock; Ferber was in close touch with the painters and approached Kline's style around 1956. In the eyes of the critics, however, these few similarities between sculpture and Abstract Expressionist painting were enough to subordinate the sculpture to the painting style.

In retrospect, then, Abstract Expressionist painting appears to have followed an evolutionary path that coincides quite well with a number of traditional theories of the way art develops. In the progression from the mode of Pollock to that of De Kooning and Rothko there are traces of Wölfflin's polar theory, a concept that Greenberg seems to support; Robert Rosenblum, on the other hand, in order to explain the demise of Abstract Expressionism, has applied to it the life-cycle theory that sees every style of art passing through phases of youth, maturity, and old age. There are also certain beliefs differentiating painting from sculpture that have favored the grouping of painters by their fidelity to the quality of paint, which has been to the discredit of sculptors, since they have so frequently departed from what sculpture is traditionally supposed to be. Barbara Rose, for instance, seems to be still looking for mass, volume, and space in sculpture, and has also tried to unify the new sculpture that was shown at the Jewish Museum in 1964 by writing that all these works were derived from Abstract Expressionism—even though the show included works of Stankiewicz and Segal, whose styles, both in relation to Abstract Expressionism and to each other, are too remote to be categorized.

The radicalism of modernist sculpture is only disconcerting to those whose historical orientation demands stylistic grouping and continuity. The belief that sculpture in this country since the late Forties has followed painting is now a cliché, resulting from the fact that the history of modern art has been written about painting. Neither the role of sculpture in Cubism, Futurism, and Constructivism, nor the object-imagery of Dada and Surrealism has been adequately described. Likewise, the essential parallel between American carve-direct sculpture and painting in the Thirties and Forties remains to be studied, as does the impact of sculpture on American painters after 1956.

Is there any tradition at all in the four decades of modernist sculpture in this country, or shall we concede to a series of a few isolated inventions in the midst of cliché-ridden, skittish divertissements? In the Thirties, amidst a milieu of carve-direct and expressionist sculptors, there were Calder, de Rivera, Noguchi, Roszak, and Lassaw. Calder's work in the late Twenties and Thirties and its sources are well known; his influence among later serious sculptors is hard to find, however, for the important kinetic imagery of the late Fifties and the Sixties reflects more the earlier innovations by Duchamp, Gabo, Moholy-Nagy, and others. But unlike the other Americans of his decade, Calder turned his art on itself, in contrast to Smith, de Rivera, and Roszak, whose work was made to reflect something outside itself. Like Calder, Smith evolved his first imagery from the Cubist collage, but he infused his process with the social implications of material and technique, using boiler plate and welding as symbols of the industrial process. DeRivera's machined sculptures of about 1930 and Roszak's hitherto unnoticed sculpture of

1934 and 1936, which involved the full range of machine-shop processes—welding, screw cutting, machining, and so on—paralleled Smith's in this respect, while differing greatly in specific ideology and in formal results. Like the stone carvers of the same decade, these sculptors were true to their material and process (though their materials and processes were very different); only to this extent did they fit into the general picture of modern sculpture in the Thirties, when the work of the carve-direct and expressionist sculptors represented fading phases of earlier styles.

What did unify the best American modernist sculpture was its surrealist bent in the second half of the Forties. In that respect it paralleled painting, but the diversity was still very much apparent. Calder continued to remind us of Miró and Arp; Smith held to the surrealistic mode of Picasso and Gonzalez; Noguchi was looking to Tanguy; Hare was in touch with Breton (and the style of Matta); Roszak had resumed the style found in his earlier paintings, which had been inspired by de Chirico; Lipton's work was aggressively surrealistic, as was Ferber's, who had also been influenced by Gonzalez in the late Forties. An important innovation in the first half of the Forties occurred in the work of both Lassaw and Grippe, who fused Surrealism with the Neo-Plasticism of Mondrian, producing the first wave of cage-like sculpture; Grippe developed this style through a remarkable series of terracotta "cities" (the most important open sculpture of the early Forties), while Lassaw made it his signature style of "armature" constructions that were first coated with plastic compound, and after 1950, with molten metal. The range in style, then, was from the Bauhaus configurations of Lippold, through the surrealistically transformed Neo-Plasticism of de Rivera's continuous forms, to the outright surrealism of Hare, Ferber, and Lipton.

But the first half of the Fifties did not show a uniform continuity in the development of sculpture. The emergence of such sculptors as Louise Bourgeois, Sidney Gordin, Richard Stankiewicz, Gabriel Kohn, Manuel Neri, and a dozen others widened the stylistic range and tended to divert sculpture from the direction of painting just at the time when American painting appeared to be most unified. What this situation really implied, however, depended on the observer's viewpoint. In regard to painting, which seemed to be forming a tradition of its own, critics tended to fix on those characteristics that unified it, whereas in regard to sculpture, they gave more attention to its diversity than to the continuity in the development of the older sculptors. Moreover, the departure of the new sculpture from established definitions of sculpture was drastic in a variety of ways, and contrasted the new painting, which seemed to have re-established the art of painting in the wake of the imaging, non-painterly phase of

Surrealism; thus the diversity of the new sculpture in the first half of the Fifties was exaggerated by being analysed in relation both to painting and to traditional sculpture.

After the mid-Fifties, when the sculpture of Chamberlain, Agostini, di Suvero, and Sugarman appeared, critics immediately paralleled their work to Abstract Expressionist painting. But this was precisely the period when support for Abstract Expressionism was beginning to wane, and when its tenets had been so often repeated and its styles so widely exposed that young painters were looking for new directions. The diversity that had characterized sculpture in the first half of the decade became the trend of painting in the second half. Yet by 1961, critics had fairly well defined the several painting styles and had grouped the painters, while the situation of sculpture was still similar to that of the Forties—a number of promising artists with viable styles amid some faded styles of older sculptors, and a profusion of divertissements by younger ones. For the first time, however, painting and sculpture were partners in the variegation.

I would liken the situation of sculpture in the Sixties, thus far, to that in the first half of the Fifties: talent is everywhere, and most of the production looks fresh. Yet there are important differences. A great deal of painting since the middle Fifties has drawn in sculpture, thus diminishing the unnecessary schism between the two; sculptors have begun to group; and some critics are making an effort to explain their work in other terms than those relative to painting or to traditional definitions of sculpture. The fresh visual appearance of the new sculpture has called for new insights and a critical language freed of rhetorical novelties and assumptions of a crisis. Even though Rosenberg and Alloway claimed in the early Fifties that action painting was not art, but an event, it turned out to be art; most of the divertissements in sculpture from the Fifties died ignobly, yet others have moved on to become art, as will a great deal of sculpture from the Sixties. The present apparent crisis is one of supply and demand, to which many sculptors have reacted with frantic originality, but a greater crisis within art may eventually turn out to be the lack of a real crisis. The new sculpture has met with no antagonism; there is no atmosphere of conflict in which the sculptor can feel himself at peril. Instead, the response to nearly everything produced today is "yes."

If it survives physically, each new sculpture of the Sixties will pass into history either as art or artifact, for we are not yet free of historicism or of segregating art from artifact by values involving ideas of timelessness and universality. The real problem we face as viewers of the present exhibition is, I think, not so much whether the new sculpture can be fitted into our accepted frames of reference, as whether we should even attempt to fit it. Looking back from the Sixties is the historical view; looking at the Sixties themselves precludes any viewpoint at all, for we are in the middle of what we see, and any viewpoint we would choose would be either arbitrary or prejudicial. The perils of the moment may be greater for the critic than for the sculptor.

Assemblage and Beyond

Dore Ashton

Consider the fortunes of the *Laocoön*: admired by Pliny because, as he thought, three consummate artists had carved the drama of father and sons out of one block of marble, it was rediscovered in 1506 when Michelangelo and others were impressed by the naturalism in the anatomy, though they noted that Pliny had been wrong about the single block—they found four joints. When Winckelmann, Lessing and Goethe later reflected on the *Laocoön*, technical considerations were forgotten. One block or four, what interested the late 18th century was the psychological and narrative power of the group. In the 19th century, the scorn of formalist critics fell upon the pathetic group while in the 20th, only a few isolated classical scholars consider it worth their while to perpetuate both sides of the argument.

Nowhere in the extensive literature on the *Laocoön* is the concept of the sculptured group challenged. That remained for the present century. Such high-minded arguments as flowed from the imaginations of Lessing and Goethe would be inconceivable today. The conventions accepted from antiquity to the 20th century—and particularly the convention which insists on the isolation of the group by means of its base—were not questioned.

The last great sculptor of the unified group, Rodin, was also the first to seriously undermine the hallowed tradition of the unified group. When Rodin fashioned separate members—hands, feet, heads—and tried them out here and there, and when he placed his *Burghers of Calais* on *terra firma* and said he wanted to get rid of the base, Rodin was taking the first step toward the dissolution of habitual attitudes toward sculpture.

After Rodin, the definition of sculpture, like that of painting, was energetically challenged in every detail. Each challenge since 1900 has subtracted a little more from the certitudes custom had affixed to the nature of sculpture.

It is to William Seitz's serious analysis of the nature of these 20th century questions that we owe a coherent approach to the new attitudes. Seitz focused on the changed methods of working, diametrically opposed to the *Laocoön* tradition, and designated the term "assemblage" to cover what would otherwise have been a bewildering variety of activities.

Assemblage, Seitz wrote in his invaluable catalog for "The Art of Assemblage," an exhibition at the Museum of Modern Art in 1961, is a term adapted from Dubuffet "which would include all forms of composite art and modes of juxtaposition." The word itself appears frequently both as a noun and verb in the literature of modern art. Still other words, frequent in the body of Seitz's text, help to focus on salient features of the new attitudes: destruction, dislocation, juxtaposition, disparate parts, disassociation, actualism.

With the establishment of a working method that emphatically denies the necessity of a visible binding unit, formerly associated with the plinth, the realm of sculpture extended beyond discernible boundaries. There was a tremendous urge to centrifugal movement. Thought itself was outward bound. The artist felt impelled to move his materials away from an anchoring center, but into what came to be called the living space. Paintings were built out from the wall until they assumed relief status, and sculptures took flight from the uncompromising obstacle of the base. Metaphysically, all things were still related, but the spaces between, both mental and physical, were greater, and the relationships more occult.

There were iconoclastic undertones. To move out into the living spaces, as Futurists, Dadaists, Surrealists and hosts of others advocated, meant to criticize. In many ways, art became largely critical much in the way Kant said philosophy was primarily criticism. Yet in the broad realm opened by assemblage, the sundering notions of dislocation and strange juxtaposition coexisted with constructive notions of grand spatial schemes. The much explored possibilities of discontinuity were not the only avenues of approach to the new ideals. The late Frederick Kiesler, for instance, was not radical in terms of what he destroyed but in terms of the traditions he amplified. In a sense Kiesler took the organic themes philosophically treated by Goethe and made them palpable, translating philosophy into assembled solids in a grand space.

"My sculpture," he wrote in 1952, "I also see as consisting of divergent chunks of matter, held together, yet apart, appearing like galactic structures, each part leading a life of coexistence, or correality with the others." And a year before his death he reiterated: "A new era has begun. . . The environment becomes equally as important as the object, if not more so, because the object breathes into the surrounding and also inhales the realities of the environment no matter in what space, close or wide apart, open air or indoor" (*Art International,* vol. 9, no. 2, 1965).

Goethe had said, "There is nothing inside and nothing outside, for the inside is the outside."

Kiesler's paradoxes are acted out with relatively traditional sculptural means, but other artists such as Harold Paris and Mark di Suvero have discovered different means to express what Kiesler isolated as "correality." Paris's "rooms," assembled from cast rubber forms and formica tectonic elements have been expanded and literally amplified with electronic devices. Di Suvero's insistence on the floor-plan and the ceiling-plan as part of his sculptural space has been ingeniously realized with hanging and balancing inventions. The results in all three artists express a *Weltanschauung* that leaves the problems of the *Laocoön* behind.

Not all of the problems, however: there is still the question of narrative sculpture, and narrative sculpture has survived only because of the permissions implicit in the assemblage attitude. In the early stages, as Seitz remarked, Apollinaire argued against narrative art because of its dependence on discursive logic. Latter-day assemblagists have found their way around Apollinaire's strictures by combining both discursive and non-discursive approaches.

The survival of narrative sculpture is seen in the tableau mode of Ed Kienholz. In all of Kienholz's larger ensembles the thread of narrative is as obvious as it is in the *Laocoön. Roxy's,* that grubby reconstruction of an American bordello, is replete with carefully characterized individual whores and the details of their biographies. *The Beanery* (after the painters' bar Barney's Beanery) carefully annotates the types who drink there, and Barney himself. Countless details tell a story. But Kienholz is not bound by naturalism and discursive logic. His fantasy charges in everywhere. It works to bring the viewer up short, as for instance, when he discovers that the realistic denizens of Barney's have clocks for faces. Disruption, disassociation and the other divisive diction of the 20th century is as omnipresent in Kienholz's blunt fantasies as conjunction, and, even though we stretch the point a bit, "correality." In these tableaux, the threads of old arguments are woven into a new fabric.

Kienholz's art has been called operatic and theatrical and there is some justice to the argument. The old problems of theatre such as unity of time and place appear in certain details: dated newspapers, dated letters and dated clothing. As in traditional theatre, we are located specifically and given instructions on how to look. But then, just when the logic is established, Kienholz breaks precedent. He offers bits and pieces of sculptured fantasy; he shapes and assembles inscrutable designs; he catches the viewer's attention with an isolated thrust of horrible invention (a blood clot or disparate teeth). No convention is inviolable.

The tableau narrative method is not exclusive with Kienholz. Marisol also freezes bits of representational narrative. In her *Cocktail Party* she carves and clothes the blasé participants so that their era and location are unmistakably identifiable as New York in the 1960s. But she also escapes linear logic with sculptural inventions that have little to do with a unified, story-telling ensemble. Where in Kienholz there is a flavor of authentic folklore, as John Coplans has remarked, in Marisol there is the savor of sophisticated play, sometimes called camp. Where Kienholz is a social critic in spite of himself, with the savage indignation of a Nathanael West, Marisol is an amused bystander in the manner of a *Vogue* magazine society reporter. Both artists spread and diffuse their ensembles beyond the limits of classical sculpture, and both are nevertheless attentive to individual sculptural details.

If horror and pathos, implicit in Kienholz's tableaux, may be said to be stock elements in narrative sculpture from the *Laocoön* on, black horror and humor seems to have lodged in the sculptural object only in recent times. Grand Guignol translated into museum art is a 20th century phenomenon. One of its most compelling practitioners is the sculptor and film maker, Bruce Conner. Conner's concern with the fusion of plastic and narrative values is minimal. Whatever he needs to convey dark nostalgia, repulsion, terror and a lurid sense of the ridiculous, he incorporates. Formal satisfactions enter, but only secondarily.

Out of the collage tradition with its welcoming attitude toward real talismans (the bottle label or wisp of rope as association-provokers) Conner draws the explosive atoms of thought that will jog slothful memories. He bundles and pastes and binds together a profusion of real references—stockings, underwear, garters, mirrors, jewelry, magazine photos—in a freely-associated tale of sordid or absurd existence. Often this jumble of telling clues is partially masked with stretched silks (the distended nylon stocking itself calls to mind sex maniacs, intruders, danger). Or an illusion is produced by means of a frame, a boxed episode, an altar-like construction.

The Surrealists' emphasis on libidinous fancy and startling juxtaposition nourishes Conner's art. Overtones of necrophilia and perverse fetishism are handled skillfully. Unlike Kienholz, Conner does not spell out a moral, but like him, Conner is liberated from earlier shibboleths of the modern tradition. They fear nothing, recognize no limitations and are impervious to charges of being "literary."

The same can be said for the younger artist Lucas Samaras. His aggressive imagery often spells out his obsessions with rather obvious Freudian symbols, knives, pins, boxes. Like Kienholz, Samaras acts out erotic fantasies in his art with varying degrees of subtlety. Both artists are inordinately impressed with the tools of the medical profession and have used sinister arrays of surgical instruments in their assemblages.

Samaras, however, is given to more surrealist juxtapositions to make his uneasy points. He will incorporate stuffed birds, compasses, shells and photographs in a single image, relying on unaccustomed associations wherever possible. He likes to accumulate minute detail in great profusion, but his emphasis is always on the object as a complete, startling, isolated unit. His relationship to folk art is ironic. Even the bright wool yarn adorning his false caskets, peasant style, is only there to pique uneasy associations.

Profusion of detail, so common in the assemblage method, often leads to expansion to larger objects. Harold Paris moved from profuse small sculpture to rooms. Samaras moves from caskets and partly opened boxes to a mirror palace that can only be called hallucinatory, no matter how much abused that old surrealist term has become. Samaras' eight foot enclosure, mirrored inside and out, provides an hallucination of infinity. The sections of mirror within reproduce themselves countlessly, endlessly, towering as far as the eye can see. Within the room the surrounded viewer will experience a sensation of reverse vertigo and possibly, he will make erotic associations. The mirrored ceiling is, after all, an old, effete dream.

Although the enclosed construction, the box, is a rather frequent device among assemblagists, no one has made it as personal or as lyrical as Joseph Cornell. Cornell occupies a space which can never be given a name. His working method is decidedly that of a poet: he takes a theme, evokes apposite images, and then works within a formal limit. Like a poet he is able to travel far in time, space and place without forsaking the formal limits of his art.

On the other hand, Cornell is a consummate craftsman, and is a maker of concrete objects. His poesy results from the juxtaposition of carefully selected detail. He constructs and makes, and is therefore as much a sculptor (if sculpture consists in three-dimensional objects, or real presences in space), as he is a poet.

Still another characteristic of Cornell is his profound interest in theatre and films. He has made films himself, and is something of an expert on the drama and opera of the 19th century. Many of his more literary boxes allude to great actresses and historical theatrical detail. These boxes may be said to be theatrical in format: the glass window is equivalent to the proscenium, and the settings within are environments within environments. A modern Palladio working in intimacy...

The film has fed his method also, for Eisenstein's careful definition of montage admirably fits certain of Cornell's compositions. There is a flattening out of imagery, as there would be on film, and there is the estrangement paradoxically induced by the close-up.

Time, also, enters Cornell's tableaux in various modern ways. There are the boxes that are to be handled, with colored sands silting slowly downward and up. There are boxes with sand clocks. There are rings which slide on bars and balls which roll. Here, movement, or time, is induced by spectator participation. But in other boxes—those in which Cornell introduces a series of symmetrically arranged forms, as in the dovecot series—the psychology of metrical procession prevails.

The physical limits of Cornell's boxes are scrupulously preserved, but the psychological limits are hard to deter-

The New Sculpture and Technology

John Coplans

mine. Cornell benefits from the powerful modern movement toward a fusion of the arts. He is given to including inscriptions, quotations, signs, symbols and objects that add a dimension to his theme. Allusiveness is the essence of his art.

In this sense, Cornell, and all the others practising some form of assemblage, hold true to the thrust toward centrifugal concepts that made its revolutionary appearance early in our century.

Understanding of current art can be deepened if, in addition to examination of the work, the artist's strategy in response to changes in the world surrounding him is also examined. Although it is not unusual for the artist to envisage his art as a persuasive factor in changing society's view of itself, it may well be considered that, ultimately, reality shapes and changes art's viewing itself as well. Whatever the nature of his individual ambition for art, the psychic and sociological pressures exerted by the world the artist inhabits are powerful forces; they eventually play an important—if not dominant—role in shaping response.

Currently exerting what is probably the most dominant pressure upon the younger artist's approach is a keen awareness and appreciation of the potency of science and the scientific mind. This, of course, is by no means new. Since the emergence of Cubism, numerous artists have endeavored, for a variety of reasons, to effect some kind of integration between art and science, but always with limited success. Despite the various theories advanced in support of this approach, in actual practice much of the work produced has qualitatively not lived up to the verbalized theoretical framework. Significant gains in art, of course, are not dependent on theory, but application. A more topical resurgence of this earlier interest is the recent emergence of Optical and Kinetic art; in one form or another both these styles once more aim to integrate art and science but, with rare exceptions, what has so far been produced has been artistically insipid and scientifically commonplace. In short, both styles can be seen as a coarse oversimplification of the issue. But there is a deeper and subtler reaction of art to science taking place among younger American artists, particularly centered around recent developments in sculpture.

The dominance of science and its handmaiden, technology, is obviously having a pervasive effect upon the shape of our culture. Correctly or incorrectly this is felt to be a threat to the continued existence of art as we know it. It engenders the feeling that if art fails to compete with science, art may very well cease to exist in the near future. On the other hand, many of the younger artists feel more at home in a world dominated by science than their elders; they do not feel out of step. In addition to the introduction of an almost breathtaking spectrum of new materials, the new technology has, in several other ways, altered the perspective of younger artists, and this, it should be emphasized, in manners which they feel neither threaten nor diminish their capacity to create art.

Art, like science, today has a tremendously rapid communication system. Not only is what is now being done disseminated so rapidly, but there is also available a much more complete picture of the past as a whole than hitherto. Unnerving to an elder generation who took until their

21

forties to reach maturity and an art of consequence is the manner in which very young artists nowadays produce work of a high quality. Obviously, the period of recapitulation is now shorter. The development of the younger artist seems to parallel the increasing number of mathematicians who very often produce their best work before they are thirty—their contribution after this age being slower, more deliberate, and not quite as free.

Not only has the whole educational basis of art changed, but art has also become increasingly intellectual as a pursuit. The artist today neither needs nor desires to see the originals to *know* what they are about. It is not necessary to see Duchamp's urinal to know what it represents, nor is it necessary for the artist to see a Pollock to know in what manner Pollock's painting changed art. This is not to imply that the artist does not *enjoy* looking at art, but only to make clear that in recent art it is no longer necessary to sit for hours carefully looking at each dab of pigment on a painting or every inch of modeling on a sculpture to *understand* the art. It is looked at, and then later it arouses a whole new spectrum of thoughts.

Whatever new opinions the artist may wish to express concerning the nature of reality he cannot concretize them except through techniques and materials. A scientist concretizes his concepts through some system of logic, for example, mathematics, and when an existing system is unsuitable he has to invent a new one. Einstein, for example, had to create a whole new system of mathematics to concretize his Theory of Relativity. Likewise, if the existing methods of concretizing art, i.e., techniques and materials, are exhausted or unsuitable, the artist has to seek and find new ones. The artist, of course, does not invent the technique or the material; they are in common usage in industry and very often in commercial art long before the painter and sculptor think of applying them to art.

A sculptor who has been educated to work within a traditional technique is bound and limited by that technique. In contrast, younger artists will not only employ any means they consider necessary to do what is required, but they are obviously not bound by a specific technique. They not only treat technique and technology with great ease and assurance, but they also use whatever aspect of technology is required, according to need, and without inhibition. In other words, they are not at all self-conscious about techniques; if they haven't either the skill or equipment, they go out and acquire them. What is important about technique and material is that it can be used for the purpose of making the work in the simplest and most direct way that is possible. Thus the new techniques and materials are no more or less than a convenient mechanical extension of the human eye and hand, and the artists' employment of them becomes almost as habitual, for once the artist becomes involved with tech-

nology, and dependent on it, he is to some extent forced to keep up with research, development and application. Thus many artists are often constantly on the hunt, seeking and storing technical information for current or future application.

Techniques and materials convey a whole stream of information concerning the artist and the environment. The employment of certain aspects of technology can sometimes clearly mark the work as being conceived and executed in the Sixties, say, rather than the Fifties or earlier. The use of new techniques will not only very often accurately locate the work in time, but, in addition, cause the artwork to reflect some of the "look" of the time. The manner, for example, in which a consumer society is constantly driven to update the look of and function of its products by ceaselessly absorbing the new advances of technology in itself makes the new techniques and materials readily available and relatively inexpensive for the artist to exploit. Aspects of this "look," particularly when synthetic materials are used, become reflected in the artwork; this is especially so, for example, in Claes Oldenburg's sculpture. The use of a certain combination of techniques and materials will, obviously, locate the artwork as a product of a technology which is restricted geographically. Larry Bell's use of rare optical coatings— a product of space technology—is readily available in Los Angeles, but it would be impossible for an artist to be able to use a technology of this order, for instance, in Barcelona or Buenos Aires, and it would probably be extremely difficult, if not impossible, in London or Paris.

The intensity with which artists involve themselves in technological matters varies greatly from artist to artist. Sometimes, an artist may want to become identified by the use of a particular process; that is, to take over its artistic identity entirely for himself. Larry Bell's coated glass boxes are very representative of this kind of appropriation. Bell takes a wide variety of techniques and extends them to a point beyond even industry's interest, to produce something that has never been seen before. This is a very different kind of idea from that of an artist who takes the commonplace, something which is seen every day, and then proceeds to use it as art in a way that is completely new; Dan Flavin's use of fluorescent tubes and Carl Andre's use of bricks are instances of this approach. Both these artists seem to be extremely indifferent to technology and may very well be perplexed by the amount of trouble Bell goes through to produce his sculpture. Donald Judd, on the other hand, involves himself in technology in the most minimal terms: his metallic sculpture is made to order by a tinsmith. Although John McCracken's sculpture is handcrafted and he uses as many as twenty or thirty coats of paint sprayed upon the surface to produce a sensuous finish with a very high degree of color luster, his work, like Bell's, represents the ultimate visualization of an idea. David Gray, like David Smith, employs a sturdy industrial technique. David Smith (in his later work) transformed the surface of the stainless steel by burnishing, grinding and polishing. This recorded upon the surface a nervous, flickering calligraphy of kinesthetic marks. In contrast, Gray's chromed and painted surfaces are more specific. He uses, in a dead-pan way, common industrial finishes for their appearance of durability and strength. These qualities add weight to the metallic structure; the blunt finishes evoke toughness and power by association. Tony DeLap is relatively indifferent to material; his identity emerges much more through a sense of detail, of rightness of proportion, and perfection of shape.

Similarly, the expressive function of new materials varies greatly from artist to artist. The assemblagists tend to work with existing objects or parts of objects. Their parts generally incorporate a history of use in some way by visual metaphor. (An exception is H. C. Westermann, who very often will construct some of his objects from raw material.) Larry Bell, Tony DeLap, Judy Gerowitz, John McCracken, Ronald Bladen, Anthony Caro and many others are definitely fabricators—they construct shapes. Bell, Flavin and McCracken, however, utilize material as matter rather than form. Bell's coated glass boxes look infinitely empty. They could be likened to anti-energy boxes; they appear capable of absorbing fantastic amounts of light—energy without reaching a saturation point. There seems to be a big difference between those artists that use light and movement. Flavin's work seems to deal with the emanation and radiation of energy and it has no existence until it is switched on. Charles Mattox's sculptures, on the other hand, although kinetic, have a full sculptural existence when immobile. In this sense, his work is not truly kinetic. The appearance of Flavin's work, however, once it is switched on is always the same, it never fluctuates. In contrast, Len Lye's work is cyclic and climactic, and it also incorporates sound, movement and light-glitter. Flavin's work is much more connected to John McCracken's, who makes a three-dimensional skin of radiant layers of color.

In this new work our whole notion of medium is upset. In the past, different materials and processes were regarded as different media; for example, wood and carving, bronze and casting, steel and welding. Not only does this not apply in this work, but even the idea of painting and sculpture being two different media is foreign to the whole outlook of most of these artists. Painting and sculpture have been regarded as two different media because of an aesthetic tradition which defined sculpture as a haptic art and painting an optic art. Now, however, whether a work is two- or three-dimensional is irrelevant. Nor is it critical anymore whether a work carves, encloses, divides or displaces space, or whether the surface is painted or not. Factors of this nature are merely incidental. The surface qualities of the material, on the other hand, *are* important. Obviously there are better means available today to utilize color, light, sound and movement, and the new technology is employed to these ends, regardless of the havoc that might be wreaked on traditionally discrete categories.

Even the exhibition space can be appropriated as part of the "medium." The most emphatic change that has taken place is in the traditional framework of the studio. Two kinds of art can now be distinguished: gallery art and studio art. If, previously, all art that could conveniently be exhibited in a gallery could be called "gallery art," a distinction must now be made for those works of art which are specifically designed to *employ the exhibition space as a part of the work of art*. Only that art that specifically utilizes the gallery space as a *component*, or which is dependent upon the simultaneous exhibition of a number of works can at this time be regarded as gallery art. Carl Andre's art is a very pure example of the kind of art that employs the gallery space as a component, utilizing the gallery space as a three-dimensional container, serving somewhat the same purpose as the rectilinear canvas of a painting. His modular components, whether they be bricks, wood or some synthetic material, are incidents in a whole; they are used to modify the space of the gallery and can be likened to the forms in an abstract painting. (Andre's art is extremely radical and very daring; it completely upsets many criteria of traditional methods of judging and evaluating art.[1] For example, the very nature of his works severely limits their potential market. The whole idea of a precious object to be collected and treasured—to be bought and sold—goes overboard. However daring Duchamp's innovations, they remained tied to a transportable object; thus Andre's notion of purity, in more ways than one, is very different from Clement Greenberg's!) Andre, Bladen, Flavin and Edward Kienholz (in his tableaux) use the gallery as a container. Serial Image artists, such as DeLap, McCracken and Bell employ the gallery space to achieve simultaneous viewing of several works at one time. In DeLap's work sequence and relationship between each part is critical. In McCracken's and Bell's work, repetitious images take on enhanced qualities when seen within a set. In contrast, David Smith's sculptures are not only self-contained, but were specifically created for an open, natural environment. In this sense, they are studio art.

23

---

[1]The contribution of the late Yves Klein, who took a radical step in this direction in about 1958, should not be forgotten. In an exhibition at the Iris Clert Galerie, Paris, he texturized and monochromed in an identical manner all the walls of the gallery. Thus the gallery walls became the painting.

Recentness of Sculpture

Clement Greenberg

Advanced sculpture has had more than its share of ups and downs over the last twenty-five years. This is especially true of abstract and near-abstract sculpture. Having gathered a certain momentum in the late Thirties and early Forties, it was slowed down in the later Forties and in the Fifties by the fear that, if it became markedly clean-drawn and geometrical, it would look too much like machinery. Abstract Expressionist painting, with its aversion to sharp definitions, inspired this fear, which for a time swayed even the late and great David Smith, a son of the "clean-contoured" Thirties if there ever was one. Not that "painterly" abstract sculpture was necessarily bad; it worked out as badly as it did in the Forties and Fifties because it was too negatively motivated, because too much of it was done in the way it was done out of the fear of not looking enough like art.

Painting in that period was much more self-confident, and in the early Fifties one or two painters did directly confront the question of when painting stopped looking enough like art. I remember that my first reaction to the almost monochromatic pictures shown by Rollin Crampton in 1951 (at the Peridot Gallery) was derision mixed with exasperation. It took renewed acquaintance with these pictures (which had a decisive influence on Philip Guston at that time) to teach me better. The next monochromatic paintings I saw were completely so—the all-white and all-black paintings in Rauschenberg's 1953 show (at the Stable). I was surprised by how easy they were to "get," how familiar-looking and even slick. It was no different afterwards when I first saw Reinhardt's, Sally Hazlett's, and Yves Klein's monochromatic or near-monochromatic pictures. These, too, looked familiar and slick. What was so challenging in Crampton's art had become almost over-night another taming convention. (Pollock's and Tobey's "all-overness" probably helped bring this about too.) The look of accident was not the only "wild" thing that Abstract Expressionism first acclimatized and then domesticated in painting; it did the same to emptiness, to the look of the "void." A monochromatic flatness that could be seen as limited in extension and different from a wall henceforth automatically declared itself to be a picture, to be art.

But this took another ten years to sink in as far as most artists and critics in New York were concerned. In spite of all the journalism about the erased difference between art and non-art, the look of both the accidental and the empty continued to be regarded as an art-denying look. It is only in the very last years, really, that Pollock's achievement has ceased being controversial on the New York scene. Maybe he had "broken the ice," but his all-over paintings continued to be taken for arbitrary, aesthetically unintelligible phenomena, while the look of art as identifiable in a painter like de Kooning remained the cherished look.

Today Pollock is still seen for the most part as essentially arbitrary, "accidental," but a new generation of artists has arisen that considers this an asset rather than a liability. By now we have all become aware that the far-out is what has paid off best in avant-garde art in the long run—and what could be further out than the arbitrary? Newman's reputation has likewise benefited recently from this new awareness and from a similar failure of comprehension—not to mention Reinhardt and his present flourishing.

In the Sixties it has been as though art—at least the kind that gets the most attention—set itself as a problem the task of extricating the far-out "in itself" from the merely odd, the incongruous, and the socially shocking. Assemblage, Pop, Environment, Op, Kinetic, Erotic, and all the other varieties of Novelty art look like so many logical moments in the working out of this problem, whose solution now seems to have arrived in the form of what is called Primary Structures, ABC, or Minimal art. The Minimalists appear to have realized, finally, that the far-out in itself has to be the far-out as end in itself, and that this means the furthest-out and nothing short of that. They appear also to have realized that the most original and furthest-out art of the last hundred years always arrived looking at first as though it had parted company with everything previously known as art. In other words, the furthest-out usually lay on the borderline between art and non-art. The Minimalists have not really discovered anything new through this realization, but they have drawn conclusions from it with a new consistency that owes some of its newness to the shrinking of the area in which things can now safely be non-art. Given that the initial look of non-art was no longer available to painting, since even an unpainted canvas now stated itself as a picture, the borderline between art and non-art had to be sought in the three-dimensional, where sculpture was, and where everything material that was not art also was. Painting had lost the lead because it was so ineluctably art, and it now devolved on sculpture or something like it to head art's advance. (I don't pretend to be giving the actual train of thought by which Minimal art was arrived at, but I think this is the essential logic of it.)

Proto-Pop (Johns and Rauschenberg) and Pop did a lot of flirting with the third dimension. Assemblage did more than that, but seldom escaped a stubbornly pictorial context. The Shaped Canvas school has used the third dimension mainly in order to hold on to light-and-dark or "profiled" drawing: painters whose canvases depart from the rectangle or tondo emphasize that kind of drawing in determining just what other inclosing shapes or frames their pictures are to have. In idea, mixing the mediums, straddling the line between painting and sculpture, seemed the far-out thing to do; in actual aesthetic experience it has proven almost the opposite—at least in the context of painting, where even literal references to the third dimension seem inevitably, nowadays if not twenty-five years ago, to invoke traditional sculptural drawing.

Whether or not the Minimalists themselves have really escaped the pictorial context can be left aside for the moment. What seems definite is that they commit themselves to the third dimension because it is, among other things, a co-ordinate that art has to share with non-art (as Dada, Duchamp, and others already saw). The ostensible aim of the Minimalists is to "project" objects and ensembles of objects that are just nudgeable into art. Everything is rigorously rectilinear or spherical. Development within the given piece is usually by repetition of the same modular shape, which may or may not be varied in size. The look of machinery is shunned now because it does not go far enough towards the look of non-art, which is presumably an "inert" look that offers the eye a minimum of "interesting" incident—unlike the machine look, which is arty by comparison (and when I think of Tinguely I would agree with this). Still, no matter how simple the object may be, there remain the relations and inter-relations of surface, contour, and spatial interval. Minimal works are readable as art, as almost anything is today—including a door, a table, or a blank sheet of paper. (That almost any non-figurative object can approach the condition of architecture or of an architectural member is, on the other hand, beside the point; so is the fact that some works of Minimal art are mounted on the wall in the attitude of bas-relief. Likeness of condition or attitude is not necessary in order to experience a seemingly arbitrary object as art.) Yet it would seem that a kind of art nearer the condition of non-art could not be envisaged or ideated at this moment.

That precisely is the trouble. Minimal art remains too much a feat of ideation, and not enough anything else. Its idea remains an idea, something deduced instead of felt and discovered. The geometrical and modular simplicity may announce and signify the artistically furthest-out, but the fact that the signals are understood for what they want to mean betrays them artistically.[1] There is hardly any aesthetic surprise in Minimal art, only a phenomenal one of the same order as in Novelty art, which is a one-time surprise. Aesthetic surprise hangs on forever—it is still there in Raphael as it is in Pollock—and ideas alone cannot achieve it. Aesthetic surprise comes from inspiration and sensibility as well as from being abreast of the

artistic times. Behind the expected, self-canceling emblems of the furthest-out, almost every work of Minimal art I have seen reveals in experience a more or less conventional sensibility. The artistic substance and reality, as distinct from the program, turns out to be in good safe taste. I find myself back in the realm of Good Design, where Pop, Op, Assemblage, and the rest of Novelty art live. By being employed as tokens, the "primary structures" are converted into mannerisms. The third dimension itself is converted into a mannerism. Nor have most of the Minimalists escaped the familiar, reassuring context of the pictorial: wraiths of the picture rectangle and the Cubist grid haunt their works, asking to be filled out—and filled out they are, with light-and-dark drawing.

All of which might have puzzled me more had I not already had the experience of Rauschenberg's blank canvases, and of Yves Klein's all-blue ones. And had I not seen another notable token of far-outness, Reinhardt's shadowy monochrome, part like a veil to reveal a delicate and very timid sensibility. (Reinhardt has a genuine if small gift for color, but none at all for design or placing. I can see why he let Newman, Rothko, and Still influence him towards close and dark values, but he lost more than he gained by the desperate extreme to which he went, changing from a nice into a trite artist.) I had also learned that works whose ingredients were notionally "tough" could be very soft as wholes; and vice versa. I remember hearing Abstract Expressionist painters ten years ago talking about how you had to make it ugly, and deliberately dirtying their color, only to render what they did still more stereotyped. The best of Monet's lily-pad paintings—or the best of Louis' and Olitski's paintings—are not made any the less challenging and arduous, on the other hand, by their nominally sweet color. Equations like these cannot be thought out in advance, they can only be felt and discovered.

In any case, the far-out as end in itself was already caught sight of, in the area of sculpture, by Anthony Caro in England back in 1960. But it came to him as a matter of experience and inspiration, not of ratiocination, and he converted it immediately from an end into a means—a means of pursuing a vision that required sculpture to be more integrally abstract than it had ever been before. The far-out as end in itself was already used up and compromised by the time the notion of it reached the Minimalists: used up by Caro and the other English sculptors for whom he was an example; compromised by Novelty art.

Still another artist who anticipated the Minimalists is Anne Truitt. And she anticipated them more literally and therefore, as it seems to me, more embarrassingly than Caro did. The surprise of the box-like pieces in her first show in New York, early in 1963 (at Emmerich's), was much like that which Minimal art aims at. Despite their

25

[1]Darby Bannard, writing in *Artforum* of December 1966, has already said it: "As with Pop and Op, the 'meaning' of a Minimal work exists outside of the work itself. It is a part of the nature of these works to act as *triggers* for thought and emotion pre-existing in the viewer.... It may be fair to say that these styles have been nourished by the ubiquitous question: 'but what does it mean?' "

being covered with rectilinear zones of color, I was stopped by their dead-pan "primariness," and I had to look again and again, and I had to return again, to discover the power of these "boxes" to move and affect. Far-outness here was stated rather than merely announced and signalled. At the same time it was hard to tell whether the success of Truitt's best works was primarily sculptural or pictorial, but part of their success consisted precisely in making that question irrelevant.

Truitt's art did flirt with the look of non-art, and her 1963 show was the first occasion on which I noticed how this look could confer an effect of *presence*. That presence as achieved through size was aesthetically extraneous, I already knew. That presence as achieved through the look of non-art was likewise aesthetically extraneous, I did not yet know. Truitt's sculpture had this kind of presence but did not *hide* behind it. That sculpture could hide behind it—just as painting did—I found out only after repeated acquaintance with Minimal works of art: Judd's, Morris', Andre's, Steiner's, some but not all of Smithson's, some but not all of LeWitt's. Minimal art can also hide behind presence as size: I think of Bladen (though I am not sure whether he is a certified Minimalist) as well as of some of the artists just mentioned. What puzzles me is how sheer size can produce an effect so soft and ingratiating, and at the same time so superfluous. Here again the question of the phenomenal as opposed to the aesthetic or artistic comes in.

Having said all this, I won't deny that Minimal art has brought a certain negative gain. It makes clear as never before how fussy a lot of earlier abstract sculpture is, especially that influenced by Abstract Expressionism. But the price may still not be worth it. The continuing infiltration of Good Design into what purports to be advanced and highbrow art now depresses sculpture as it does painting. Minimal follows too much where Pop, Op, Assemblage, and the rest have led (as Darby Bannard, once again, has already pointed out). Nevertheless, I take Minimal art more seriously than I do these other forms of Novelty. I retain hope for certain of its exponents. Maybe they will take still more pointers from artists like Truitt, Caro, Ellsworth Kelly, and Kenneth Noland, and learn from their example how to rise above Good Design.

The Poetics of Softness

Max Kozloff

One of the typical approaches to problems and accomplishments in a contemporary art is to set them off and judge them in the light of the form history of that art. This may be a characteristic perspective, but it is not necessarily or always the most relevant one. The criteria it develops are self-referring, for change is measured generally against a concept of internal continuity. In the case of American sculpture, for instance, current phenomena are evaluated to a great extent insofar as they relate to the post-Cubist outcrop of the "central," volumetrically clear style of David Smith. Implicit in this perspective is the asumption that *serious* sculptors use a common vocabulary of forms. It may allow them a wide array of alternatives, in color, material, texture, spatial impulse (monolithic or disaggregate), as long as they still make a reference, however oblique, to these forms. Yet one thing sculpture is quite simply not allowed to be, if it has any pretensions to the mainstream, or any claim to historical necessity, is soft.

I mean soft in the literal sense of easily yielding to physical pressure. A soft thing can be poked, molded, squeezed, scrunched. In a word, its surface is elastic, and its densities are scandalously rearrangeable. Even kinetic sculptures and three dimensional works that incorporate artificial light, remain safely within the category of the modern, for if they tamper with effect, they do not usually subvert structure. Unaware that they were doing so, for it had scarcely become an issue until recently, critics have always been talking about *hard* sculpture, much as Molière's character was all along speaking prose. Among so many affirmations, it was never considered that all modern sculpture expresses one implacable negation—of gravity. Not that it fights free of it, as in Andy Warhol's helium filled, aluminum foil pillows—but that it deliberately opposes itself to the force from below by the very tensile strength of its presence. In this respect, sculpture in general is an incurably alert production, stressing fixity, endurance, and power—all that which man himself cannot maintain, except in intermittent defiance of gravity. On the other hand, a soft sculpture, in various proportions, might suggest fatigue, deterioration, or inertia. It mimes a kind of surrender to the natural condition which pulls bodies down. No matter how figurative, then, sculpture in general must be seen as, in an important sense, escaping the anthropomorphic. And regardless of how abstract is a soft sculpture, it will unavoidably evoke the human.

The correlations and analogies we make between our bodily condition or tone, and a sculptural statement, therefore, are natural—and revealing. For sculptures are inevitably emphatic and concrete presences, to which we have responded legitimately, and so far, optimistically, as anagrams of our energies in differing hypothetical states. It is the affront of the soft sculptural mode to have introduced a pessimistic, and even more, a rather unflattering note into this aesthetic transaction. The "organic" has up to now been acceptable precisely because it was a metaphor imposed stylistically upon a *rigid* or solid material. However, when it becomes a factor of the material itself, it takes on an alarming correspondence to our own transient mortality. A more "professional" objection, of course, is that the necessarily indeterminate or provisional nature of the soft image precludes any stable formal invertebrate relationship. The invertebrate sculpture, slipping out of tether, has the potentiality of translating itself into chance shapes which defy the usual formal critique. It does not so much partake of a vocabulary of forms as it "accepts" form. Not even the Surrealist precedents for this phenomenon, most noticeably in the painting of Dali (but also in certain assemblages by Tanguy, Miró, and Duchamp), lend soft sculpture any tradition. For, rather than a Surrealist device, we are dealing with a somatic re-construction in sculpture: more mechanistic than it is literary, and yet far more metaphorical than it is abstract.

Needless to say, there can be variations on this theme of softness. Assemblages such as Ed Kienholz's, which include stuffed animals or their parts, bear the relationship to soft sculpture that taxidermy has to creaturely life. They are the dead habiliment of something once breathing and fleshy, which now excite a dreading response in the mind. John Chamberlain's recent foam rubber sculptures, on the other hand, function as recollections of his twisted metal car part pieces that will register any passing probe and then resiliently bounce back to original shape. Less elastic in their surface tensions are works by Keith Sonnier, transparent plastic bags, suspended between wall and floor, that resemble large diaphragms, waiting for some dire inhalation. In the various effects produced within this mode, there evidently can be qualities of nostalgia or expectancy. For the very malleability of soft materials, slightly inflated or drooping, focusses on the way an action will, or possibly already has, altered a substance in time. In this sense, a soft sculpture is an object becalmed, something like Georg Christoph Lichtenberg's watch which "had been lying in a faint for some hours."

The chief explorer (rather than exponent) of soft sculpture in the United States is Claes Oldenburg.[1] In the physiology of this new mode, he occupies a mid-point between such extreme solutions as external and internal pressure, metaphor and concreteness, invocation of past, and imminence of future action. And, if one holds his entire production of the last five years up for view—the sketches of household items, both technical and impressionistic, the engineering models and ghostly maquettes—all this in addition to the final, soft sculpture, whether typewriters or toilets, then one has a spectacle of such radical, almost Ovidian transformation, that it throws in question the very nature of matter, and our relation with all the familiar objects around us. It is a dizzying task to sort out that

in his work which has surprisingly gone dead and brittle, from that which is implausibly glamorous and re-animated. For the reason that transubstantiation of this order can only be perverse, his results are hallucinating, even if his processes themselves are far from illusory. The midpoint I mention is perhaps an unconscious strategy of equivocation, but the outright manufacture of his work, the sewing of fabrics, is rationalized in the extreme. Finally, there can be discerned a conceptual structure in all this, in which physical de-tumescence is countered by a magniloquence of scale and aggressiveness of color, as if the artistic organism is descending in vitality from some impossibly larger (larger, that is, than the level on which we live) intenseness of life. Or more modestly, it gives the impression of a poignant displacement, like that of the last wriggles of a fish, lying aghast out of the water.

So prescient is this somnolence—actually a disquieted somnolence—that it has led one critic of the artist to make some remarkable observations.

"Many of Claes Oldenburg's works" writes Ulf Linde (in the introduction to the catalogue of the Oldenburg exhibition in Stockholm's Moderna Museet, 1966), "are concerned with sleep. The most obvious, of course, is his *Bedroom Ensemble*. But he has also depicted the ante-chamber in which much of the ritual [of sleep] is enacted—the *Bathroom*; and the *Wall Switches* which produce darkness; the shirt hung on the back of a chair . . . the association of pillows, the most essential of all sleep-articles, is certainly meaningful . . . . During sleep, man is reduced to nature. This reduction also occurs in the soft sculptures. Oldenburg thus states in a new way the ancient problem of the relation of art to nature . . . . The artist operates in the area between consciousness and unconsciousness; so does the person preparing to fall asleep . . . it belongs to their roles. Consciousness opens towards unconsciousness, the non-natural towards nature . . ."

In this little analysis, which sweeps from simple iconography through a philosophy of nature to a more complex analogy between aesthetic effect and creative role, Linde surely penetrates the secret of Oldenburg's comatose objects. They are taken out of, or removed from "life," and are yet found to be preternaturally welling up with it—but life of a different sort, rioting in a stunned or dreaming matter. Such is the alibi of a sculpture whose real lack of animation is camouflaged by a kind of ostentatious trance. Oldenburg puts his bet on both the formal and psychological faces of the coin of modern art. Heads, the spectator becomes aware of new tensions and physical correlations in the outer world as he responds to those set up in the work; tails, he senses in the work some analogy to his own internal propensities, whether voluntary or not. The first might be illustrated by a haptic intuition of space being eased out, or "backed away" by the slow advance of one of creations; the second is exemplified by any number of things the artist himself says, "Sanding the wooden typewriter keys, I feel like a manicurist."

In such a light, he emerges as among the most protean of contemporary artists. Landscape, still-life, genre are all almost as ready to be executed as they are to be conceived. If Linde's simile about nature goes far, it can be pushed further still. Harris Rosenstein (in "Climbing Mt. Oldenburg," *Art News*, February, 1966) postulates, for instance, a tri-fold behavioral pattern relevant, he thinks, to Oldenburg, or rather, his various operations: "visceratonia (relaxation, love of food and sociability, extraversion of affect and conservation of energy); somatonia (the need for assertive muscular activity and expenditure of energy); cerebrotonia (suppression of both other tendencies in favor of hyperattentive consciousness)." Although it may be difficult to find a human temperament or sensibility that would comprehend all three drives, consecutively or simultaneously, they can, and I think, have, been given crypto-embodiment all at once in Oldenburg's sculpture. Or rather, it is enough to say that they do not seem mutually contradictory in his work. The Swedish rye-krisps cast countlessly in lead, the shoestring potatoes spilling Baroquely out of their bag; what are these if not psychosomatic hybridizations, oral-anal figurations that have gone berserk in cross-bred ecstasies? Yet the stifled gaiety of the results demonstrates that the artist is still in control—that his disconnections are expressively self-aware . . . intentional. For everything in Oldenburg takes the form of maximum, monstrous equivalence. Digestion equals excretion, city equals nature, frustration equals liberation, sub-conscious equals conscious, and lifelessness equals animism. Or, as he himself says, "Newspaper equals drawing. Food equals painting. Furniture equals sculpture." This glutton for experience seems incapable only of making such distinctions as those between activity, affect and object.

But it is a simulated incapacity. One is increasingly impressed by the canniness with which each of his forms and elements is fitted into a consistent vision. They become inevitable constituents, rather than gratuitous motifs, of a creative principle. That principle, as hinted at often by the artist, is the rehabilitation of falsity—that grin of glamour imposed upon any article intended for mass consumption. Monuments, architecture, furniture, food, products, magazines are all, for him, not so much stigmatized, as interestingly colored by being dolled up with bad faith. As the only ambitious Pop art sculptor, he seizes upon kitsch with that combination of alacrity and detachment found also in the painting of Lichtenstein and Rosenquist. Unlike them, however, "I am only one who persists in creating my own form and I always look bad by comparison with those who rely on commercial techniques or found objects." That is, the point of departure

for the painters is always the hard sell "routine" itself, from which they diverge in terms of structure, and greater pictorial intensity. Oldenburg, rather, runs a parallel to the mass-cult affect, without indulging in any of its routines. One does not sense in him, as with his colleagues, a burrowing within and subversion of a technique, all the while holding on to its particularities. On the contrary, he operates quite as if he were an independent creator, who generalizes all objects within view to such an extent that their preposterous inflation or glossy materials are the only recollections of the fraudulent claims that surround them in the real world. His art is a kind of spilled kitsch.

A real critical problem in Oldenburg is the extent to which one can call his outlook caricatural. If this issue comes up, it does so because it is hard for spectators to make a distinction between inflation and exaggeration. The former exists primarily as a factor of scale, the condition being that we get more of it then we expect or perhaps think reasonable in any one instance. The latter defines itself quite baldly as overstatement, with a concomitant moral evaluation. I make the further proviso that exaggeration must always be *of* something, that it demands an original or recollected object, a *donné*, by which to gauge it as an activity. Inflation is much the more inclusive process, and a more open one, for which reason Oldenburg would expectedly be drawn toward it. As the "distortion" of his pieces appears to be quite naturally the result of their construction, so too does their scale, innocent, in the deeper level, of any parody. It is not too far-fetched to think of his choice of scale as motivated by the same reasons as those of certain abstractionists, like Olitski (whose earlier, e.g. 1964, globule, or "cyclops eye" pictures are not dissimilar in content from Oldenburg). In both instances, immense areas are needed to convey the expressive extent of a sensation. That one does not accept an Oldenburg sculpture in the spirit, say, of a mammoth Ronald Bladen, that the one seems implausibly enlarged, and the other formally assimilated to its dimension, is the result of residual "appearances" in Oldenburg. Yet the identities of things are precisely what have diminished in importance for him over the years. Of his work, he can say that

its use of appearances, frankly and directly, is offered as an alternative to the elimination of appearances . . . which is not possible . . . but saying I hope more effectively that appearances are not what count. It is the forms that count . . . my art is the constant enemy of meaning . . . or you could say I have aimed at neutralizing meaning (which is unexpungable). . . . To eliminate appearances seems to me impossible . . . simply grasp them and show how little they mean.

These subtle remarks are not those of a Pop artist, still less would a caricaturist have uttered them. Instead of being

28

artifacts laughingly putting on airs, his objects are inconveniently large icons in which specificity of reference has diminished in proportion as their symbolic or talismanic value has increased. In principle, his pneumatic fantasies know no limit. Not for nothing has he plotted monuments of the future, such as a giant ironing board (for New York's lower east side), or a hot dog straddling Ellis Island, or a rabbit as big as the Plaza, that want to sum up the psyche of a local environment.

Appearances, then, have been pre-empted or relatively extruded by a kind of creative blatancy. Often it is even extremely difficult to grasp the original source of an image, like the water in the sink, or the ketchup on the french fries, or the blotches of "wet" tea in their rather prophylactic bag. Such presences have always been considered "impure," except by sculptors of the most degradedly illusionist bent. Without the slightest hint of illusion, and in the manner of a child who finds the most direct and clear equivalent of his sensation, Oldenburg gives bundled proxies of objects, with sewed-in or colored identification cues. Doubtless it is easy to lose one's bearing before images of liquidity that have now simplistically congealed. But more frequent has been the opposite situation, in which very coherent or complex structures, all with at least a nominal attention paid to their various parts, have lost their armature, and have viscously crumpled. The soft telephone and wall switches, the striking *Two Bats*, and above all, the *Airflow 5, Soft Engine with Fan and Transmission*, are examples. Their folds and lumps, their wrinkles and limp volumes, may evoke a response between compassion and ridicule, but they are, before that, objects challenging to recognize. As such, they initially produce a certain disorientation and anxiety, not least because they work against the fitting into previous mental patterns, or even simple naming. The relief which their lesser if familiar aspects bring, therefore, is only a qualified one. On this titular level, Oldenburg's sculptures "resist meaning," but they illuminate it, despite themselves, and in unexpected ways, on other levels. The *Light Switches*, for instance, are like giant nipples, and the handles of the models of the *Dormeyer Blenders* come to resemble incriminating phalluses. Involuntarily, it would seem, the erotic latency, or possibly the secondary sexual characteristics, of the most unassuming objects is played up in a vast recall of an American obsession (by now an old story in Pop art). Yet even this is incidental to the overarching curiosity of the artist to see what new form combinations arise whenever his "manufacturing" processes meet various object ideas. The results often invoke a pathos, without, however, the intrusion of the pathetic fallacy.

On the question of his attitude to American technology, Oldenburg appears just as complex and paradoxical as in the dissolution of his subject matter. An archaeologist of the future would find in his creations only the most lugubrious reflections of an industry and wealth that once dominated the world. In would still be possible to image a gleam of hopefulness from rusted chrome, but what could conceivably be said about paunchy canvas and kapok? In everything that we touch or use, the artist gives us a spectacle of an artifact that has been deserted by pride, an object, in fact, which shrinks away from the contours of its normal dignity. This is quite different from the numbed and intractable blocks of a Judd or Morris, whose immobility is affirmed rather than merely acknowledged, as in Oldenburg, and whose sense of impasse is a direct, if abstracted, formal, concomitant of a perception of the American scene. With his colleagues, whatever psychological relationship betwen objects and people have been divested of structure, with Oldenburg, the physical structure itself, of objects, has so melted away, that our connection with them has weirdly altered. And all this occurs in a context in which, as Oyvind Fahlstrom says (the catalog of the Stockholm show, 1966), objects are ecstatic fetishes to make better mothers, millionaires, prize-fighters, etc. Juxtaposed solely with their environment, Oldenburg's works act as a harsh social indictment. They subvert every premise upon which the cajoling, commercial culture is built; they are monumental bad news, emphasizing the unworkability and the obsolescence of machines, and, above all, a lack of control over matter that American society is pledged not to mention. Moreover, to the degree that we pride ourselves on our youth and virility, our progressive viewpoints and conceptual ordering of sense data and communications, he shows their outcomes to be floundering and spastic.

But in their own terms, these works are just as convincing as evidence of the view of the man-made as one more product of nature. Oppositions between the artificial and the natural, the inanimate and the organic, are dissolved in a metaphor in which loathing or acceptance of the object becomes irrelevant. With this option at our disposal, I don't see why we have to restrict our interpretation of Oldenburg to that of a commentator. Perhaps at point, one understands better his statement, "I am a technological liar." It means not merely that he undermines the manufacturing process for his own ends, but that he sees mechanical and natural regeneration to be indistinguishable—a view unacceptable to modern reasoning. Despite the humanoid quality of his sculptures, they represent an activity that is outside the human, or better, indifferent to the human. Even machines are the products of our imaginative and conceptual faculties. It does not matter that his fat toilets and foodstuffs fall under the same category: they *presume* to do otherwise. Such is the final lie. They symbolize forces that go on quite literally without us, even as they operate internally, biologically, one might say, to bring us low. Such an intuition of the presences in the world as devoid of mind (yet rife with change) is extraordinarily contemporary. Yet, unlike many assemblagists, Oldenburg does not present abandoned artifacts that have been, or will be subject to, natural action, like decay or oxidation, in an effort to force their poetry or picturesqueness. This is a sentimentalism absolutely foreign to his hardheaded outlook. Rather, he pricks the balloon of egocentrism in art (and secondarily all the human affairs that it may allude to), as if he did not even recognize that any sacrifice was implied. As a result, the experience of Oldenburg's work is colored, on the one hand, by a nightmare sense of conspiracy in which the spectator almost feels himself less organic than the creaturely squirming of all the dead things around him, while, on the other hand, he receives a premonition of psychological rebirth, in which there is extended to him the possibility of a liberation from the conceit of having to dominate all material circumstances.

Fahlstrom, in the essay mentioned before, says that an object that *gives in* is actually stronger than one which resists, for which reason it also permits the opportunity to be oneself in a new way. This dream is Oldenburg's ultimate, and perhaps not altogether deliberate, subject. Here it might be well to recapitulate the stages of inquiry with which it has been possible to formulate such a speculation. Initially, one saw how inappropriate was the concept of modernist sculpture as applied to three dimensional works of art which were soft. Their surrender to gravity introduced a pessimistic inflection into our sculptural empathies; and their acceptance of chance shapes contradicted formalist criteria. Within this anthropomorphic mode, in which, alone among his generation, he shows no prejudice for any shape over another, Claes Oldenburg establishes an equilibrium between extremes of density and the capacity of the work to change physical character. But he reveals himself to be such an astonishingly comprehensive artist, that he not only encompasses a metaphor of sleep in all his work, but establishes interconnected levels between psychosomatic states in our groping responses. Further still, he abolishes distinctions between classes of objects, like furniture and sculpture, and classes of activities, such as growth and degeneration. Preoccupied by social perceptions, he rehabilitates the public falseness of the American scene by the endorsing of synthetic materials like vinyl, and the aping of manufacturing methods in an ironically rationalized production outlook. Yet this has led, not to caricature, but to a kind of monstrous, yet strangely innocent, inflation of the scale in all his creations. If the actual appearance of the articles he purveys suffers a loss of identity, he merely sees an unexpected formal advantage in this new incoherence. Despite possibilities of viewing his work as a savage jibe at the technological order, it is more pertinent to consider his art as an amalgam of the idea of nature into the mechanistic gear and tempo of the industrial complex. That this dislocates our fondly held notion of human control over matter, introduces an hallucinating element into an aesthetic encounter that may slide downward into a sense of menace, or upward to a greater potentiality in accommodating ourselves to our own "nature." Always, one is struck by such extreme oscillations and blurrings of import in Oldenburg's sculpture, that its reference to slumber becomes the only appropriate domain in which, finally, to locate it. One of the finest analyses of sleep that I know occurs in the novel *Hadrian's Memoirs* by Marguerite Yourcenar, in which the emperor is made to say:

> I grant that the most perfect repose is almost necessarily a complement to love, that profound rest which is reflected in two bodies. But what interests me here is the specific mystery of sleep partaken of for itself, alone, the inevitable plunge each night by the naked man, solitary and unarmed, into an ocean where everything changes, the colors, the densities, and even the rhythms of breathing, and where we meet the dead. What reassures us about sleep is that we do come out of it, and come out of it unchanged, since some mysterious ban keeps us from bringing back with us in their true form even the remnants of our dreams. What also reassures us is that sleep heals us of fatigue, but heals us by the most radical means in arranging that we cease temporarily to exist. There, as elsewhere, the pleasure and the art consist in conscious surrender to that blissful unconsciousness, and in accepting to be slightly less strong, less light, less heavy and less definite than our waking selves.

Surely the voluptuousness which is the impression Oldenburg's sculpture finally leaves is a blend, though he would hardly have recognized it, of Hadrian's special pleasure and art.

---

[1]Since about 1959, he had shown a continuous affinity for the use of cloth and paper as sculptural materials. For the execution of some "silly" cloth doll, or toy-like pieces, sewing first became necessary about this time. And, of course, cloth, crumpled and spattered, was one of the major constituents of properties in Oldenburg's celebrated early happenings. Later, in 1961-62, he began to employ cloth dipped and wrinkled in plaster, that is to say, "stiffened," on chicken wire armatures, to surface rather bumptious creations that had something in common with the aesthetics of poverty and street detritus which also characterized the work of his fellow artists at the Reuben Gallery, Lucas Samaras and George Segal. Eventually, Oldenburg became interested in a kind of upholstering initiated by the necessity to provide internal support for a rather heavy duck canvas integument. The original solution was newspaper wadding, but, in 1962, he switched to kapok as a more effective ingredient for his purposes. During his association with the Green Gallery, he was using cloth, coated with tempera (*Hamburger*, etc.), but, finding this too matte in effect, he began coating the cloth with enamel, and finally introduced vinyl, which became, in its shininess and softness, the material that he has most favored in the last four years. The first vinyl piece was the *Telephone*, followed by the *BLT*. Oldenburg's wife, Pat, has become the ever more present, and indispensable, devil's seamstress for this enterprise.

As Painting is to Sculpture: A Changing Ratio

Lucy R. Lippard

> *Ad Reinhardt: "A definition of sculpture: something you bump into when you back up to look at a painting."*

The relationship between two- and three-dimensional art has changed radically over the last few years, and not only because color has been broadly reintroduced into sculpture during that time. At the moment, there is considerably more interest in sculpture than in painting simply because there seems to be more interesting sculpture than painting being made. Formally and non-formally oriented sculptors are now exploring aesthetic areas either exhausted or rejected by painters over the last half century. Sculpture has long been considered a more or less subsidiary art, following painting's innovations and docilely translating them into three-dimensional versions. When one categorized sculpture, one did so, awkwardly and often ridiculously, in the context of painting; there has been Cubist sculpture, Abstract Expressionist sculpture, even "hard-edge sculpture" and "painterly sculpture." Now the relationship is more complex. In several important ways, sculpture is gaining its independence from painting and painting, in turn, frequently finds itself the follower. "Structural painting" borrows from primary structures. In the present exchange and occasional confusion between painting and sculpture and the structural "third stream" (which includes some shaped canvases), three interacting points seem particularly pertinent: the relationship of painting and sculpture as physical objects, as vehicles for formal or sensuous advance, and as vehicles for color.

Although non-representational painting has progressively eliminated all attributes not consistent with its imposed flat, rectangular surface, the result of this total emphasis on two-dimensionality has been, paradoxically, a concomitant emphasis on painting as three-dimensional object, a fact leading directly to sculpture. With Neo-plasticism in the Twenties and Thirties, this progression had already reached the point where sculpture could not effectively follow painting, for while Cubist sculpture could treat directly the volumes that Cubist painting's shifting planes attempted to subdue, there was little that Neo-plastic sculpture could achieve within the de Stijl and Bauhaus programs that could not be better achieved in painting, architecture or design. It could only echo painting's colored, asymmetrical surfaces. While a handful of Suprematist and Constructivist sculptors managed to escape briefly these painting-regulated strictures, their accomplishments, though important, were few and isolated. Geometric sculpture from then on was a pallid reflection of geometric painting. In the early Sixties, this situation surfaced again, so to speak, but under entirely different conditions, and in America, where younger artists had reason to be overwhelmed and dissatisfied by the successes, dominance and inexorable progression of painting over a twenty year period. There was, and is, no Movement, nor even much agreement between the artists on what they are doing; it is a general phenomenon that a good many painters began to "escape" to sculpture, though their lack of sculptural habits and training made the results peculiarly non-sculptural in effect. In all probability, the possibilities of painting per se only *seem* limited at this time, but this notion is prevalent enough to urge many artists into three dimensions.

Mark Rothko's insistence upon the painting as an independent object in the early Fifties, bolstered by his habit or making stretchers deeper than usual, painting around the side edges, and dispensing with frame and stripping, was part of this development. The painting stood away from the wall as a separate entity, free of the transitional and taming agent of frame to isolate pictured reality from everyday reality. With others of his generation, notably Pollock, Newman and Still, he also used large size and scale to force a picture's "presence" to dominate the space in which it was hung. Ad Reinhardt's black rectangles and stringently rejective program further contributed to the process in which painting became more than a decoration, illustration or conversation piece. The break away from easel painting provoked a new sculpture as well, for the great self-consciousness and growing self-assurance of the New York School's heroic period permitted freedom of scale and the consequent conceptual freedom to revise conventional definitions of sculpture as well as painting. From around 1960, this attitude was implemented by a growing body of new sculptural directions.

The notion of the painting as object has two interpretations. First as a specific surface, but without connotations of volume and physicality, second as an actual three-dimensional thing. Both contributed to the idea of a non-sculptural sculpture, that is, a sculpture which rejects the history of sculpture as precedent in favor of the history of painting, and at times, of architecture and engineering. The notion of the sculpture as object is equally equivocal. Until recently, the "object" implied an additive, Dada or Surrealist or assemblage work made of non-traditional materials or found items. Structures, or as Don Judd has called a broader grouping—"specific objects"—are, on the other hand, simple, single or strictly repetitive, serial or modular, with a quality of inertia and apparent (superficial) abdication of the transforming powers of art. In this context, the object or objectness is directly opposed to the additive premise on which most post-Cubist works are founded. But its connotations, like those of the Dada object, are non-sculptural and even anti-sculptural. In that many of the artists are former painters who have rejected painting, this is also an anti-painting idiom, though most of these artists are far more interested in recent painting than in recent sculpture. For all the magnitude of David Smith's achievement, and his historical importance as the only major American sculptor to emerge since the war, the extent of his influence on the current young generation has been much overstated. His polychromed *Zigs* as well as his *Cubis* are less relevant to recent developments than to the tradition preceding him; he can be seen as the culmination of an area of post-Cubist sculpture, though an area which presents suggestions for further, if minor developments.

Many of Smith's apparent successors were not influenced by him so much as they were subjected to the same influences he was—namely New York School painting and that of the younger "color painters." Anthony Caro knew Noland and Olitski as well as Smith at Bennington; Weinrib, Doyle, di Suvero, and a somewhat older group, reached artistic maturity in the late Fifties, when Abstract Expressionism and related idioms were at their exposure peak. Di Suvero's debt is to Kline, and De Kooning's broad color swatches have appeared in many sculptural guises. Similarly, the concurrent rejuvenation of the collage medium, which also dealt with overlapping planes and flat irregular patches of color was important to American sculptors in the Fifties just as it had been years before to Picasso, Gonzalez and the ensuing line of "junk sculptors."[1] A parallel pictorial mainstream—the ideographic image—was translated into the open but increasingly rigorous sculpture of the Fifties and at the same time found its way into Sugarman's, Weinrib's and Doyle's more experimental "space sculpture" of the early Sixties, which has, in turn, had successors. Still another contribution of the New York School—Newman's quasi-geometric single images—was later to become important to Don Judd and Robert Morris.

Around 1963, the structurists and structural painters actually paralleled each other's efforts to advance formally with their chosen means. Frank Stella's use of a very deep stretcher and "deductively" shaped supports, Dan Flavin's lighted "icon" boxes, Ronald Bladen's flat forms projecting from panels, Donald Judd's ribbed and striated reliefs and Richard Smith's canvas constructions all demonstrated a preoccupation with expanding the dimensions and formal possibilities of painting, or wall-hung pieces. The fact that all but Stella further approached or moved into free-standing structures and all but Stella and Smith are now considered sculptors is significant. Perhaps the most important aspect of the increasing attraction of sculpture today is its apparent potential as a vehicle of advance—both formal and evocative, or sensuous. This comprises its most crucial relationship to painting, for it is only with the avant-garde's

decreasing interest in painting that sculpture has come to the fore. This is a very literal period. Sculpture, existing in real space and physically autonomous is *realer* than painting. Yet sculpture also has its own peculiar kinds of illusionism which it has not, like painting, had to give up in the interest of fidelity to medium. For instance, a laquered wooden surface disguises the color and texture of wood, but retains a mellowness characteristic of wood, whereas a hard, shiny, enameled wooden surface disguises wood to the point of making it an illusion of metal. A shiny, reflecting metal surface gives the illusion of insubstantiality or transparency by reflecting its surroundings, and a burnished metal surface like that of David Smith's *Cubis* can give the illusion of several atmospheric depths as well as asserting the surface. By painting their materials, whether masonite, wood, steel, plaster, most abstract and some figurative sculptors are trying to avoid the connotations of the materials—naturalistic or industrial or academic—and give the illusion of something autonomous and new in itself without reference to its antecedents—physical or historical.

Smith himself was not averse to painting his sculptures in much the same manner that one might paint a canvas. His *Zigs* often combine strong sculptural form with a frontal, centralized image, polychromy, and even brushwork that was frankly allied to painting. It was only Smith's knowledge of sculpture which kept some of them from looking like one-image painting peeled off the wall. One-image painting, in turn, could be said to imitate (unconsciously) the singleness and self-sufficiency of sculpture; when Barnett Newman made an exaggeratedly tall, thin monochrome painting as well as bronze sculptures out of the stripe which divides all his canvases, he was admitting in effect that the stripe was the unit by which his painting existed, denying, at least temporarily, the importance of that stripe's placement on the supporting surface. There has been other single-image planar sculpture (structures are generally imageless), such as Ellsworth Kelly's flat monochrome shapes which, like Newman's stripes, seem to have been freed from their canvas grounds to exist rather precariously in three dimensions. The "thin" idiom itself, in more hierarchal form, can be traced to Calder's stabiles and perhaps to Matisse's late cut-outs. Such works could be said to mimic and even parody the necessary flatness of a painted image by their own unnecessary flatness. The kind of color Kelly uses, for instance, so sharp and positive in a painting when juxtaposed against another color or the white of a wall, becomes far more ambiguous when isolated in actual space.

For that matter, very little of the new sculpture—from assemblage to "space sculpture" to structures—is anything but ambiguous as a vehicle for color, though the effectiveness of color should not be underrated. Color in sculpture

[1]See Clement Greenberg, "The New Sculpture" and "Modernist Sculpture, Its Pictorial Past," *Art and Culture*, Beacon, Boston, 1961, pp. 139-145, 158-163.

is more difficult to work with than color in painting because so many factors must be taken into consideration. It is also more difficult to assess from a critical point of view. Whereas color in painting can be judged within a relatively understood system of theory or experience, such a system, fortunately, is not yet established for sculpture. No matter how large a painting is, the surface can be taken at a glance, and while the form and color action may be extremely subtle and engender different effects after different viewing times, it can be perceived initially as a unity. A sculpture must hold its own in space and from different angles; color must be so thoroughly controlled that it is both absorbed by and heightens the purpose (formal or psychological) of the sculpture itself. Because of this, and because color had largely disappeared from sculpture for so long, its development is in a much earlier stage.

The quite sudden prevalence of color in sculpture occurred when color in painting was at a high point of brilliance and dominance. The Whitney Museum Annual of December, 1964, devoted to sculpture, reflected this trend and may even have been influential, for the non-colored (naturally colored) sculptures, with some exceptions, looked dull and obsolete in the company of brightly painted pieces which were of equal aesthetic quality. In the heyday of Hard-edge and Pop and Op art, assertiveness and aggression were valued effects; colored sculpture could hold its own with painting. Since that time, sculptors' use of color has rapidly become more sophisticated and recently has paralleled the preoccupation of certain structural paintings with an "off-color"—greyed, neutral, metallic, sweet tones in preference to the extreme brilliance and decorative obviousness of the primary hues. An initial enchantment with hit or miss application of any old bright color gave way to a more serious consideration of the formal role color could play. It is used illusionistically to disperse and minimize volume, to separate shapes in space, making heavy forms seem weightless, light ones heavy, near forms farther away and far ones closer. And it is used to unify, to make a form more "real," isolating it from the environment and asserting the piece as a self-contained whole. Yet unless the material is colored to begin with, like certain plastics, color is applied after form and too often comprises an arbitrary "envelope" apparently chosen for neither a metaphorical nor a formal reason, but merely as an attracting, eye-catching device. Clement Greenberg's complaint about Anthony Caro's color could be applied to any number of other sculptors: "I know of no piece of his, not even an unsuccessful one, that does not transcend its color, or whose specific color or combination of colors does not detract from the quality of the whole (especially when there is more than one color). In every case I have the impression that the color is aesthetically (as well as literally) provi-

sional—that it can be changed at will without affecting quality."[2]

Monochromatic color especially tends to represent an abdication of its formal positive virtues, as well as a rejection of aspects of painting carried over to sculpture. The planar surfaces of the structurists are not in any sense surfaces for decoration, though other sculptors, including David Smith, Kenneth Price and Robert Hudson, have painted images on their surfaces either to stress or to contradict the underlying forms. John McCracken is perhaps the only structurist for whom surfaces are literally vehicles for color, though Judd has made isolated pieces of which this is true. The problems inherent in a polychromed object are quite different from those of monochrome. At best a polychrome sculpture is colored in such a specific way that it approaches the pictorial; justice of form and color are inseparable from each other. Price, for instance, is able to color relatively small and similar forms so that each is invested with a highly particular aura—too detached to call a mood, but certainly of some psychological importance. An ovoid of one red seems to *mean* something different from a slightly dissimilar ovoid of a slightly dissimilar red. Of course assemblagist, figurative, or abstract post-Surrealist sculptors use color in necessarily more specific manner than the formalists. The fact that a recognizable object referential image is its "natural" color, or not, has to be important, whereas in wholly abstract sculpture, color has more of a chance of standing for its own properties. The question of meaning in non-objective art is intricately involved with the question of color, and while this aspect remains to be clarified both from the angles of achievement and criticism, the psychological effects are important even when unintended.

Color in painting is always added color; in sculpture it can be inherent in the material. Sidney Geist has asked some basic questions about this aspect: "Does all sculpture, by virtue of being material, have color? Does a touch of color or the use of subtle or quiet color qualify for the title of colored sculpture? Is a sculpture painted all blue more 'colored' than a white marble?"[3] Obviously touches of color or quiet color do qualify and are often more important to the work than a large area or bright hue. Yet naturally colored traditional materials such as wood, bronze, marble, stone, no matter how much color they may provide, would not make colored sculpture in the strict sense, partially because of their long acceptance and consequent low level of visibility, but mainly because other characteristics of these materials, such as grain,

[2]Clement Greenberg, "Anthony Caro," *Arts Yearbook*, no. 8, 1965, pp. 106-109.
[3]Sidney Geist, "Color It Sculpture," *Arts Yearbook*, no. 8, 1965, pp. 91-98.

reflectiveness, surface, texture, are likely to be more important than their color. Thus a sculpture *painted* gray is more "colored" than a gray stone sculpture because the color is a positive, added factor, an agent of change that disguises or regulates all other properties of the material. A good many new materials such as opaque and translucent plastics, vinyl, neon and fluorescent light, cloth synthetic rubbers, have color qualities that are entirely new and therefore dominate their other properties, though here too, one is eventually aware of the material *qua* material as much or more than one is aware of its color. For this reason, they are difficult to manipulate and control on a formal basis, lending themselves more aptly to evocative or sensuous goals. The color of Oldenburg's vinyl objects is far less important to the result than the color of his painted plasters were.

As new materials are tested and found viable, the kind of color opens to sculpture expands and is in turn often picked up by painting. Metal-flecked, day-glo and other commercial paints, sprayed color, professional "fabrication" and color application, garish Pop derived hues, are examples of this feedback. The constant introduction of new media is one reason that sculpture seems to bear more possibilities for originality than painting at the moment, even in the nonformalist idioms to which "advance" is beside the point. These materials liberate forms previously "used up" in painting and traditional sculpture. A vinyl biomorph is an entirely different sight and experience than approximately the same biomorph in marble by Arp, or in paint by Gorky. Every object employing labyrinthine wires, threads, ropes, all-over linear patterns can be tenuously traced to Pollock and therefore accused of being unoriginal.[4] However, this attitude seems unnecessarily exclusive, and finally invalid. Exact use of color alone, as evidenced in Kenneth Price's work, transforms shapes previously used by Brancusi and Arp into something new, just as Sol LeWitt's structural frameworks of a square within a square bear no visual resemblance to Albers' *Homage to the Square* paintings, nor Bruce Nauman's random, rubbery shapes to Masson's automatism. Three-dimensional objects can, I believe, return to the vocabulary of previous painting and sculpture and, by changing the syntax and accents, more fully explore avenues exhausted in two dimensions or conventional materials and scale, without risk of being unoriginal or reactionary.

Bagless Funk*

James Monte

Since the mid-Forties, partially in New York but more emphatically in the San Francisco Bay Area, an attempt, perhaps only partially conscious, has been made to meld into a single expression two sensibilities antagonistic in origin and in intention. The first is the mythic, abstract surrealism of Clyfford Still and Mark Rothko, especially as it has filtered through the work of Frank Lobdell, Jack Jefferson and Julius Hatofsky, among others. The second is the funky, Dadaistic attitude, with its vestiges of social protest and its predilection for art as action or event as well as art as object.

Documentation of the early stages of the evolution of this synthesis, especially in the Bay Area, is fragmentary, but it would appear that artists like Clay Spohn and Hassel Smith were key figures in the early stages. Spohn created bizarre assemblages with banal materials, and the tradition was helped along with the almost incomprehensible (at the time) early work of Wally Hedrick and Bruce Conner. The undiluted version of the tradition which their work represents currently finds expression in the work of James Melchert and Dennis Oppenheim. Another Bay Area figure whose art has consistently struggled to combine the two sensibilities is Jeremy Anderson.

Anderson's earliest efforts in the middle and late Forties follow the direction of Alberto Giacometti's surrealist works. Anderson's fragile cage forms of plaster or cement over metal armature continue the mythic Surrealist tradition and, as new materials, such as redwood and bronze, are added to his sculptural repertory, new ideas are pursued. The visual rhetoric is obliquely literary and often includes whimsical or poetic sentences carved into the redwood material. Emblems appear and disappear. Totems carved and doweled into the main mass of wood give the spectator the curious space and scale relationship sometimes found in Giacometti and often found in De Chirico's early paintings. A fastidiously funky quality grows in Anderson's work even to the present moment.

Jeremy Anderson's accomplishments, as one of the very few who bridged the gap in the Bay Area between Adeline Kent and Robert Howard's generation of thoroughly modernist sculptors remains, as yet, both underrated and misunderstood.

The blending of mythic signs and symbols to a Dadaist stance occurs in William Geis' sculpture. Highly personal forms coming out of Clyfford Still's legacy are blended with unexpected polychrome base areas. Geis' forbidding plaster shapes, recalling Gothic Beasties, have a compelling mystical aura. The mystical and irreverent are combined as the plaster shapes are situated on rectangular environments gaudily painted and in some cases overlaid

---

[4]As did Hilton Kramer in the *New York Times*, Sunday, September 25, 1966.

*Bagless Funk—Funk is used throughout this writing as it is used by jazz musicians i.e. a sound or a look that is unsophisticated, powerful and draws deeply on folk tradition.

with black velour. Because of the dualism in the pieces one is tempted to extemporize on the giddy romanticism of the pieces.

Another artist, akin to Anderson in his free-wheeling use of materials, forms and color and who has had a powerful impact on young sculptors throughout the United States is H. C. Westermann. Perhaps more than any single American sculptor working today, Westermann's multi-directional body of work presents younger artists with a multitude of clues about what is possible in sculpture today. Essentially Westermann's pieces are three-dimensional repositories of ideas. To explain further one must begin by noting that sculptural form as an end product in his work is not what he wants or achieves. Westermann employs a hobbyist's attitude about making *things*. A Westermann placed next to an Arp bronze creates an uneasy tension, because the Arp fulfills the requirements of a sculptural tradition extending from the Hellenistic Greek artists to the present. Westermann, on the other hand, refuses *any* high art tradition, but rather draws heavily from the parallel artifact cultures which throughout recorded history have been present if not always accounted for. Westermann has made art out of the clumsy aspects of twentieth century American culture. His bent cylindrical pieces with an all-over marbling of their painted surfaces pre-figure Pop art and draw more subtly on banal sources. Westermann's poker-faced exploitation of the cheapest vinyl tile design is altogether in keeping with Lichtenstein's comic book iconography. And yet if a hierarchy of subject matter were set up, Lichtenstein's contemptible sources seem heroic next to Westermann's tile designs, which are *beneath* contempt and therefore virtually invisible. So, in a sense, Westermann renders visible what everyone knows is around yet refuses to acknowledge because it is simply too distressing.

William Wiley's sculpture is closely related to Westermann's curious oeuvre. Wiley, at 29, is a younger artist than Westermann and arrived at sculpture through painting. Besides painting and sculpture he makes prints, but uses a Verifax office copying machine rather than the traditional printing methods.

The pyramid pieces chosen for this exhibition represent a body of work largely completed in 1964. They can be called typical in the sense that they represent Wiley in a working posture best termed sequential. Wiley has painted triangles in series, often using the form to structure a given painting. The pyramid shapes grow out of a concern for tightly delineated triangles set within heavily painted expressionist surfaces. A desire to explore a shape or series of shapes again and again in two dimensions and carry the idea into the palpable space of the third dimension has been and is a major concern of Wiley's artistic life.

Since his auspicious student work in painting and graphics Wiley has become increasingly aware of the need to explore new avenues of expression at the expense of careerist ambitions. His work has, out of necessity, been made in recent years of ephemeral materials since he has tried to maintain an essentially painterly speed in making sculptural objects.

Wiley's dilemma is shared to some extent by Agostini, Nauman and Harris, all of whom remain artistically tense in the face of a difficult choice. These three artists want to maintain the speed that a painter has in terms of changing a picture and yet remain object makers. Bruce Nauman's sculpture, like William Wiley's, is made for the most part of fragile plastics, cardboard or fabrics. His reductive shapes are usually loosely crafted and create an intellectual as well as visual anomaly because they deviate from what one has quickly come to expect in reductive post-constructivist sculpture. Nauman has chosen the sculptural sketch and elevated it to the highest position within his work. This in itself is not so curious but within the tradition of the new sculpture his position is heretical. Nauman's intellectual place in American sculpture is curious because he singlehandedly created the first viable mutation of the new structural American sculpture.

Paul Harris, another of the sculptors chosen for the exhibition, remains difficult to characterize in the normal, "he-comes-out-of-so-and-so," or such-and-such a tradition. When his upholstered women emerge from their upholstered plinth chairs the viewer experiences a jerky, visual dislocation. The chintz material used to cover the figures and the chairs unifies each piece as an ensemble. Usually Harris paints the various segments of chairs, limbs, clothing, shoes, etc., to give the viewer a better opportunity to differentiate between them. In so doing, he deliberately permits a certain feckless nonchalance to permeate the finished pieces. By grouping four or five pieces together, a tableau effect is created making one acutely aware of the multiplicity of levels on which Harris' work affects the onlooker.

Of all the sculptors working in the United States today, Claes Oldenburg is the most persuasive in turning younger artists' heads. An object maker who literally takes the stuffing out of depicted solids, he relentlessly pursues an ever-widening area of sculptural endeavor, reminding one of the lyrics in a Bob Dylan song, ". . . she's an artist and she don't look back . ." His maddeningly funny variations on the wall telephone characterize his transvestite approach to sculpture. The solid vinyl telephone becomes a canvas telephone which becomes a soft vinyl telephone and so on. His art emotionally parallels the slapstick comic Buster Keaton who could bring both pathos and outrageous humor simultaneously to the fore.

Since 1962 with the naming of a widespread sensibility, now called Pop, it has become evident that the power of a catchword, phrase or slogan will stick and even influence the working habits of artists who should know better. Of all the sculptors in the show only Claes Oldenburg, George Segal, Marisol, and Paul Harris fit, however uncomfortably, into the Pop category. The works of Peter Agostini, William Wiley, Frank Gallo and H. C. Westermann pre-date the Pop ascendance and, in the case of Westermann and Agostini, actually jelled a number of key ideas that were later incorporated into much Pop painting and sculpture. Agostini's balloons, rubber balls, paper cups and inner tube molds used for casting his plaster pieces pre-date by years the common use of the common object for uncommon ends. The blatant *thereness* of Pop imagery actually obscured the contribution of such artists whose work didn't fit the orthodox confines of Pop.

Amy Goldin in an extremely useful article on Dada and its present day usage in American art says:

> The Dadaists, painters, poets and intellectuals spelled out the failure of "the Great Tradition" and articulated the conditions that art must meet in order to be modern. The demand for novelty is a part of the aesthetic tradition that the Dadaists left for us. It has been in force for fifty years, and there is no excuse for the continued critical failure to recognize its existence and to discriminate between contemporary theory, style and fashion. Once the Dadaist accomplishment is understood we may gain a view of the past which does not isolate the present in a limbo of anxiety.... Artists had repudiated the claims of their patrons before, but they did so in the name of God or nature; the Dadaists, repudiating everything quite indiscriminately, clung only to the practice of art (some of them) and the artistic relevance of power—that is, the idea that art that doesn't *do* something to its audience is a failure. This very up to date, extreme and unreasonable demand on art was first articulated by the Dadaists.[1]

If Miss Goldin's thesis is correct, the Dada legacy is everywhere, not only in obvious cases such as the work of Edward Kienholz or Bruce Conner but in the paintings of Pollock and De Kooning as well as in the wrenching tonalities of a Poons abstraction. There hasn't been a dilution of Dada or Dada gestures, rather there has been a widespread acceptance of Dada theory and practice in the context of other received ideas from art history such as Expressionism, Fauvism, Surrealism and so on. To further understand the rich vein younger American artists are mining at the present moment, one can look to such varied cultural phenomena as custom automobile metal workers with their half-naïve, half-sophisticated designs. Closely allied are the folk-engineers who design and build drag racing machines which perform at fantastic speeds in standing quarter mile racing events. The design criteria for these machines is radically functional with emphasis on light construction and rearward distribution of essential weight. These cars are usually fitted out with unique paint jobs and other body and chassis decorations, making European Grand Prix and Sports machines appear inhibited and stuffy by comparison. This tradition of unique workmanship of the highest standards of craftsmanship lavished on the smallest details of painting and construction, has had a powerful impact on young artists, especially those having contact with the West Coast.

It must be remembered that one of the main forces of new art is the availability of new materials with which to make it. The do-it-yourself tradition has had a powerful primary impact on the sculptors of the United States. The availability of the local lumberyard, scrap dealer or even hardware store is a new phenomenon in European countries. The European artist is not totally handicapped on an imaginative level, but his imagination is seriously limited by the materials available to him. The United States, blessed or cursed with a plethora of castoff objects of everyday usage such as clothing, furniture, auto parts and used building materials, also has an entire range of government surplus components of the most complex and diverse nature. As one sculptor said recently, "Why, hell, the government surplus stores are more valuable to me than any federal sponsorship of the arts could ever dream of being."

So, in a sense, in America there is a ready-made Dada climate complete in every way except on the ideological level. The artistic heritage in America has been further shaped by a traditionally anti-conceptual and at times anti-intellectual climate radically different from that of the self-consciously grouped Europeans whose articulate manifestos ring through the first half of the twentieth century. In contrast, the American artist shares the deep suspicion of dialectics and ideology so much a part of Anglo-American thinking in religion, art and politics.

A further spiritual boost in American art is supplied by the ambience surrounding the unique musical developments in the United States since the eighteenth century. As the folk singer, Pete Seeger, has pointed out, the development of a new musical form came into being when the traditional Irish ballads were re-made and crossed with West African rhythms. The resultant combinations since the earliest phases of American history have been important in terms of Western musicology, but perhaps more importantly have helped shape attitudes, behavior and intuitive impulses of more than six generations of Americans.

The contemporary soul sound presents the young person with a whole mode of personal identification completely outside the middle class value system in the

---

[1] "Dada Legacy," *Arts*, vol. 39, September 1965, p. 26.

United States. As a microcosmic world replete with its own set of saints, martyrs, heroes and heritage, this demi-monde affects millions of people throughout the world. It is quite natural, in fact inevitable, that an ever-growing number of artists should feel an affinity with such a rich spiritual force as an alternative to the vacuity to be found in the materialist Western societies, not to mention the artificially vised-in cultures of the Neo-Byzantine Eastern European states.

Post-Cubist Sculpture

Barbara Rose

"After cubism, who cares about form? It's planes."
—David Smith, in an interview with Katharine Kuh

One way of seeing the best new sculpture is in its relationship to David Smith's work. Smith's late work seems to have opened avenues for exploration as rich as those originally unlocked by Gonzalez and Picasso, which Smith himself explored. In several important respects, the best new sculpture either continues Smith's researches or finds its identity in reaction to his work. All of it follows Smith in its close rapport with painting, interest in industrial materials and techniques, and formal clarity. One must insist on Smith's seminal influence because his was the only sculptural genius of the Abstract Expressionist generation; hence he was the only one capable of generating work which would inform a new generation of sculptors.

Although his interpretation of the technique of "drawing in air" with welded metal rods relates Smith to the gestural aspect of Abstract Expressionism, Smith was the first sculptor to understand the potential meaning of Post-Painterly Abstraction for sculpture. The structural emphasis in Post-Painterly Abstraction, particularly as it was manifested in the intuitive geometry of Smith's friend, Kenneth Noland, provided Smith with a fresh basis for a broad, monumental sculptural style. In his last three series, the *Voltri-Bolton*, *Zig*, and *Cubi* series, Smith made sculpture that went beyond Cubism in scale, directness, clarity of execution, and use of color. From that point on, his was a mark that the most ambitious young sculptors had to either challenge or accept; in either event it was a mark they were forced to acknowledge, in one way or another, in all future work.

At the recent exhibition of Primary Structures at the Jewish Museum, where many examples of the best new sculpture were shown, the works of Anthony Caro and Tony Smith flanked the entrance like twin heralds of the exhibition inside. Their position as "elder statesmen" of the new sculpture seems entirely justified. Such a statement must be modified, however, by pointing out that Caro's influence on a whole generation of younger British sculptors such as Philip King, Isaac Witkin, Michael Bolus, David Annesley and Derek Woodham, a number of whom studied with him, is greater than any direct influence Tony Smith may have had on younger American sculptors. This is so because the latter's reputation, though substantial, was mostly an underground, word-of-mouth phenomenon because his work was not shown in New York. Only recently have photographs and exhibitions begun to fill out the picture. Thus, it is perhaps more accurate to see the development of single-image *gestalt* sculpture as parallel with, rather than deriving from Tony Smith's work in a similar vein.

It is mainly in their view of the importance of the plane that British sculpture and the new American work divide. For the English sculptors, including Caro, the plane remains the decisive factor, and open, additive, frequently linear form the dominant mode of composition. In this way they are the executors of David Smith's legacy, rather than its challengers. This is by no means to minimize the originality of Caro's statement; for Caro, in the largeness and depth of his vision has come closer than anyone to assuming Smith's mantle. The burden of expression in Caro's work, as Michael Fried has pointed out, resides in his ability to use gesture abstractly to convey feeling. In so doing he charges the relationship of individual members to each other and to the body of the work with abstract analogues of tension, drama, and poignancy. Without recourse to symbolism, these works managed to sustain a level of lyric intensity which the straightforwardness of their forms might seem to belie.

Like David Smith, Caro has had special success in using standard structural parts (in Caro's case, mostly rods, girders and I-beams) with a direct and matter-of-fact objectivity that keeps the work happily free from triteness or sentimentality. Again like Smith, Caro paints his metal constructions. Caro's use of color, however, is perhaps more successful than Smith's because it seems more necessary to the expressiveness of the work, and less an applied finish. In this respect, Caro has been uniquely able to choose colors of a certain weight and density that seem appropriate to sculpture, and, for reasons I find hard to qualify, less obviously pictorial than the snappier hues of his younger colleagues. Wisely restricting himself to one unifying color per work, Caro integrates color with structure rather than complicating or weakening his statement by superimposing pattern on form.

One of the basic ways Caro's work is unlike David Smith's is in its horizontal orientation. Often hugging the earth, or twisting and turning abruptly to cover a large territory, Caro's recent works achieve a kind of openness and free flow in sculpture the Cubists never even dreamed of. Most of Smith's late works, on the other hand, were essentially verticals, their uprightness underlining their latent anthropomorphism.

As the exhibition at the Jewish Museum, which lumped all of the new sculpture together, proved, certain common denominators exist which link British and American sculpture today. Large scale, free use of geometry, and rejection of anthropomorphism and alusive or symbolic content are the three major similarities one may discern. Beyond this, there are more differences than similarities. As opposed to the openness and flow, the pictorial effects, and the dependence on the function of plane of English sculpture, young American sculptors have developed a kind of three-dimensional structure that challenges

exactly these qualities. Replacing the flat plane with the closed volume and the blocky mass, sculptors like Don Judd, Robert Morris, Ronald Bladen, John McCracken, and Robert Grosvenor are challenging the basis of the Cubist aesthetic in sculpture. As they see it, the guiding principle of Cubist composition was the hierarchical ordering of parts. Rejecting the relational basis of Cubism, they are making works which are integral *gestalts*: bold, aggressive, volumetric structures which demand to be seen all at once, as a single image.

Large scale and non-relational composition are principles generalized from recent American painting, specifically the paintings of Pollock and Newman. Now that Tony Smith's work has become public, one can see how his single-image sculpture is a conception very much related to Pollock's all-over paintings and Newman's wholistic chromatic abstractions. It is not surprising that Smith's thinking should have taken such a turn at an early date since he was personally close to both Pollock and Newman. The arrival at a similarly wholistic conception of sculpture based on the formal innovations of Pollock and Newman by the group of young artists variously referred to as "minimal" or "reductive" or "ABC" seems coincidental, rather than dependent on Smith in any way. Although chronologically Smith's work preceded the new work, his influence could scarcely have been felt since the work itself was not known. Its appearance at this time seems less an historic precedent than a kind of mutual validation of similar solutions independently arrived at. I should, however, hasten to add that the little I've seen of Smith's work seems to me qualitatively superior to most if not all of "primary structures" by younger artists.

Even if one cannot point to Tony Smith directly as a precursor of "primary structures" or single *gestalt* sculpture, one can still at this juncture disengage its roots from the complex tangle of recent art history. Not a movement (any more, for example, than Pop art was to begin with), the new sculpture has only recently coalesced—particularly since the Jewish Museum show focussed on it as a general development—into some kind of coherent, recognizable sculptural style about which certain generalizations can be made. Originally, its intensions appeared to be negative and subversive; recently, however, it seems to be more positive and constructive in its approach as it gains adherents.

The new sculpture arose out of two dissatisfactions: one with painting and the other with Cubist aesthetics. It represents, on the one hand, a rejection of the necessarily illusionistic space of painting, and on the other, a rejection of Cubist composition which depends on the relationship and subordination of parts to a whole. After painting had become as flat as possible, in the work, for example, of Kenneth Noland and Frank Stella, there was nowhere to move except laterally toward the perimeter or forward into three-dimensional space. By the late Fifties, Stella and Noland had chosen to do the first in laterally expanding concentric bands and rings, whereas others, notably Rauschenberg and Johns, began doing the second by affixing objects to the surface of paintings, allowing them to spill out into three-dimensional space. In addition, "specific objects"—Don Judd's term for three-dimensional objects which are not precisely painting or sculpture—began to be made. These included works by Rauschenberg, Johns, Oldenburg, and Bontecou. Of primary importance in this context were Johns' beer cans and Oldenburg's colossal food and clothing.

Since Cubism, painters have been increasingly preoccupied with asserting the literal character of the painting surface, i.e., that it is two-dimensional. This assertation made painting, which now corresponded more closely to real experience, more actual and concrete. Pursuing this issue to its logical conclusion, in 1960 Frank Stella notched the corners and cut out the center of a series of aluminum paintings in order to squeeze out any remaining illusionistic depth. Soon after, a number of painters including Sven Lukin, Neil Williams, and more recently, Charles Hinman, began experimenting with the shaped canvas. As a result, the gap between painting and sculpture started filling up as quickly as Rauschenberg's now legendary gap between art and life. Among the first to make shaped canvases, and to my mind the most original artist in the genre, was the young English painter, Richard Smith, whose casual geometry has affinities with the new English sculpture. His influence in helping to generate the climate in which the new sculpture was born ought to be noted. Ellsworth Kelly is another whose activity ought to be cited in this context. Using roughly the same hard-edge shapes familiar from his paintings since the late Fifties, Kelly has been making a remarkable series of free-standing flat and bent plane sculptures, which call to mind both Matisse's cut-outs and Calder's stabiles.

In conjunction with his sculpture, Kelly also made reliefs in which geometric cut-outs are detached and float free in front of flat painted backgrounds. Others who made reliefs which, not precisely painting or sculpture, had elements of both, include Larry Bell, Claes Oldenburg, Don Judd, Robert Morris, and Ronald Bladen. In the past few years all have made the leap into fully three-dimensional work. The reliefs in retrospect seem to represent some point of no return from which it was not possible to go back to illusionistic pictorial space but rather was necessary to go forward into the actual space of sculpture.

Art history has never been the simple linear progression the orderly Germanic mind would have it. It is even less so today, when a multiplicity of styles, from Abstract Expressionism, to Hard-edge, to Pop to Post-Painterly Abstraction coexist. The historical moment in which the new sculpture was born was that of the reaction against Abstract Expressionism around 1960 which produced Pop and the new abstraction. Both Johns' and Oldenburg's object sculpture and the non-relational composition and emphasis on immediacy of impact of the new abstraction have influenced its development. If one wishes to be even more precise, the specific cradle of the new sculpture was the nexus formed by the Castelli and Green galleries from 1960-65. Here, Johns, Stella, Chamberlain, Bontecou, Oldenburg, Morris, and Judd showed regularly. Di Suvero, whose influence has been primary for the Park Place group, also had his first one-man show at the Green gallery during this period. Although by now a far broader development including both older sculptors who were working earlier in unrelated styles, such as David von Schlegell and Peter Voulkos, as well as younger sculptors like Judy Gerowitz, David Gray, and John McCracken, the new sculpture began to take on a definable identity in the reliefs and constructions of Robert Morris, Don Judd, and Ronald Bladen which were shown at the Green gallery in the early Sixties.

Originally painters, all three found painting lacking in some vital respect. Judd has spelled out his quarrel with painting. In *Arts Yearbook*, no. 8, he wrote: "Oil paint and canvas aren't as strong as commercial paints and as the colors and surfaces of materials, especially if the materials are used in three dimensions. Oil and canvas are familiar and, like the rectangular plane, have a certain quality and have limits. The quality is especially identified with art." According to Judd, the new work can be more powerful than painting because, "Three dimensions are real space. That gets rid of the problem of illusionism and of literal space, space in and around marks and colors—which is riddance of one of the salient and most objectionable relics of European art."

Both Judd and Robert Morris have written lengthy theoretical defenses of their own positions in particular, and by association of the new sculpture in general. Although they obviously disagree on certain central points—Morris rejects reliefs and color out of hand as being too closely related to pictorial, non-sculptural values—they are in accord about several major issues. For example, they are especially adamant about having their work judged in terms that no longer apply, that is, those of Cubist sculpture. They object especially to the labels "minimal" and "reductive" being applied to their work. Such judgments arise, they feel, out of a misunderstanding of the terms of the new aesthetic, which sets total impact at a premium above internal relationships.

Because its antecedents lie more in the range of the

Gesture and Non-Gesture in Recent Sculpture

Irving Sandler

three-dimensional objects produced in reaction against the limitations of painting, than in sculpture itself, the new work seems to have disconcertingly little in common with conventional sculpture. Although it operates in the area of closed form, it cannot properly be equated with the monolithic. Mainly this seems to be so because one knows that the monolith is solid, but what one knows or senses about the new sculpture is that it is hollow. (In Larry Bell's glass boxes and certain of Don Judd's works, for example, this hollowness is made explicit.) This awareness of the interior space which contained within the hollow volume does not allow us to treat the new sculpture as a monolith. A strange play between contained and displaced space is set up that is one of the complex subtleties of the new work. Another new consideration is the degree to which the new sculpture interacts with its environment. In his brilliant plywood show at the Green gallery in 1964, Robert Morris explored a number of extraordinary original new ways sculpture could relate to the floor, ceiling, or walls of a room. The extent to which this show inspired many recent converts to "primary structures" cannot be overestimated. Not only the pieces themselves, but photographs of them seemed to act as the catalyst necessary to fill galleries with a raft of imitative and frankly not very good work.

Like any kind of art, the new sculpture is as good as the best works of its originators and as poor as the derivative or misunderstood work of its imitators. At its best I find it subtle, provocative, and sometimes beautiful, although beautiful in new terms we need to become better acquainted with.

The dominant tendency in abstract sculpture during the Fifties was open, welded construction. The metalworkers who matured in that decade—Herbert Ferber, David Hare, Ibram Lassaw, Seymour Lipton, Theodore Roszak—generally drew ambiguous, organic images in space. Since then, a number of sculptors, including John Chamberlain and Mark di Suvero, have extended this gestural vein. Others, such as Robert Morris and Donald Judd, have reacted strongly against it. George Sugarman, David Weinrib, Ronald Bladen, Tom Doyle and Robert Grosvenor have veered off in new directions between the two poles.

These sculptors of the Sixties have developed highly varied styles, yet they share certain formal concerns. All are disposed to articulate structure and to clearly define form. Therefore, they tend to favor simple volumes, signaling a rebirth of monolithic sculpture. However, they differ from traditional carvers and modelers in that they construct mass, continuing the constructival aesthetic, the most fruitful in twentieth century sculpture. But in their desire for structural lucidity and volume (a classicizing bent), they also diverge from the metalworkers of the Fifties who preferred to assemble intricate and active linear elements and to use the oxyacetyline torch like a brush, producing richly detailed textures, erupting crusts that focus attention on the surface, thereby denying mass and the immediacy of structure. The recent inclination to monolithic construction has even affected those younger artists who build open or semi-transparent sculptures. The rectilinear scaffolds of Sol LeWitt and Larry Bell section and contain space, turning it into masses of air—negative solids—unlike the constructions of the Fifties which pierce and cut into space vigorously.

Classicizing sculptors today have been influenced by the strict forms preferred by David Smith, notably in his late polychromed and stainless steel pieces, and Alexander Calder, in his stabiles rather than in the mobiles. The younger sculptors are also interested in the ideas of contemporary painters. There are strong affinities between Morris, Judd and Frank Stella; and between Sugarman, Weinrib, Bladen, Doyle, Grosvenor and Al Held. In fact, as in the case of Smith, several (Bladen, Judd, Grosvenor, Morris) began their careers as painters.

*   *   *

The most provocative of the sculptors who have emerged in the Sixties are occupied with non-relational design. The idea of shaping a form so that it exists in its own isolated space has been developed in two antithetical directions. It is carried to an extreme in the unitary objects of Morris and Judd, on the one hand, and on the other, in the disassociated, extended sculptures of Sugarman, Weinrib and Doyle. The two kinds of non-relational organization are new, and both differ from earlier Cubist-oriented abstraction, including welded construction of the Fifties, the unifying principle of which is the rhythmic iteration of sculptural elements about a central core.

As an alternative to balancing varied shapes and colors, Morris and Judd build a single geometric solid or repeat identical units in symmetrical arrangements. As Judd remarked, he aims to create sculptures which are "seen at once and not part by part." Morris also tries to affect a total apprehension of a volume, to make its *gestalt* immediately apparent. "Characteristic of a gestalt is that once it is established, all the information about it, qua gestalt, is explained." To stress the factual attributes of objects, Morris and Judd favor elementary polyhedrons, because these are instantaneously visualized.

In contrast, Sugarman, Weinrib and Doyle juxtapose disparate, polychromed masses, unfolding them in sequence. Their approach requires the invention of a great variety of forms, and they improvise organic as well as geometric ones. It enables them to incorporate into a single sculpture a surprising diversity of spatial and emotional events. In unitary objects, parts are eliminated to emphasize the whole; in disassociated structures, the whole tends to be subordinate to the parts. (To a degree, Sugarman's *Two in One*, 1966, the largest and most complex piece he has created, is a polemic against the idea of minimal sculpture.)

Unitary objects convey a different order of feelings and thoughts from disassociated sculptures. The inert, contained volumes of the one are impassive and aloof. The off-axis, extended masses of the other are dynamic, "conquering" the space the viewer is in dramatically, instead of "occupying" it, to borrow two of Lucy Lippard's words. Dissimilar, individuated shapes appear less self-effacing than generalized, geometric ones. Like the gestures in Action Painting, they become signs of the artist's particular creative process and temperament. In this sense, Sugarman, Weinrib and Doyle continue the self-affirming, romantic spirit of Abstract Expressionism, but in a fresh classicizing vein.

Forms that move into space actively resemble human gestures. But Judd spurns as outworn what he calls "anthropomorphic sculpture," that is, sculpture reminiscent of bodily motions. Furthermore, T-square shapes are less evocative of human physiology than biomorphic masses. One naturally associates geometry with "the man-made world . . . one that man constructs and upon which he meditates—abstractly, from a position once removed," as William Rubin has observed.

However, Judd and Morris deny that their objects relate to architecture, technology or mathematics. Instead, they emphasize their occupation with formal problems, with the "autonomous and literal nature of

sculpture," as Morris has written. "This approach was summed up by dancer Yvonne Rainer: "In the studio, I work with aesthetics like a shoemaker works with leather."

Unitary objects appear as if they were reduced by the logic of purist aesthetics, by the subtraction of any references—to image, painting, relief and architecture—that are not deemed intrinsic to sculpture. (Morris derived his purist ideas from Ad Reinhardt and Clement Greenberg, but the latter has opted for a Cubist-oriented open construction, "liberated" from the monolithic, and allowed "to be as pictorial as it pleases." Conversely, Morris has insisted that sculpture be massive, indivisible, tactile and stable, and approach the object, an intention "diametrically opposed to Cubism.")

The bareness of unitary objects forces attention to the irreducible limits of sculpture, to qualities and allusions which have been renounced. These matter-of-fact pieces seem thought-up rather than felt-through in the process of working. Coolly intellectual, they strike one as the opposite of art, which in Jacques Barzun's words, simulates "life . . . throbbing in your veins or panting in your face." Neutral in shape, color and surface, they reveal no trace of the artist's hand, has active presence. Stringently ABC, as Barbara Rose characterized them, they seem vacant. But much as Morris and Judd try to construct things that assert their physical attributes only, these do invite contemplation and evoke extra-aesthetic associations in an understated way. Judd's hollow, galvanized iron cubes call to mind mass-produced artifacts. Morris' polyhedrons are like Pandora's box; their off-white finish, though blank, has an enigmatic cast, Surrealist rather than Purist.

*　　*　　*

To Morris, color has no place in sculpture, for as an "optical element," it "subverts the physical." Not so to Sugarman, Weinrib and Doyle, for to disassociate the parts of their sculpture, they paint each a different, generally strong hue. They recognize that the wedding of color and mass raises difficult problems—the possible incompatibility between the bulk of a shape and its thin skin of pigment. But the difficulties only make the attempt to fuse the two more challenging.

They, along with Calder, Smith, Chamberlain, Bladen, Robert Hudson and a few others, have projected color in three dimensions with a daring unprecedented in Western sculpture since the Gothic era. With the exception of Hudson, they apply pigment in uniform coats to conceal surface effects which would blunt the visual (and emotional) impact of color and mass. Hudson uses color to disguise volume, not to clarify it. His metal structures, which derive from Smith, Richard Stankiewicz and the early Chamberlain, are coherent and sturdy, but he covers them with painted forms that fool the eye. Flat planes are made to appear curved or bulky; protuberances, to dissolve; the concave or convex, to flatten out. To these optical illusions are added a variety of contradictory images—anatomical, geometric, hard-edge, pop and op. The zany dislocation here, curiously literary, is surrealist, as is the incongruous juxtaposition of volumes and their polychromed surfaces.

*　*　*

Chamberlain, di Suvero, Sugarman, Weinrib, Bladen, Doyle and Grosvenor often work on a huge scale. All share a desire for immediacy and grandeur, to which their massive forms contribute. They also dislike sculpture which looks like precious, coffee-table *objets*. Amy Goldin has written, "Sugarman believes that if a piece of sculpture feels like a *thing*, even a beautiful thing, it's a failure. He wants a more energetic relationship between the work and the space it creates, for the sake of vivid response."

There are, however, varied motives for essays into outsize construction. Bladen and Grosvenor want epic sculpture that has a powerful impact. Sugarman and Weinrib are not interested in monumentality, but their disassociated structures require extended space. Grosvenor and Doyle are attracted by the idea of environmental sculpture that can be walked into or over. Grosvenor plans his mammoth pieces for specific places; he conceives them as "ideas which operate in the space between the floor and the ceiling. They bridge the gap."

By working large, these artists can eliminate pedestals, which they feel are meant only to carry pieces and are sculpturally meaningless. By preference, they place their works directly on the floor or suspend them from the walls or ceiling. Sugarman in his sprawling *Inscape* and *Two in One* and Doyle in his ramp-like construction *Over Owl's Creek* are interested in a low center of gravity. The manner in which these pieces hug the ground suggests the floor as the logical base. Morris also rests his pieces on the floor. "The ground plane . . . is the necessary support for the maximum awareness of the object." Conversely, Weinrib and Grosvenor, in order to defy gravity, project their forms off the wall or ceiling.

*　*　*

Chamberlain's assemblages of smashed automobile parts, executed from 1958 to 1964, and di Suvero's constructions of huge, weathered timbers, the guts of demolished buildings, tires, chains, rope, barrels, ladders, are close in look and feeling to Action Paintings. Chamberlain's mangled fenders slice into and about each other in ambiguous relationships. They call to mind de Kooning's interpenetrating, overlapping and colliding slashes of paint which open up space violently and generate energy. Chamberlain is a bulldozer Bernini. His torn and beat-up

scrap metal planes, conveying the force needed to crumple and to jam them together, are like drapery, but are more savage than any of his Baroque forerunners. Di Suvero's roughly splintered and hacked beams, joined to form jutting and tilting open angles—like Kline's muscular black and white swaths—are even rawer.

Both sculptors have affinities to the metalworkers of the Fifties in that their structures are relational. But they differ in their preference for massive elements and the sense of brute strength that these impart. Furthermore, Chamberlain's color and di Suveros' kinetics are departures. Unlike most past sculptors who merely ignored color, aside of course, from a small interest in the tones of their materials, Chamberlain chooses to assemble fenders because of the fresh palette built into them. It enables him to compose directly in the ready-made enamel and lacquer hues and, later, in sprayed hot-rod colors, or as the Fauves liked to say, to orchestrate color. The color does not render the shapes solid, even though they are space enclosing, but acts as painting in three dimensions, articulating the impacted complexes of forms, their rhythms and the flow of space. Di Suvero's introduction of motion was prompted by the manner in which the beams of his stationary pieces were flung outward. The viewer can mount tires attached to the heavy timbers and propel them about a pivot to take an exhilarating trip around and into the construction.

The two artists' use of found objects almost exclusively is akin to that of Stankiewicz, Jason Seley and a few of their contemporaries, but has no precedent in earlier sculpture. These chunks of environment assert their origin, evoking the automobile graveyards or wrecked buildings from which they were resurrected. Such allusions are unavoidable, but they are countered by the highly formal quality of the pieces. The detritus, despite its haphazard appearance, is cut and shaped into desired forms which are thoughtfully balanced, and it is the cogency of structure which makes the lasting impression.

*　*　*

Sugarman, Weinrib and Doyle are as romantic as Chamberlain and di Suvero, but since the early Sixties, they have preferred volumes that are neither indeterminate nor organized centripetally. Sugarman, who pioneered the disjunctive approach, has been the most audacious in the use of it. He laminates pieces of wood to build unrelated, weighty forms which evolve in open-ended progression. He paints each segment a different hue to further isolate it and to render its gesture unique, although all are robust, a quality that has always characterized his style. The coating of liquitex is not an added or decorative element but augments the masses and helps clarify their positions in space. Recently, Sugarman has modified the principle of disassociation. His forms are still distinctive, but they are also variations on a theme, unfolding like an abstract narrative, embodying continuity as well as change.

To achieve an effect of buoyancy, Weinrib has floated sinuous, vividly colored shapes, none of which is repeated, off the walls or ceiling. In the past, he used a great variety of materials, but during the last few years, he has limited himself to plastic. No sculptor who has worked in this medium can make it come alive as Weinrib can. His opulent volumes, the progeny of Arp and Miró, are light-hearted. The translucent and polychromed plastic adds to this mood, for he uses it to produce a play of dissonant colors and bouncing lights.

Lately, Weinrib has cast plaster into luminescent, bulbous shapes, which he stands on ground planes. Casting has enabled him to create a quality of color new in art—a colored light that at once articulates contour and is volumetric, visible in the depths of mass. Semi-transparency also acts to dissolve solids, making them seem to levitate. Weinrib accents this volatility by poising the parts on points, enhancing the airiness of his sculpture.

In 1964, Doyle simplified the rough-hewn wood and rock forms of his earlier carvings. He began to assemble curved planes of masonite reinforced with fiberglass, and to disjoin and paint them in the manner of Sugarman and Weinrib. But unlike the other two, he wrapped his planes around space, partly enclosing it, sweeping air (and the viewer's imagination) into ample hollows. Doyle extends his massive, sail-like sheets so that they seem about to keel over—to look "impossible," as he puts it. And they are painted in equally improbable colors—exotic pinks, purples, grasshopper green.

In some of his wood constructions, Bladen has used color to disassociate his forms, and so he relates to Sugarman, Weinrib and Doyle. However, he favors geometric volumes which tend toward unitary objects, particularly in his latest work, a row of three free-standing, nine-foot high rhomboids. Nevertheless, in spirit, this work is poles apart from Minimal sculpture. Bladen's rhomboids (they are actually rectangular volumes whose bottoms are cut off at a 65° angle) are more particular and individuated than Morris's or Judd's simple polyhedrons. The asymmetrical thrust of his masses causes them to appear dynamic, precariously balanced and on the verge of toppling. The slant is a human gesture, suggesting falling or bowing, signs of vulnerability, or marching, more the latter, for together, the giant rhomboids in a line form an awesome procession of anthropomorphic menhirs. The incline of Bladen's monoliths is also past art's heroic diagonal in a contemporary vein. Indeed, they loom like a section of Stonehenge, geometricized as if conceived by a master of International Style architecture.

Although Bladen does not intend it, his sculpture evokes modern buildings and industrial structures. Such allusions are suggested by the rectangular forms, painted in ordinary red, yellow, black or white, and by the enamel or lacquer finish, a paint-job polish which looks machine-made. In one untitled piece, Bladen, engineer-like, cantilevers elements over a distance of eighteen feet, employing a system of weights, structural stresses and counter-stresses to hold an off-balance plane in suspension.

Grosvenor has also explored the possibilities of suspension in sculpture. In *Transoxiana*, he spans a bulky, red and black V over a distance of thirty-one feet. Bolted to a single point on the ceiling, it trajects down, almost to the floor, then up, stopping just short of the ceiling. To stretch a form as far as it will go, and Grosvenor does just that, is a feat of engineering. In fact, he treads the line where art and engineering meet. *Transoxiana* is a big gesture, like Bladen's monuments, dramatic and heroic. Its thrust is physical and forceful, dominating the space occupied by the viewer; its torsion, excruciating; and its loftiness, elating.

*   *   *

Inherent in the idea of modernism is the continual challenging of accepted ways of seeing. Chamberlain's and di Suvero's use of massive found objects, color and kinetics has led to one kind of expansion of perception. The non-relational aesthetic has provided other means of breaking habits, of forcing art out of the known into the unknown, of evolving fresh forms to embody insights into art and life. It is largely responsible for the continuing vitality of contemporary sculpture.

Postscript: After this essay was completed, I saw Tony Smith's black constructions of 1961 to 1966 in Hartford and Philadelphia. These shows, his first, reveal him to be one of the most powerful of contemporary sculptors. Several of Smith's pieces are elementary rectangular volumes, akin to Morris's and Judd's unitary objects. Others, enormous in size, are close in feeling to Bladen's three-part sculpture. Each of the last group is based on a module, mostly the tetrahedron, a carry-over perhaps from Smith's earlier career as an architect. The simple volumes are combined to form complicated, jutting and twisting, asymmetrical, massive structures, the awesome twentieth century descendants of ancient megaliths.

Artists' Statements

Carl Andre

January, 1967

Fletcher Benton

My work at this time is involved primarily with controlled motion and in most cases transformation of one simple shape to another. I am working with purity of form and its relationship to motion . . .

Most kinetic devices that I am familiar with are very simple and unsophisticated statements. The visual time-space involvement from a technical standpoint is fairly uncomplicated. Being first-generation kineticists, we must acquire a great amount of technical information that second and third-generation kineticists will find more readily available. . . . The ultimate in space-time involvement will be the assimilation of the computer, data processing and other highly complex electronic equipment. For it is here that one may have the ultimate visual experience. . .

from Peter Selz, *Directions in Kinetic Sculpture*, Berkeley, University of California, 1966, p. 19.

Ronald Bladen

My involvement in sculpture outside of man's scale is an attempt to reach that area of excitement belonging to natural phenomena such as a gigantic wave poised before it makes its fall or man-made phenomena such as the high bridge spanning two distant points.

The scale becomes aggressive or heroic. The esthetic is a depersonalized one. The space exploded or compressed rather than presented. The drama taut in its implication is best described as awesome or breathtaking. In rare moments I think these things can be gathered to produce a particular beauty.

from Barbara Rose, "ABC Art," *Art in America*, vol. 53, no. 5, October-November 1965, p. 63.

Anthony Caro

. . . I think part of the trouble—part of the disadvantage of sculpture, and also part of the advantage of it is the fact that it's heavy and real; I don't want to make sculpture which has an unreality. I want to make sculpture which is very corporeal, but denies its corporeality. I don't want to make sculpture which is like a . . . conjurer's trick.

. . . I would really rather make my sculpture out of "stuff" —out of something really anonymous, just sheets maybe which you cut a bit off. Angle-iron and rolled-steel joists and all that, I think, are irrelevant: they are a thing I'd like to get away from in the end. . . . They'll bit by bit creep away out of the sculpture. The only thing is that certain things like those heavy joists from which I think I've taken most of the bridge connotations, do have a weight about them, they do have the effect of being able to punctuate, they are a bit like a blob of colour in a Monet painting or something like this. Much of the sculpture that I'm doing is about extent, and even might get to be about fluidity or something of this sort, and I think one has to hold it from becoming just amorphous.

. . . I have been trying, I think, all the time to eliminate references, to make truly abstract sculpture. It is using these things like notes in music. But the note must not remind you too much of the world of things, or of parts of noses or breasts or ears or anything—perhaps it's impossible to make a sculpture out of clay at this moment, at the moment it's too difficult for me anyway—there are too many reminders in it. And I think therefore one tries really to get a material with not too much art history in it. Although I think steel's got plenty of art history now, unfortunately. But I would be very happy to use another material.

from "Anthony Caro Interviewed by Andrew Forge," *Studio International*, vol. 171, no. 873, January 1966, p. 7.

John Chamberlain

My involvement is with a
Wadding, Compression, surfacing,
Techniques,
Applied to various materials in that
Uncommon, particular way to

Expose under articulation its
Content slant yield

from a letter to John Weber, Santa Fe, New Mexico, January 1967.

Chryssa

Years ago, when I first came to America, I was very drawn to Times Square. I used to go walking there, as people go searching for certain moods. I wanted to be a signmaker then, but I couldn't because of the union. Now I would rather visit Brooklyn.

Signs, the very good signs, like some of those in Times Square, have solved the basic problem of sculpture: How to be static, yet have motion.

Some things about art can't be explained. Somehow, I *know* when they work and when they don't. I am inspired, like a scientist, to study the nature of materials just as I study letters, the alphabet, the basis of communication. But I can't use just any letters. The right ideas come only after an agony of searching.

from Chryssa, "The Artist Says," *Art Voices*, vol. 4, no. 4, Fall 1965, p. 62.

Walter DeMaria

I think both art and life are a matter of life and death.

December 1966.

Dan Flavin

. . . By 1961, I was tired of my three year old romance with art as tragic practice. I found that all my small constructions, with the exception of "mira, mira," were memorial plaques and that the numerous pages and folding books of watercolor and poetry which I had made were drowned in funereal black ink.

My four room flat had shrunk to a closet around my mind. . . . I had to abandon it. . .

In time, I came to these conclusions about what I had found in fluorescent light, and about what might be done with it plastically:

Now the entire spatial container and its parts—wall, floor, ceiling, could support this strip of light but would not restrict its act of light except to enfold it. Regard the light and you are fascinated—inhibited from grasping its limits at each end. While the tube itself has an actual length of eight feet, its shadow, cast by the supporting pan, has none but an illusion dissolving at its ends. This waning shadow cannot really be measured without resisting its visual effect and breaking the poetry.

Realizing this, I knew that the actual space of a room could be broken down and played with by planting illusions of real light (electric light) at crucial junctures in the room's composition. . .

from Dan Flavin, ". . . In Daylight or Cool White," *Artforum*, vol. 4, no. 4, December 1965, pp. 20-24.

. . . Electric light is just another instrument. I have no desire to contrive fantasies mediumistically or sociologically over it or beyond it. Future art and the lack of that would surely reduce such squandered speculations to silly trivia anyhow. . .

. . . the lamps will go out (as they should, no doubt). Somehow I believe that the changing standard lighting system should support my idea within it. I will try to maintain myself this way. It may work out. The medium bears the artist. . .

from Dan Flavin, "Some Remarks," *Artforum*, vol. 5, no. 4, December 1966, p. 27.

William R. Geis, III

I think in the patterns that are available. I just think, about what it doesn't matter, I just think. And I find variations and twist them around and twist them up and tie them up in order to compress more meaning into the smaller space. It is like being an artist, it's not what it is, it's how you make it. It has nothing to do with what it is, because it all comes out different, I can't make the same thing twice.

From an interview with Joe Raffaele, December 1966.

Robert Grosvenor

I don't want my work to be thought of as "large sculpture," they are ideas which operate in the space between floor and ceiling. They bridge a gap.

from The Jewish Museum, New York, *Primary Structures: Younger American and British Sculptors,* 1966.

Donald Judd

Three dimensions are real space. That gets rid of the problem of illusionism and of literal space, space in and around marks and colors—which is riddance of one of the salient and most objectionable relics of European art. The several limits of painting are no longer present. A work can be as powerful as it can be thought to be. Actual space is intrinsically more powerful and specific than paint on a flat surface. Obviously, anything in three dimensions can be any shape, regular or irregular, and can have any relation to the wall, floor, ceiling, room, rooms or exterior or none at all. Any material can be used, as is or painted.

A work needs only to be interesting. Most works finally

have one quality. In earlier art the complexity was displayed and built the quality. In recent painting the complexity was in the format and the few main shapes, which had been made according to various interests and problems. A painting by Newman is finally no simpler than one by Cézanne. In the three-dimensional work the whole thing is made according to complex purposes, and these are not scattered but asserted by one form. It isn't necessary for a work to have a lot of things to look at, to compare, to analyze one by one, to contemplate. The thing as a whole, its quality as a whole, is what is interesting. The main things are alone and are more intense, clear and powerful. They are not diluted by an inherited format, variations of a form, mild contrasts and connecting parts and areas. European art had to represent a space and its contents as well as have sufficient unity and aesthetic interest. Abstract painting before 1946 and most subsequent painting kept the representational subordination of the whole to its parts. Sculpture still does. In the new work the shape, image, color and surface are single and not partial and scattered. There aren't any neutral or moderate areas or parts, any connections or transitional areas. The difference between the new work and earlier painting and present sculpture is like that between one of Brunelleschi's windows in the Badia di Fiesole and the façade of the Palazzo Rucellai, which is only an undeveloped rectangle as a whole and is mainly a collection of highly ordered parts.

from Donald Judd, "Specific Objects," Contemporary Sculpture, New York, The Art Digest, (Arts Yearbook 8), 1965, pp. 79-80.

. . . Pollock and those people represent actual chance; by now it's better to make that a foregone conclusion—you don't have to mimic chance. You use a simple form that doesn't look like either order or disorder. We recognize that the world is 90 percent chance and accident. Earlier painting was saying that there's more order in the scheme of things than we admit now, like Poussin saying order underlies nature. Poussin's order is anthropomorphic. Now there are no preconceived notions. Take a simple form—say a box—and it does have an order, but it's not so ordered that that's the dominant quality. The more parts a thing has, the more important order becomes, and finally order becomes more important than anything else.

. . . (We're) getting rid of the things that people used to think were essential to art. But that reduction is only incidental. I object to the whole reduction idea, because it's only reduction of those things someone doesn't want. If my work is reductionist it's because it doesn't have the elements that people thought should be there. But it has other elements that I like . . .

. . . I don't consider (my work) nihilistic or negative or cool or anything else. Also I don't think my objection to the Western tradition is a positive quality of my work. It's just something I don't want to do, that's all. I want to do something else.

from Bruce Glaser, "Questions to Stella and Judd," Art News, vol. 65, no. 5, September 1966, pp. 58-60.

Ellsworth Kelly

. . . I don't like most Hard Edge paintings. I'm not interested in edges. I'm interested in the mass and color, the black and white. The edges happen because the forms get as quiet as they can be. I want the masses to perform. When I work with forms and colors, I get the edge. In a Chamberlain, the edges of the forms are hard but you don't think about the edges. In my work, it is impossible to separate the edges from the mass and color.

I like to work from things that I see whether they're man-made or natural or a combination of the two. Once in a while I work directly from something I've seen, like a window, or a fragment of a piece of architecture, or someone's legs; or sometimes the space between things, or just how the shadows of an object would look. The things I'm interested in have always been there. The idea of the shadow of a natural object has existed, like the shadow of the pyramids and the pyramids, or a rock and its shadow and the separation of the rock and the shadow; I'm not interested in the texture of the rock, or that it is a rock but in the mass of it, and its shadow.

from Henry Geldzahler, "Interview with Ellsworth Kelly," Art International, vol. 8, no. 1, February 1964, pp. 47-48.

Edward Kienholz

THE STATE HOSPITAL 1964. This is a tableau about an old man who is a patient in a state mental hospital. He is in an arm restraint on a bed in a bare room. (The piece will have to include an actual room consisting of walls, ceiling, floor, barred door, etc.) There will be only a bedpan and a hospital table (just out of reach). The man is naked. He hurts. He has been beaten on the stomach with a bar of soap wrapped in a towel (to hide tell-tale bruises). His head is a lighted fish bowl with water that contains two live black fish. He lies very still on his side. There is no sound in the room.

Above the old man in the bed is his exact duplicate, including the bed (beds will be stacked like bunks). The upper figure will also have the fish bowl head, two black fish, etc. But, additionally, it will be encased in some kind of lucite or plastic bubble (perhaps similar to a cartoon balloon), representing the old man's thoughts.

His mind can't think for him past the present moment. He is committed there for the rest of his life.

from the descriptive portion of the "Concept Tableau" entitled "The State Hospital" 1964-1967.

Frederick J. Kiesler

. . . You see, the sculptor's wings are really made of clay and his work is earthbound. It is the breathing of the intervals between details that makes his materials live and expand visually. Isn't the dimensioning which space-distances, the exactitude of intervals, the physical nothingness which links the solid parts together so powerfully—isn't this the major device for translating nature's time-space continuity into man-made objects? . . .

from Solomon R. Guggenheim Museum, New York. *Frederick Kiesler: Environmental Sculpture*, 1964.

Len Lye

Perhaps, deep in our hearts, we would all like to be impervious to change of moods, opinions and environment. The static element in painting, sculpture and architecture may, therefore, unconsciously and symbolically anchor this deep desire to something as human and innately individual as art. And, as it is, only the static work of art can hold the emotional mark of its creator in one instantaneously perceived image, one that may invoke an immediate aesthetic response.

On the other hand, no one exists without some form of motion occurring in his makeup. From conception to death some form of motion is part of life; every waking moment is directed to enacting behavioral patterns of motion. . .

I eventually came to look at the way things moved mainly to try to *feel* the movement, and *only* feel it . . . I wanted to put the feeling of a figure of motion outside of myself to see what I'd got. I came to realize that this feeling had to come out of myself; not out of streams, swaying grasses, soaring birds. So, instead of sketching lines and accents described by things in motion, I now tried to tie and plait their particular motion characteristics into my bones and into my sinews—to get a kind of inner echo of their feeling . . .

from Peter Selz, *Directions in Kinetic Sculpture*, Berkeley, University of California, 1966, p. 43.

John McCracken

I think of color as being the structural material I use to build the forms I am interested in. The fact that in another sense I use plywood, fiberglass and lacquer as structural materials is of less importance. I have found that a certain range of mainly primary and some secondary colors and a certain combination of color intensity and transparency and surface finish provide me with the expressive means I want, at least for the present.

from "New Talent USA," *Art in America*, vol. 54, no. 4, July-August 1966, p. 66.

47

Charles Mattox

The work I am doing now is a development that has come in the last two years. From primary interest in motion and feedback mechanics I have become more interested in new sculptural forms and an integration of other dimensions such as sound into the new work. Motion can be an obsession and is not enough in itself. To get more random motion and less predictable movement in the work is important.

The forms, color, sound and motion are all necessary and should all function to the intent or meaning of the work. The spirit of play is a part of the creation of my work and the intent is for the viewer (player) to respond as to a toy or game. To make a toy for a child, not a mass-produced object, but a single toy for a particular child, is close to my approach. I am interested in technology and science of this era and its effect on our culture, particularly as it is reflected in the popular movements of drag racing, slot racing, popular music and dance.

February, 1967

Robert Morris

Mondrian went so far as to claim that "Sensations are not transmissible, or rather, their purely qualitative properties are not transmissible. The same, however, does not apply to *relations* between sensations . . . Consequently only *relations* between sensations can have an objective value. . . ." This may be ambiguous in terms of perceptual facts but in terms of looking at art it is descriptive of the condition which obtains. It obtains because art objects have clearly divisible parts which set up the relationships. Such a condition suggests the alternative question: could a work exist which has only one property? Obviously not, since nothing exists which has only one property. A single, pure sensation cannot be transmissible precisely because one perceives simultaneously more than one as parts in any given situation: if color, then also dimension; if flatness, then texture, etc. However, certain forms do exist which, if they do not negate the numerous relative sensations of color to texture, scale to mass, etc., they do not present clearly separated parts for these kinds of relations to be established in terms of shapes. Such are the simpler forms which create strong gestalt sensations. Their parts are bound together in such a way that they offer a maximum resistance to perceptual separation.

. . . The simpler regular and irregular (polyhedrons) maintain the maximum resistance to being confronted as objects with separate parts. They seem to present lines of fracture by which they could divide for easy part-to-part relationships to be established. I term these simple rectangular and irregular polyhedrons "unitary" forms. Sculpture involving unitary forms, being bound together as it is with a kind of energy provided by the gestalt, often elicits the complaint among critics that such works are beyond analysis.

Characteristic of a gestalt is that once it is established all the information about it, qua gestalt, is exhausted. (One does not, for example, seek the gestalt of a gestalt.) Furthermore, once it is established it does not disintegrate. One is then both free of the shape and bound to it. Free or released because of the exhaustion of information about it, as shape, and bound to it because it remains constant and indivisible.

Simplicity of shape does not necessarily equate with simplicity of experience. Unitary forms do not reduce relationships. They order them. If the predominant, hieratic nature of the unitary form functions as a constant, all those particularizing relations of scale, proportion, etc., are not thereby canceled. Rather they are bound more cohesively and indivisibly together. The magnification of this single most important sculptural value, shape, together with greater unification and integration of every other essential sculptural value makes on the one hand, the multipart, inflected formats of past sculpture extraneous, and on the other, establishes both a new limit and a new freedom for sculpture.

from Robert Morris, "Notes on Sculpture," *Artforum*, vol. 4, no. 6, February 1966, p. 44.

The object is but one of the terms in the newer esthetic. It is in some way more reflexive because one's awareness of oneself existing in the same space as the work is stronger than in previous work, with its many internal relationships. One is more aware than before that he himself is establishing relationships as he apprehends the object from various positions and under varying conditions of light and spatial context. Every internal relationship, whether it be set up by a structural division,

a rich surface, or what have you, reduces the public, external quality of the object and tends to eliminate the viewer to the degree that these details pull him into an intimate relation with the work and out of the space in which the object exists.

While the work must be autonomous in the sense of being a self-contained unit for the formation of the gestalt, the indivisible and undissolvable whole, the major esthetic terms are not in but dependent upon this autonomous object and exist as unfixed variables which find their specific definition in the particular space and light and physical viewpoint of the spectator. Only one aspect of the work is immediate: the apprehension of the gestalt. The experience of the work necessarily exists in time. *The intention is diametrically opposed to Cubism with its concern for simultaneous views in one plane.* Some of the new work has expanded the terms of sculpture by a more emphatic focusing on the very conditions under which certain kinds of objects are seen. The object itself is carefully placed in these new conditions to be but one of the terms. The sensuous object, resplendent with compressed internal relations has had to be rejected. That many considerations must be taken into account in order that the work keep its place as a term in the expanded situation hardly indicates a lack of interest in the object itself. But the concerns now are for more control of and/or cooperation of the entire situation. Control is necessary if the variables of object, light, space, body, are to function. The object itself has not become less important. It has merely become less *self*-important. . .

from Robert Morris, "Notes on Sculpture, Part II," *Artforum*, vol. 5, no. 2, October 1966, pp. 21, 23.

Robert Murray

To some extent, I feel I am involved with volumes. In fact, I like to work with a kind of contradiction in my sculpture. When I worked for a short time in bronze, I made sculpture that was meant to be seen in a two-dimensional way. That is, strong in silhouette. They were simple cylinders stacked irregularly on top of each other which made a configuration I thought of as being more linear than volumetric. When I went back to fabricated sculpture, I tried to use plate in such a way as to suggest volume without actually boxing-in the form. In other words, I wanted to activate more space than I could actually fill. . .

from Barbara Rose, "An Interview with Robert Murray," *Artforum*, vol. 5, no. 2, October 1966, p. 45.

Reuben Nakian

The difference between Picasso and the ordinary artist, the reason Picasso is great, is because he knows a thousand and one ways of finishing a picture, and he knows how to try them all. The average artist knows about five. To be a good artist you not only have to understand this but you've got to live long enough to achieve it. The secret of being a great artist is not to drop dead too soon.

from H. H. Arnason, "Nakian," *Art International*, vol. 7, no. 4, April 1963, p. 37.

Bruce Nauman

I suppose some work has to do in part with some of the things the Dadaists and Surrealists did. I like to give the pieces elaborate titles the way they did, although I've only been titling them recently. That all came from not trying to figure out why I make those things. It got so I just couldn't do anything. So like making the impressions of knees in a wax block [*A Wax Mold of the Knees of Five Famous Artists*] was a way of having a large rectangular solid with marks in it. I didn't want just to make marks in it so I had to make this other kind of reasoning. It also had to do with trying to make a less important thing to look at.

from an interview with Joe Raffaele, December 1966.

Claes Oldenburg

. . . I have found myself the last two years or so (1963) in a specific perverse relation to my surroundings. . . I have combined my unworldly fantasy in a shock wedding to banal aspects of everyday existence . . . so completely . . . the thing is likely to burst either way, as it has arrived at a point where the cohabitation is no longer possible . . . either into banality or the other way into poetry. . .

People's lack of detachment about themselves surprises me. They operate—how one should say it . . . contained as if the machinery would fall apart if they could take a removed view of themselves and become self-conscious. . . . People believe themselves. . . It is possible for me to treat my subjectivity and that of others objectively and this is a unique thing in my art: the emotion in it is the observation of emotion. I am both committed and not committed and man must learn, when forces make him more and more self-conscious, how to be self-conscious and still effective, how to be intellectual and still not "cold."

The imagination of horror exceeds the experience of horror . . . or is a disguise for something else (like a nightmare). The representation of horror is not necessarily connected with what is being represented.

Horror in reality is too impersonal and the natural body is too quick to protect itself. . . Imagined horror is absolutely limitless. . .

from "Claes Oldenburg: Extracts from the Studio Notes (1962-64)," *Artforum*, vol. 4, no. 5, January 1966, pp. 32-33.

. . . you might ask what is the thing that has made me make cakes and pastries and all those other things. Then I would say that one reason has been to give a concrete statement to my fantasy. In other words, instead of painting it, to make it touchable, to translate the eye into the fingers. That has been the main motive in all my work. That's why I make things soft that are hard and why I treat perspective the way I do, such as with the bedroom set, making an object that is a concrete statement of visual perspective. But I am not terribly interested in whether a thing is an ice cream cone or a pie or anything else. What I am interested in is that the equivalent of my fantasy exists outside of me, and that I can, by imitating the subject, make a different kind of work from what has existed before. . .

from Bruce Glaser, "Oldenburg, Lichtenstein, Warhol: A Discussion," *Artforum*, vol. 4, no. 6, February 1966, p. 22.

Robert Rauschenberg

Someone asked me yesterday: "Do you really see modern life as all made up of hell?" Of course not. But if one is illustrating hell one usually uses the properties of hell. I've never thought that problems were so simple politically that they could be tackled directly in art works, not by me anyway, although in my personal life I do take stands on atrocities of all kinds. But everyday, by doing consistently what you do with the attitude you have, if you have strong feelings, these things are expressed over a period of time as opposed to, say, one *Guernica*. That's just a different attitude. . . . When you just illustrate your feeling about something self-consciously—that is for me almost the only way the political scene can come into my work—and I believe it's there. Consistently there has been an attempt to use the very last minute in my life and the particular location as a source of energy and inspiration rather than retiring into some other time or dream or idealism. I think that cultivated protest is just as dreamlike as idealism.

from Robert Rauschenberg and Dorothy Gees Seckler, "The Artist Speaks: Robert Rauschenberg," *Art in America*, vol. 54, no. 3, May-June, 1966, p. 84.

George Rickey

To design with movement itself, as distinct from adding movement to a design, has been my preoccupation for the last fifteen years. Movement reveals itself most clearly in very simple forms, for example in a single line moving through space. Combined with a second line, moving contrapuntally, the two may cut each other; may divide, squeeze, and define space; and, moving at different speeds, may measure time in a surprisingly complex way.

I have thus far worked with lines in combinations up to six. I have also, in another mode, assembled constellations of very numerous parts, sometimes lines and sometimes other forms. These groups exploit a different kind of phenomenon, where the *many* become a new *one*, and complexity and simplicity develop simultaneously.

I have worked with lines for some six years now, on various scales, from a few inches long to over thirty feet, both indoors and outdoors. I have not exhausted linear themes (in fact they seem inexhaustible); but a line has in it to become a plane. Planes do not simply repeat linear themes with one added dimension; they are another world with its own laws and language. With moving lines, space is cut; when it is planes which move, space is compressed, stretched, twisted, and compartmented. Planes can be assembled into more extensive undulating surfaces or into containers of unstable and indeterminate volumes.

Any material will reflect or absorb light; a line will thus be light or dark. A surface has a greatly augmented response to light; its reflection or absorption almost adds another dimension. If the surface is polished like a mirror it disappears and becomes space instead, as it receives and retransmits, in altered form, the surrounding world. A moving mirror-surface renders the dismembered images of the environment unstable and endows them with velocities of their own.

These phenomena are unimportant in themselves, but may become a vocabulary for expressive statement.

January 1967.

Lucas Samaras

. . . At the moment I'm interested in the mirror. . . . I started working with mirrors a long time ago, but now I'm constructing a mirror room. It's completely mirror on the outside, and 8 by 10 by 8 feet high. You open the door, go in, and it's completely mirror inside, too; floor, ceiling, walls, everything, and there's just a table and a chair. Just the skeleton of them, you might say, and they are mirror too, and nothing else. No light, only the light that comes through the door. . .

. . . First I wanted to do a real room, and I did that, and then, I wanted to do more abstract rooms; this is an abstract room. I suppose people paint with their bodies when they enter the room; you know, they inspect themselves, "paint" themselves; they scribble. Then they go away and the scribble goes away too, so that they don't leave their marks. Kind of an instant erasure.

from Alan Solomon, "An Interview with Lucas Samaras," *Artforum*, vol. 5, no. 2, October 1966, pp. 42-43.

George Segal

. . . Once you begin to deal with the everchanging aspects of three-dimensional encounters the number of formal solutions is countless. The largest problem lies in the emotional choice of the most moving or the most revelatory series of experiences. The peculiar shape and qualities of the actual empty air surrounding the volumes becomes an important part of the expressiveness of the whole piece. The distance between two figures or between a figure and another object becomes crucial. My pieces often don't end at their physical boundaries.

from Henry Geldzahler, "An Interview with George Segal," *Artforum*, vol. 3, no. 2, November 1965, p. 29.

David Smith

. . . My realities giving impetus to a work which is a train of hooked visions arises from very ordinary locale. The arrangement of things under an old board, stress patterns, fissures, the structure pattern of growth, stains, tracks of men, animals, machines, the accidental or unknown order forces, accidental evidences such as spilled paint, patched sidewalks, broken parts, structural faults, the force lines in rock or marble laid by glacial sedimentation. Realistic all, made by ancient pattern or unknown force to be recorded, repeated, varied, transformed in analogy or as keys to contemporary celebrations. Some works are the celebration of wonders. After several of these a spectre. In my life, joy, peace, is always menaced. Survival; not only from commercial destruction but from the threat of daily existence, the battle of money for material—and welfare during. I date my esthetic heritage from impressionism.

from David Smith, "The Language is Image," *Arts and Architecture*, vol. 69, no. 2, February 1952, p. 33.

I cannot conceive a work and buy material for it. I can find or discover a part. To buy a new material—I need a

50

truckload before I can work on one. To look at it every day—to let it soften—to let it break up in segments, planes, lines, etc.—wrap itself in hazy shapes. Nothing is so impersonal, hard and cold as straight rolling-mill stock. If it is standing or kicking around, it becomes personal and fits into visionary use. With possession and acquaintance, a fluidity develops which was not there the day it was unloaded from Ryerson's truck.

from David Smith, "Notes on My Work," *Arts*, vol. 34, no. 5, February 1960, p. 44.

... Painters don't "come upon" subjects for a still-life; the Impressionists didn't come upon their subjects. They found their trees; they chose their apples; those are all "found objects"—flowers, fruit, everything.

I find many things, but I only choose certain ones that fit a niche in my mind, fit into a relationship I need, and that relationship is somewhat of a geometric nature. They aren't meant to relate to the art. But there is a certain romantic relationship in my mind to the old hand-made objects that have ceased to function...

... There is a kind of vision, usually, which is a meditated vision—as against premeditated. But I would rather call it a continuation. And then sometimes I need the contradiction to the kind of work I'm doing. Sometimes I work in what people call lines or drawing. Sometimes I need big strong cubic shapes. Sometimes I need total disrespect for the material and paint it as if it were a building...

... You know who I am and what I stand for. I have no allegiance, but I stand, and I know what the challenge is, and I challenge everything and everybody. And I think that is what every artist has to do. The minute you show a work, you challenge every other artist. And you have to work very hard, especially here. We don't have the introduction that European artists have. We're challenging the world... I'm going to work to the best of my ability to the day I die, challenging what's given to me.

from interview with Thomas B. Hess, "The Secret Letter," *David Smith*, Marlborough-Gerson Gallery, New York, October 1964.

Tony Smith

I view art as something vast. I think highway systems fall down because they are not art. Art today is an art of postage stamps. I love the Secretariat Building of the U. N., placed like a salute. In terms of scale, we have less art per square mile, per capita, than any society ever had. We are puny. In an English village there was always the cathedral. There is nothing to look at between the Bennington Monument and the George Washington Bridge. We now have stylization. In Hackensack a huge gas tank is all underground. I think of art in a public context and not in terms of mobility of works of art. Art is just there. I'm temperamentally more inclined to mural painting, especially that of the Mexican, Orozco. I like the way a huge area holds on to a surface in the same way a state does on a map.

from Samuel Wagstaff, Jr., "Talking with Tony Smith," *Artforum*, vol. 5, no. 4, December 1966, p. 17.

Robert Smithson

Many architectural concepts found in science-fiction have nothing to do with science or fiction, instead they suggest a new kind of monumentality which has much in common with the aims of some of today's artists. I am thinking in particular of Donald Judd, Robert Morris, Sol LeWitt, Dan Flavin, and of certain artists in the "Park Place Group." The artists who build structured canvases and "wall-size" paintings, such as Will Insley, Peter Hutchinson and Frank Stella are more indirectly related. The chrome and plastic fabricators such as Paul Thek, Craig Kauffman, and Larry Bell are also relevant.

The works of many of these artists celebrate what Flavin called "inactive history" or what the physicist calls "entropy" or " energy-drain." They bring to mind the Ice Age rather than the Golden Age, and would most likely confirm Vladimir Nabokov's observation that, "The future is but the obsolete in reverse." In a rather roundabout way, many of the artists have provided a visible analog for the Second Law of Thermodynamics, which extrapolates the range of entropy by telling us energy is more easily lost than obtained, and that in the ultimate future the whole universe will burn out and be transformed into an all-encompassing sameness...

Instead of causing us to remember the past like the old monuments, the new monuments seem to cause us to forget the future. Instead of being made of natural materials, such as marble, granite, or other kinds of rock, the new monuments are made of artificial materials, plastic, chrome, and electric light. They are not built for the ages, but rather against the ages. They are involved in a systematic reduction of time down to fractions of seconds, rather than in representing the long spaces of centuries. Both past and future are placed into an objective present. This kind of time has little or no space; it is stationary and without movement, it is going nowhere, it is anti-Newtonian, as well as being instant, and is against the wheels of the time-clock...

This kind of nullification has re-created Kasimir Malevich's "non-objective world," where there are no more "likenesses of reality, no idealistic images, nothing but a desert!" But for many of today's artists this "desert" is a "City of the Future" made of null structures and surfaces. This "City" performs no natural function, it simply exists between mind and matter, detached from both, representing neither. It is, in fact, devoid of all classical ideals of space and process. It is brought into focus by a strict condition of perception, rather than by any expressive or emotive means. Perception as a deprivation of action and reaction brings to the mind the desolate, but exquisite, surface-structures of the empty "box" or "lattice." As action decreases, the clarity of such surface-structures increases. This is evident in art when all representations of action pass into oblivion. At this stage, lethargy is elevated to the most glorious magnitude. . .

from Robert Smithson, "Entropy and the New Monuments," *Artforum,* vol. 4, no. 10, June 1966, pp. 26-27.

Kenneth Snelson

My concern is with nature in its most fundamental aspect: the patterns of physical forces in space.

January 1967.

Robert Stevenson

. . . It was necessary to cut through fuzzy amorphous outlines, to clear images and burn through to harsh simple shapes. While introducing the use of direct and powerfully uncomfortable color, it became important to use what might be termed "designedness" to unify and to keep . . . control. This bothered some, and continues to bother some—the sure evidence of rational thinking alongside a dissonant element. . .

from the artist's dissertation, June 1965.

George Sugarman

In my sculpture, the color is as important as form and space. The important thing is that it has a tremendous emotional impact, and the experience of the spectator, in seeing color allied to a three-dimensional form, is something that is quite novel at first, in fact, quite shocking. An important aspect is that the color is not used decoratively. It's not used to be pretty or attractive. It is used to articulate the sculpture in space.

from Bruce Glaser, Lyman Kipp, George Sugarman and David Weinrib, "Where Do We Go from Here?" *Contemporary Sculpture,* New York, The Art Digest (Arts Yearbook 8), 1965, p. 154.

David Von Schlegell

With new sculpture, there is an intellectual clarity that comes from new materials and new ideas about their use. I have developed a way of making sculpture that includes what I have practiced in the past, but goes beyond that practice. My wish is to take hold of the invisible feelings one has toward form, space and motion and to make them visible. In this way sculpture cannot be ponderous, but must be fragile, as well as large.

from "New Talent USA," *Art in America,* vol. 54, no. 4, July-August 1966, p. 38.

David Weinrib

. . . To me, environmental is enclosural, and I feel that, whether or not we like it, the materiality of a sculpture is still more important than all the space we grab. I think we're involved in something more basic than an environmental idea. It's true, the reason I push my sculpture into space physically, to try to attach it to a ceiling rather than the floor, for example, is that I want it to partake of the space more. But unfortunately, as it sits there, it still is an object. One of the things I'd like to get to is that feeling that the space in and around the sculpture is a little more important than the object materiality of the sculpture itself, but the space cannot be activated without the sculpture, and ultimately we must come back to the fact that it is the sculpture that is most important. . .

from Bruce Glaser, Lyman Kipp, George Sugarman and David Weinrib, "Where Do We Go From Here?" *Contemporary Sculpture,* New York, The Art Digest (Arts Yearbook 8), 1965, p. 154.

William T. Wiley

I think my work is about the past, in a spiritual way. Everybody I know has a real nostalgia about something which happened a long time ago, like Dada. Part of what I do and who I am is that I can't bear to give that up, the nostalgia, all that past stuff. The good stuff is always present no matter when it was done. Seems like I'm always looking for a way to work which doesn't exclude anything . . . any possibility.

from an interview with Joe Raffaele, December 1966.

Catalog of the Exhibition

Height precedes Width precedes Depth
†Denotes color reproduction

Arlo Acton

1. *Ball*, 1966,
mixed media, 102″ x 29″ x 90″
Lent by the artist

Peter Agostini

2. *Burlesque Queen (Swells/Woman Series)*, 1965,
plaster, 7′ x 6′
Lent by Stephen Radich Gallery, New York

Jeremy Anderson

3. *Altar*, 1963,
enamel, redwood, pine, privet,
89″ x 31″ x 33½″
Lent by Dilexi Gallery, San Francisco

4. *Temptation of St. Anthony*, 1965,
redwood, masonite, plastic,
19½″ x 101½″ x 34¾″
Lent by Dilexi Gallery, San Francisco

†5. *Early Morning Hours*, 1966,
enamel, redwood, fruitwood,
45″ x 35″ x 23½″
Lent by Dilexi Gallery, San Francisco

Carl Andre

†6. *Lock*, 1967,
painted chipboard, ½″ x 16′ x 16′
Lent by Dwan Gallery, Los Angeles

Stephen Antonakos

7. *Orange Vertical Floor Neon*, 1966,
neon and metal, 9′ x 6′ x 6′
Lent by Fischbach Gallery, New York

Larry Bell

†8. *Untitled*, 1966,
coated glass and rodium plated brass,
20″ x 20″ x 20″
Lent by Ferus-Pace Gallery, Los Angeles
and Pace Gallery, New York

9. *Untitled*, 1967,
coated glass and rodium plated brass,
12″ x 12″ x 12″
Lent by Ferus-Pace Gallery, Los Angeles and
Pace Gallery, New York

10. *Untitled*, 1967,
coated glass and rodium plated brass,
15″ x 15″ x 15″
Lent by Ferus-Pace Gallery, Los Angeles and
Pace Gallery, New York

Fletcher Benton

11. *Synchronetic C-4400-S Series*, 1966,
aluminum and plexiglass,
70″ x 60″ x 9″
Lent by Esther-Robles Gallery, Los Angeles

12. *Synchronetic C-8800 Series*, 1966,
aluminum and plexiglass,
83″ x 70″ x 11″
Lent by Esther-Robles Gallery, Los Angeles

†13. *Tri-Hexagon, Third Phase*, 1966,
aluminum and plexiglass,
65″ x 54″ x 10¼″
Lent by Esther-Robles Gallery, Los Angeles

Tony Berlant

14. *The Marriage of New York and Athens*, 1966,
aluminum over plywood, 10′4″ x 6′ x 6′
Lent by David Stuart Galleries, Los Angeles

Ronald Bladen

15. *Untitled*, 1965,
painted wood and aluminum, three units each,
9′ x 4′ x 10′ x 21″
Lent by Fischbach Gallery, New York

Alexander Calder

16. *Hello Girls*, 1964,
painted metal, three units,
H. 8′9″; H. 15′; H. 22′11″
Los Angeles County Museum of Art,
Art Museum Council Fund

17. *Octopus*, 1964, steel plate, H. 10′
Lent by Perls Galleries, New York

†18. *Day and Night*, 1965,
painted metal, 5′ x 12′
Lent by Perls Galleries, New York

Anthony Caro

19. *Prospect*, 1964,
painted steel, 8′11″ x 8′3″ x 12″
Lent by Edwin Janss, Jr., Los Angeles

20. *Span*, 1966,
painted steel, 72½″ x 15′4″ x 11′
Private Collection, Boston

John Chamberlain

† 21. *Sweet William*, 1962,
metal, 60″ x 46″ x 62″
Los Angeles County Museum of Art.
Gift of Mr. and Mrs. Abe Adler in memory of
Mrs. Esther Steif Rosen

22. *Toy*, 1961,
    metal and plastic, 48″ x 38″ x 31″
    Lent by Dwan Gallery, Los Angeles

23. *Boydille*, 1966,
    fiberglass, 42″ x 51″ x 42″
    Lent by Dwan Gallery, Los Angeles

24. *Ta Tung*, 1966,
    urethane foam, 21″ x 49″ x 43″
    Lent by Dwan Gallery, Los Angeles

54

Chryssa

†25. *Fragments for the Gates to Times Square II*, 1966,
    neon and plexiglass, 43″ x 34 1/16″ x 27 1/16″
    Lent by Pace Gallery, New York

Bruce Conner

26. *Tick-Tock-Jelly-Clock Cosmotron*, 1961,
    mixed media, 57½″ x 53½″
    Lent by Landau-Alan Gallery, New York and
    Felix Landau Gallery, Los Angeles

27. *Couch*, 1963,
    mixed media, 31½″ x 26″ x 72″
    Lent by Landau-Alan Gallery, New York and
    Felix Landau Gallery, Los Angeles

†28. *Looking Glass*, 1964,
    mixed media, 78″ x 48″ x 12″
    Lent by Landau-Alan Gallery, New York and
    Felix Landau Gallery, Los Angeles

Joseph Cornell

29. *Celestial Navigation Box*, c. 1955,
    construction, 8½″ x 15¾″
    Lent by Allan Stone Gallery, New York

30. *Fountain Box*, n.d.,
    construction, 13″ x 8″ x 5″
    Lent by Allan Stone Gallery, New York

31. *Sun Box Series*, c. 1960,
    construction, 14″ x 10″ x 4¾″
    Lent by Allan Stone Gallery, New York

32. *Apollinaris*, c. 1960,
    construction, 14″ x 8¾″ x 5″
    Lent by Allan Stone Gallery, New York

33. *Eclipse Series*, c. 1960,
    construction, 9″ x 14″ x 4½″
    Lent by Allan Stone Gallery, New York

34. *Du Lion d'Or*, c. 1960,
    construction, 9″ x 13″ x 4½″
    Lent by Allan Stone Gallery, New York

35. *Eclipse Series*, c. 1962,
    construction, 10″ x 16″ x 5″
    Lent by Allan Stone Gallery, New York

36. *Clay Pipe Series*, c. 1962,
    construction, 10″ x 15″ x 5″
    Lent by Allan Stone Gallery, New York

Tony DeLap

37. *Houdin's House*, 1967,
    aluminum and glass, two units, each:
    6′ x 6′ x 6′
    Lent by Dilexi Gallery, San Francisco;
    Robert Elkon Gallery, New York;
    Felix Landau Gallery, Los Angeles

Walter de Maria

38. *Museum Piece*, 1966,
    aluminum, 3⅝″ x 36″ x 36″
    Lent by Cordier & Ekstrom, Inc., New York

Jose de Rivera

39. *Construction #72*, 1960,
    stainless steel, motorized, 32″ x 80″
    Lent by The Art Museum,
    The University of New Mexico, Albuquerque

Mark di Suvero

40. *Elohim Adonai*, 1966,
    iron and wood, 22′ x 30′
    Lent by Park Place Gallery, New York

Tom Doyle

41. *Over Owl's Creek*, 1966,
    wood and linoleum, W. 9′ x L 18′
    Lent by Dwan Gallery, New York

†42. *Untitled*, 1966,
    fiberglassed wood, 5½′ x 12′ x 12′
    Lent by Dwan Gallery, New York

Dan Flavin

43. *Untitled*, 1963-66,
    fluorescent light, 8′ x 8′
    Private Collection, Los Angeles

Peter Forakis

44. *1, 2, 3 Infinity*, 1966,
    acrylic lacquer and metal,
    each unit: 30″ x 34″ x 34″
    Lent by Park Place Gallery, New York

William R. Geis, III

†45. *"Want Not . . .,"* 1965,
    plaster and fiberglass, 7′ x 7′ x 42″
    Lent by the artist

Judy Gerowitz

46. *Ten Part Cylinder*, 1966,
fiberglass, ten units: 36" x 12", 60" x 12", 48" x 18",
72" x 18", 60" x 24", 84" x 24", 72" x 30", 96" x 30",
84" x 36", 108" x 36" (arranged randomly)
Lent by Rolf Nelson Gallery, Los Angeles

David Gray

47. *Irvine 4*, 1967,
painted aluminum and chrome plated steel,
85⅝" x 48" x 72"
Lent by Ferus-Pace Gallery, Los Angeles

48. *Unit Q*, 1967,
painted aluminum and chrome plated steel,
72" x 14" x 96"
Lent by Ferus-Pace Gallery, Los Angeles

Robert Grosvenor

†49. *Still No Title*, 1966,
fiberglass, steel, plywood,
13' x 8' x 24'
Lent by Dwan Gallery, Los Angeles;
courtesy Park Place Gallery, New York

Lloyd Hamrol

50. *Five by Nine*, 1966,
formica on wood, closed dimensions:
6" x 30" x 30"
Lent by Rolf Nelson Gallery, Los Angeles

51. *Five by Nine*, 1966,
formica on wood, closed dimensions:
6" x 30" x 30"
Lent by Rolf Nelson Gallery, Los Angeles

52. *Five by Nine*, 1966,
formica on wood, closed dimensions:
6" x 30" x 30"
Lent by Rolf Nelson Gallery, Los Angeles

Paul Harris

53. *Woman Laughing*, 1964,
cloth, wood, paint, 42" x 42" x 42"
Lent by Poindexter Gallery, New York

54. *Woman Giving Her Greeting*, 1964,
cloth, 72" x 18" x 24"
Lent by Poindexter Gallery, New York

55. *Woman in Green Gown*, 1965,
cloth, wood, paint, 52" x 36" x 36"
Lent by the Abrams Family Collection, New York

†56. *Woman Smelling Her Roses*, 1966,
acrylic resin, cloth, wood, paint,
60" x 24" x 42"
Lent by Poindexter Gallery, New York

Duayne Hatchett

57. *Summer Solstice*, 1966,
stainless steel, 58½" x 112" x 30"
Lent by Royal Marks Gallery, New York

58. *Largo*, 1966,
painted steel, 82" x 86" x 29½"
Lent by Royal Marks Gallery, New York

Robert A. Howard

†59. *Landscape XX*, 1965-66,
painted steel, 80" x 13' x 30"
Lent by Royal Marks Gallery, New York

60. *Landscape XXIII*, 1966,
painted steel, 37" x 74" x 26"
Lent by Royal Marks Gallery, New York

Robert Hudson

†61. *Charm*, 1964,
painted metal, H. 45½"
Los Angeles County Museum of Art,
Contemporary Art Council Fund

62. *Space Window*, 1966,
painted steel, 69" x 60" x 57"
Lent by Mrs. Sally Hellyer, San Francisco

63. *Space Wrap With a Western Cut*, 1966,
painted steel, L. 72"
Lent by Mr. and Mrs. Robert A. Rowan, Pasadena

Donald Judd

64. *Untitled*, 1965,
perforated steel, 8" x 120" x 66"
Lent by Leo Castelli Gallery, New York

65. *Untitled*, 1966,
galvanized iron and painted aluminum,
40" x 190" x 40"
Lent by Pasadena Art Museum,
Gift of Mr. and Mrs. Robert A. Rowan

66. *Untitled*, 1967,
lacquer and cold rolled steel,
eight units, each: 48" x 48" x 48"
Lent by Leo Castelli Gallery, New York

Ellsworth Kelly

67. *Gate*, 1959,
painted aluminum, 66½" x 54½"
Lent by Mr. and Mrs. Donald Factor, Beverly Hills

68. *Blue Disk*, 1963,
painted aluminum, 70" x 72"
Lent by Mr. and Mrs. Max Wasserman,
Chestnut Hill, Massachusetts

55

Edward Kienholz

†69. *The State Hospital*, 1966,
mixed media, 8′ x 12′ x 10′
Lent by Dwan Gallery, New York

Frederick J. Kiesler

70. *Arch*, 1965,
bronze and aluminum,
6′6″ x 8′3″ x 2′7″
Lent by Howard Wise Gallery, New York

Lyman Kipp

†71. *Muscoot*, 1967,
painted steel, 14′ x 6′ x 4′
Lent by Betty Parsons Gallery, New York

Gabriel Kohn

72. *Long Beach Contract #1*, 1965,
laminated redwood, 7′ x 9′
Lent by California State College at Long Beach

Gary Kuehn

73. *Untitled*, 1965,
wood, steel, bolts, enamel, tar,
7′ x 2′6″ x 12″
Lent by Bianchini Gallery, New York

†74. *Untitled*, 1965,
structolite, wood, enamel,
96″ x 96″ x 12″
Lent by Bianchini Gallery, New York

Sol LeWitt

75. *Untitled*, 1966,
enamel on aluminum,
50″ x 50″ x 50″
Lent by Dwan Gallery, New York

Alexander Liberman

76. *Ritual*, 1966,
painted steel, H. 18′
Lent by Betty Parsons Gallery, New York

Alvin Light

77. *November 1964*, 1964,
hardwoods, H. 93″
Lent by Dilexi Gallery, San Francisco

Len Lye

78. *Flip and 2 Twisters*, 1965,
steel and electricity, H. 9′; 20′ in motion
Lent by Howard Wise Gallery, New York;
courtesy of the University Art Gallery,
University of California, Berkeley

John McCracken

79. *Untitled*, 1966,
lacquer, fiberglass, plywood,
96″ x 11½″ x 1″
Private Collection, courtesy of the
Nicholas Wilder Gallery, Los Angeles

80. *Untitled*, 1966,
lacquer, fiberglass, plywood,
84″ x 46″ x ½″
Lent by Mr. and Mrs. Robert B. Mayer,
Winnetka, Illinois

81. *Untitled*, 1966,
lacquer, fiberglass, plywood,
96″ x 11½″ x 1″
Private Collection, Los Angeles

†82. *Untitled*, 1967,
fiberglass, 15′ x 27″ x 20″
Los Angeles County Museum of Art,
Gift of Friends of Leonard B. Hirsch, Jr.,
through the Contemporary Art Council

Marisol

83. *The Dealers*, 1965-66,
mixed media, 74″ x 74″ x 47″
Lent by Sidney Janis Gallery, New York

John Mason

†84. *Red X*, 1966,
clay, H. 60″
Lent by Ferus-Pace Gallery, Los Angeles

85. *Cube Form*, 1966,
clay, H. 60″
Lent by Ferus-Pace Gallery, Los Angeles

86. *Oval Form*, 1966,
clay, H. 60″
Lent by Ferus-Pace Gallery, Los Angeles

Charles Mattox

87. *Tom Tom Series #3*, 1966,
painted fiberglass, 6′ x 6′ x 15″
Lent by Nicholas Wilder Gallery, Los Angeles

88. *Opposing V's*, 1966,
painted fiberglass, 6′ x 6′ x 2′
Lent by Nicholas Wilder Gallery, Los Angeles

†89. *Green Triangle with Red Cube*, 1966,
painted fiberglass and metal, 4′ x 4′ x 10″
Lent by Nicholas Wilder Gallery, Los Angeles

Robert Morris

90. *Untitled*, 1966,
fiberglass, 2′ x 8′
Lent by Dwan Gallery, Los Angeles

91. *Untitled*, 1966,
    steel, 31″ x 106″ x 106″
    Lent by Leo Castelli Gallery, New York

Robert Murray

†92. *Track*, 1966,
    steel and painted aluminum, L. 14′
    Lent by Betty Parsons Gallery, New York

Forrest Myers

†93. *Sando's Pipeline*, 1966,
    acrylic lacquer and welded aluminum,
    12′ x 38′ x 7′
    Lent by Dwan Gallery, Los Angeles;
    courtesy Park Place Gallery, New York

Reuben Nakian

94. *Goddess of the Golden Thighs*, 1964-65,
    bronze, 6′ x 12′
    Lent by Egan Gallery, New York

Bruce Nauman

95. *Untitled*, 1965,
    fiberglass, 24″ x 11′ x 5″
    Lent by Mr. and Mrs. Melvin Hirsh, Beverly Hills

96. *Untitled*, 1965,
    rubber, 88″ x 6″ x 2″
    Lent by Mr. and Mrs. John McCracken,
    Los Angeles

97. *Platform made up of the space between two
    rectilinear boxes on the floor*, 1966,
    fiberglass, 7″ x 80″ x 36″
    Lent by Alan Power, London

Louise Nevelson

98. *Royal Tide IV*, 1960,
    painted wood, 11′ x 14′
    Lent by Martha Jackson Gallery, New York

Isamu Noguchi

99. *Khmer*, 1962,
    bronze, H. 6′
    Lent by Cordier & Ekstrom, Inc., New York

100. *Floor Frame*, 1962,
    bronze, 9½″ x 34″ x 26″
    Lent by Cordier & Ekstrom, Inc., New York

101. *Lessons of Muso Kokuchi*, 1962,
    bronze, five units: 17″ x 19″ x 19″, 5″ x 19″ x 20″,
    3″ x 25″ x 25″, 12″ x 25″ x 25″, 18″ x 20″ x 24″
    Lent by Cordier & Ekstrom, Inc., New York

Claes Oldenburg

102. *Giant Ice Cream Cone*, 1962,
    painted canvas and foam rubber,
    150″ x 50″ x 50″
    Lent by Sidney Janis Gallery, New York

103. *Pecan Pie*, 1963,
    mixed media, 15″ x 21″ x 50″
    Private Collection

104. *Baked Potato*, 1963,
    plaster and jersey, 14″ x 24″ x 14″
    Lent by Dr. and Mrs. Nathan Alpers, Los Angeles

105. *Giant Blue Shirt with Brown Tie*, 1963,
    canvas, cloth, kapok, dacron, metal,
    plexiglass, 54″ x 82″ x 12″
    Lent by Mr. and Mrs. Ian Beck, New York

106. *Light Switch*, 1964,
    formica, wood, metal, 48″ x 48″ x 12½″
    Lent by Mr. and Mrs. Harold Ladas, New York

107. *Falling Shoestring Potatoes*, 1965,
    painted canvas and kapok,
    9′ x 46″ x 42″
    Lent by Walker Art Center, Minneapolis

108. *Giant Good Humor*, 1965,
    vinyl, 86″ x 37″ x 12″
    Lent by Conrad Janis, New York

109. *Four Models, Dormeyer Blender*, 1965,
    canvas and kapok, 42″ x 36″ x 24″
    Lent by Mr. and Mrs. Eugene M. Schwartz,
    New York

110. *Soft Manhattan #2 (Subways)*, 1966,
    stenciled canvas and kapok, 68″ x 32″ x 7″
    Lent by Sidney Janis Gallery, New York

111. *Soft Toilet*, 1966,
    vinyl, kapok, wood,
    55″ x 33″ x 28″
    Lent by Victor Ganz, New York

Harold Persico Paris

112. *Pantomina Illuma*, 1965-66,
    plastic, rubber, stainless steel,
    8′ x 8′ x 11′4″
    Lent by the artist

Kenneth Price

†113. *S.L. Blue*, 1966,
    painted clay, 3½″ x 3″ x 9″
    Lent by Ferus-Pace Gallery, Los Angeles, and
    Pace Gallery, New York

114. *S.D. Green*, 1966,
    painted clay, 5″ x 4″ x 9½″
    Lent by Ferus-Pace Gallery, Los Angeles, and
    Pace Gallery, New York

Richard Randell

†115. *Blue Klacker*, 1966-67,
    enamel on aluminum, 40″ x 13′8″ x 26″
    Lent by Royal Marks Gallery, New York

116. *Five Striped Klacker*, 1967,
    enamel on aluminum, 27″ x 26′ x 27″
    Lent by Royal Marks Gallery, New York

Robert Rauschenberg

117. *Image Wheels*, 1967,
    aluminum and plastic, 7′ x 6′2″ x 2′6″
    Lent by Leo Castelli Gallery, New York

George Rickey

†118. *Two Red Lines, II*, 1966,
    painted stainless steel, H. 37′
    Lent by the artist

119. *Four Planes, Hanging*, 1966,
    steel, W. 76″
    Lent by the artist

Lucas Samaras

120. *Corridor*, 1967,
    glass mirror and crystal spheres,
    8′ x 8′6″ x 7′9″
    Lent by Pace Gallery, New York, and
    Ferus-Pace Gallery, Los Angeles

George Segal

121. *The Gas Station*, 1964,
    plaster, metal, glass, stone, rubber, L. 25′
    Lent by Sidney Janis Gallery, New York

David Smith

122. *Noland's Blues*, 1961,
    painted steel, 99⅛″ x 44¼″ x 20½″
    Lent by Estate of David Smith, courtesy
    Marlborough-Gerson Gallery, New York

123. *Circle III*, 1962,
    painted steel, 95½″ x 72″ x 18″
    Lent by Estate of David Smith, courtesy
    Marlborough-Gerson Gallery, New York

124. *Untitled*, 1962-63,
    stainless steel, 97″ x 63″ x 27½″
    Lent by Estate of David Smith, courtesy
    Marlborough-Gerson Gallery, New York

125. *Cubi VI*, 1963,
    stainless steel, H. 9′10½″
    Lent by Estate of David Smith, courtesy
    Marlborough-Gerson Gallery, New York

126. *Untitled*, 1964,
    stainless steel, 9′9⅝″ x 69″ x 16¾″
    Lent by Estate of David Smith, courtesy
    Marlborough-Gerson Gallery, New York

127. *Untitled*, 1964,
    mild steel, 82¾″ x 67″ x 29½″
    Lent by Estate of David Smith, courtesy
    Marlborough-Gerson Gallery, New York

†128. *Cubi XXIII*, 1964,
    stainless steel, H. 76¼″ x L. 14′4⅞″
    Los Angeles County Museum of Art,
    Contemporary Art Council Fund

Tony Smith

129. *Cigarette*, model: 1961;
    wood mock-up to be made in steel: 1967,
    wood mock-up, 15′ x 26′ x 18′
    Lent by Fischbach Gallery, New York

†130. *Willy*, 1962,
    wood mock-up to be made in steel: 1967,
    wood mock-up, 7′8″ x 12′ x 18′
    Lent by Fischbach Gallery, New York

131. *Die II*, 1967,
    steel, 6′ x 6′ x 6′
    Lent by Fischbach Gallery, New York

Robert Smithson

132. *Alogon #2*, 1966,
    painted steel, ten units; square surfaces:
    2½″, 3″, 3½″, 4″, 4½″, 5″, 5½″, 6″, 6½″, 7″
    Lent by Dwan Gallery, New York

Kenneth Snelson

133. *Cantilever*, 1967,
    floating compression cantilevered:
    aluminum and steel, L. 30′
    Lent by Dwan Gallery, New York and Los Angeles

Robert Stevenson

†134. *Untitled*, 1966,
    plexiglass, 8′ x 3′ x 3′
    Private Collection; courtesy Rolf Nelson
    Gallery, Los Angeles

George Sugarman

†135. *Two in One*, 1966,
    painted wood, 7′ x 11′6″
    Lent by Fischbach Gallery, New York

Michael Todd

†136. *Weehawken*, 1966,
painted wood, overall length, 14′
Los Angeles County Museum of Art,
Anonymous Gift through the Contemporary
Art Council

137. *Zees*, 1966-67,
painted wood, 6′ x 12′
Lent by the artist

Ernest Trova

†138. *Study Falling Man: Venice Landscape*, 1965-66,
silicone bronze, 90″ x 14′ x 72″
Lent by Pace Gallery, New York

Anne Truitt

139. *Thirtieth*, 1962,
painted wood, H. 7′
Lent by Andre Emmerich Gallery, New York

140. *Shrove*, 1962,
painted wood, 60½″ x 10″ x 10″
Lent by Andre Emmerich Gallery, New York

DeWain Valentine

141. *3-Silver*, 1967,
fiberglass reinforced plastic,
54″ x 78″ x 54″
Lent by Dwan Gallery, Los Angeles

142. *Double Top*, 1967,
fiberglass reinforced plastic,
54″ x 76″ x 54″
Lent by Dwan Gallery, Los Angeles

Vasa

†143. *Blue in the Middle*, 1966,
acrylic lacquer on wood, 8′ x 6′ x 22″
Lent by Herbert Palmer Gallery, Los Angeles

Stephan Von Huene

144. *The Hermaphroditic Horseback Rider*, 1966,
wood and leather, 78″ x 26″ x 29″
Lent by David Stuart Galleries, Los Angeles

145. *Pneumatic Music-Machine*, 1967,
wood, leather, pneumatic system,
75″ x 24″ x 22″ (work in progress)
Lent by David Stuart Galleries, Los Angeles

David Von Schlegell

146. *Untitled*, 1966,
polished aluminum, 88″ x 10′ x 8′
Lent by Royal Marks Gallery, New York

147. *Untitled*, 1967.
polished aluminum, 78″ x 42′ x 5′
Lent by Royal Marks Gallery, New York

Peter Voulkos

148. *Gallas Rock*, 1961,
clay, H. 84″
Lent by Mrs. Digby Gallas, Los Angeles

149. *Firestone*, 1965,
cast bronze and aluminum,
80″ x 72″
Los Angeles County Museum of Art,
Contemporary Art Council Fund

150. *Dunlop*, 1966,
bronze, 7′ x 13′
Lent by David Stuart Galleries, Los Angeles

David Weinrib

†151. *Spatial Sculpture IV*, 1964,
enameled steel, plastic, wood,
96″ x 84″ x 60″
Los Angeles County Museum of Art,
Gift of Howard Wise through the
Contemporary Art Council

152. *30 Forms*, 1966,
plastic, 18″ x 36″ x 36″
Lent by Royal Marks Gallery, New York

153. *Orange Circle*, 1967,
plastic, 27″ x 73″ x 37″
Lent by Royal Marks Gallery, New York

H. C. Westermann

154. *The Plush*, 1963-64,
wood, metal pipe, carpeting,
62″ x 29″ x 21″
Lent by Allan Frumkin Gallery, New York

155. *Untitled*, 1964,
wood, H. 70″
Lent by the Kleiner Foundation, Beverly Hills

156. *Antimobile*, 1966,
plywood and metal, 57″ x 36″ x 28″
Lent by Charles S. Jules, New York

†157. *Westermann's Table*, 1966,
plywood, bolt, books, H. 44¾″
Lent by Allan Frumkin Gallery, New York

William T. Wiley

158. *Enigma Bone*, 1964,
mixed media, 48″ x 24″ x 54″
Lent by the artist

159. *Zebra Tomb*, 1964,
mixed media, 12″ x 18″ x 66″
Lent by the artist

160. *Untitled*, 1964,
mixed media, 24″ x 36″ x 12″
Lent by the artist

Norman Zammitt

†161. *Solid Construction-Laminated*, 1966,
acrylic plastic, 19½″ x 29⅝″ x 4¼″
Lent by Felix Landau Gallery, Los Angeles and
Landau-Alan Gallery, New York

162. *Solid Construction-Laminated*, 1966,
acrylic plastic, 19″ x 23½″ x 5″
Lent by Felix Landau Gallery, Los Angeles and
Landau-Alan Gallery, New York

163. *Solid Construction-Laminated*, 1966,
acrylic plastic, 12″ x 16″ x 8½″
Lent by Felix Landau Gallery, Los Angeles and
Landau-Alan Gallery, New York

Wilfrid Zogbaum

164. *Islais Creek*, 1961,
painted steel, H. 85″
Lent by Dilexi Gallery, San Francisco

165. *II*, 1962,
metal and stone,
69″ x 37″ x 26″
Lent by San Francisco Museum of Art,
Gift of Friends of the Artist

†166. *Vincristin*, 1964,
painted steel, H. 14′
Lent by Grace Borgenicht Gallery, New York and
Dilexi Gallery, San Francisco

1. Arlo Acton. *Ball.* 1966.
Mixed media, 102″ x 29″ x 90″.

2. Peter Agostini. *Burlesque Queen (Swells/Woman Series).* 1965. Plaster, 7′ x 6′.

62

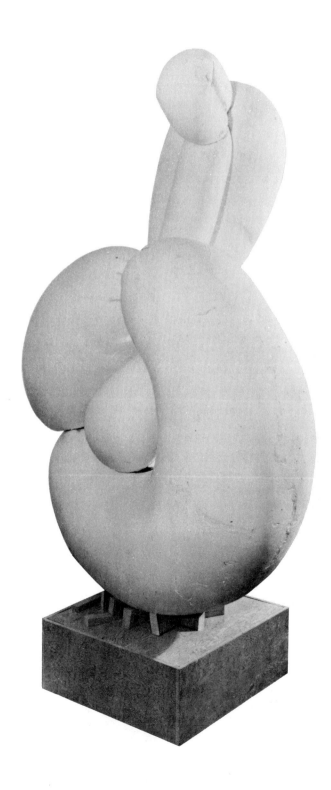

3. Jeremy Anderson. *Altar*. 1963.　　　　　　　　　　　　　Enamel, redwood, pine, privet, 89″ x 31″ x 33½″.

4. Jeremy Anderson. *Temptation of St. Anthony.* 1965. Redwood, masonite, plastic, 19½″ x 101½″ x 34¾″.

64

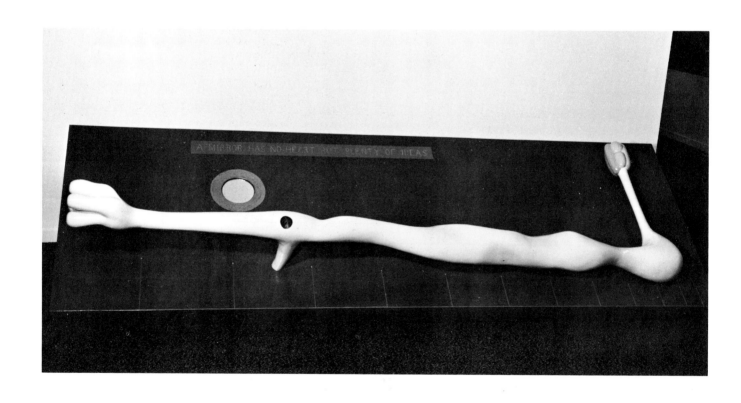

5. Jeremy Anderson. *Early Morning Hours.* 1966.　　　　　　Enamel, redwood, fruitwood, 45″ x 35″ x 23½″.

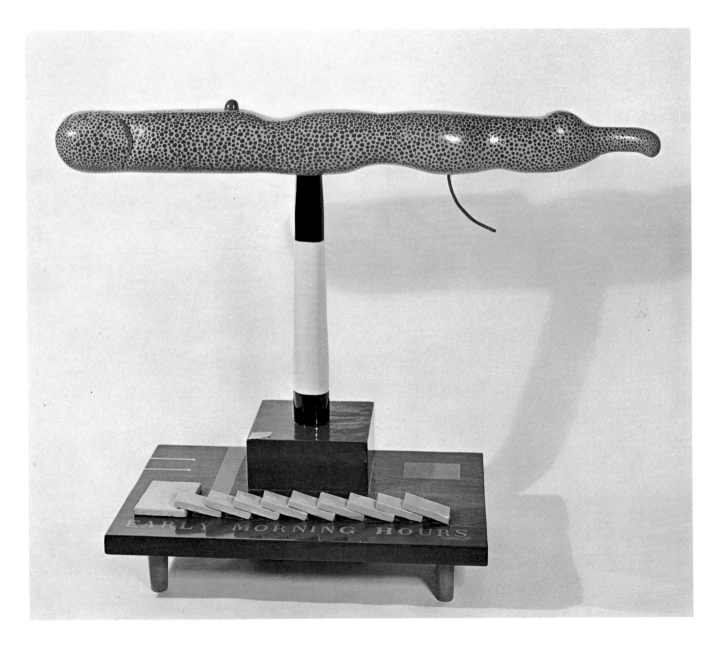

66

68

70

12. Fletcher Benton. *Synchronetic C-8800 Series.* 1966.   Aluminum and plexiglass, 83″ x 70″ x 11″.

14. Tony Berlant. *The Marriage of New York and Athens*. 1966.

Aluminum over plywood, 10′4″ x 6′ x 6′.

72

15. Ronald Bladen. *Untitled.* 1965.   Painted wood and aluminum, three units each, 9′ x 4′ x 10′ x 21″.

16. Alexander Calder. *Hello Girls.* 1964.   Painted metal, three units, H. 8'9"; H. 15'; H. 22'11".

74

76

78

79

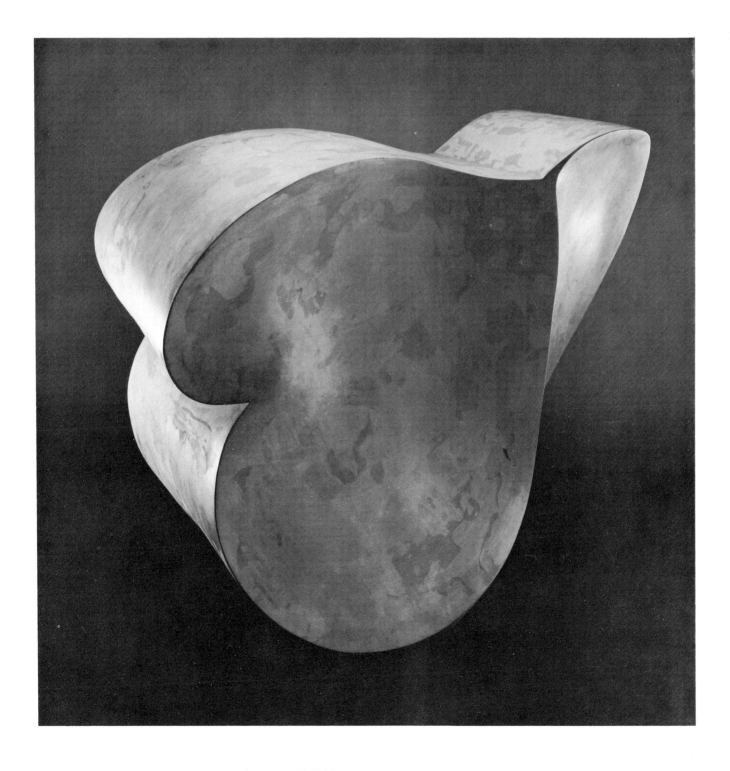

80

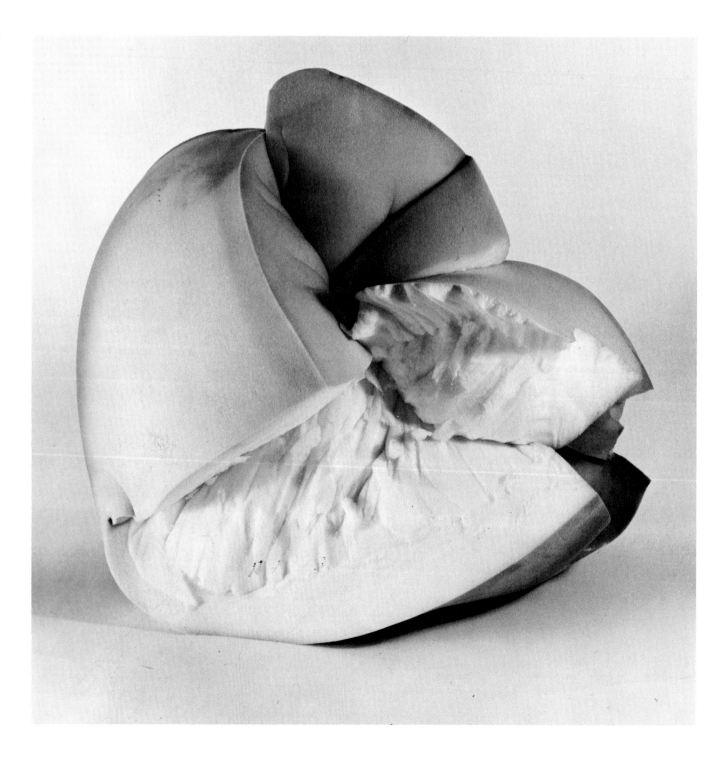

25. Chryssa. *Fragments for the Gates to Times Square II*. 1966.   Neon and plexiglass, 43″ x 34 1/16″ x 27 1/16″.

See page 103 for color reproduction

82

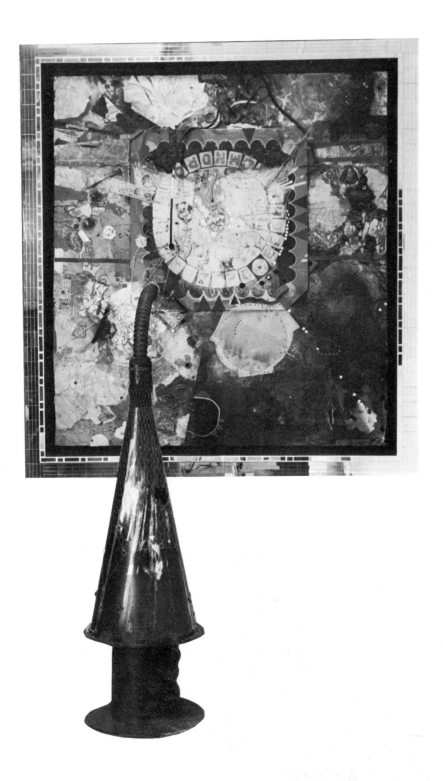

8. Larry Bell. *Untitled*. 1966.   Coated glass and rodium plated brass, 20″ x 20″ x 20″.

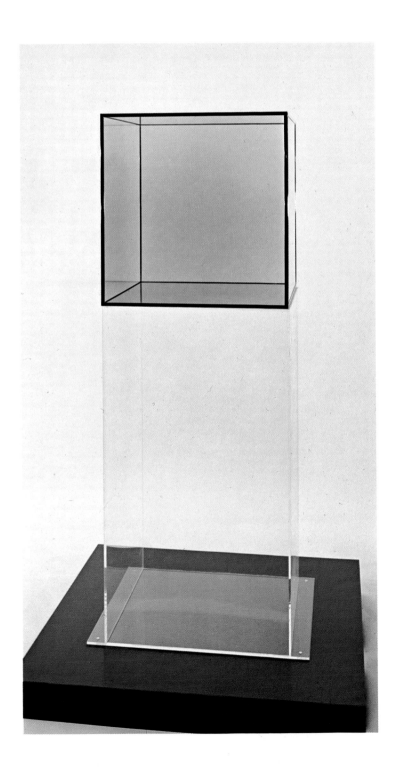

84

86

27. Bruce Conner. *Couch*. 1963.

Mixed media, 31½″ x 26″ x 72″.

88

32. Joseph Cornell. *Apollinaris.* c. 1960.   Construction, 14″ x 8¾″ x 5″.

91

92

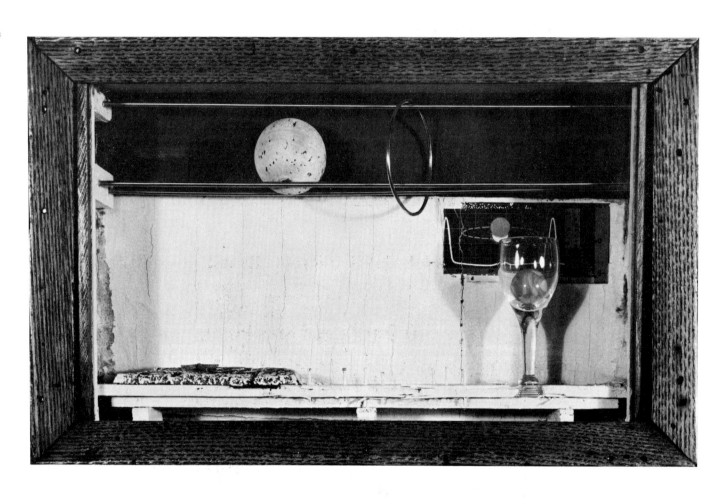

94

96

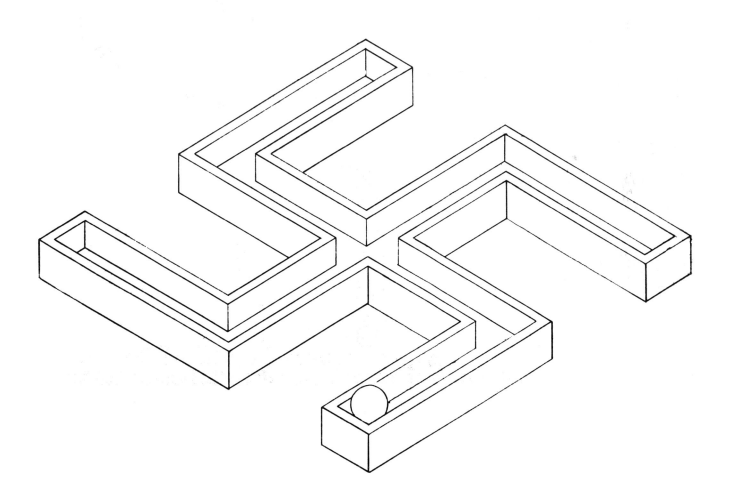

98

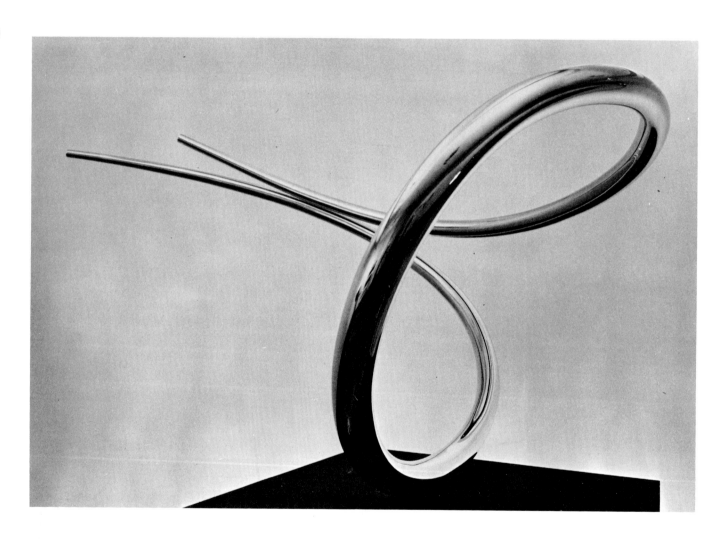

100

104

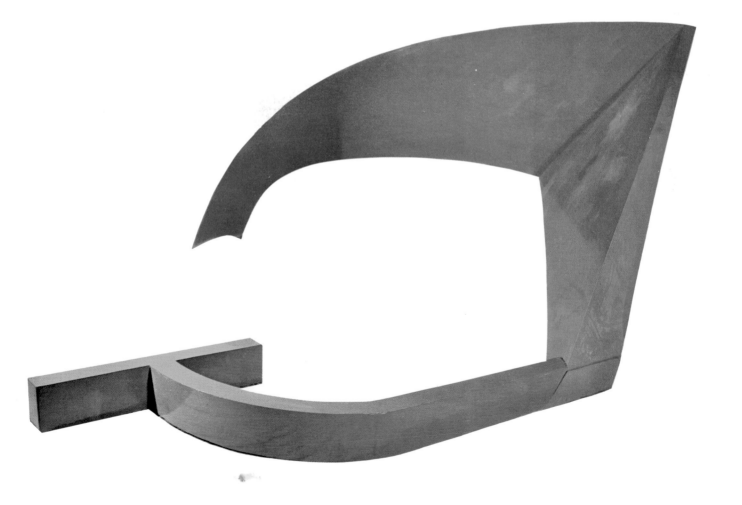

45. William R. Geis, III. *"Want Not. . ."* 1965.   Plaster and fiberglass, 7′ x 7′ x 42″.

106

46. Judy Gerowitz. *Ten Part Cylinder*. 1966.   Fiberglass, ten units: 36″ x 12″, 60″ x 12″, 48″ x 18″, 72″ x 18″, 60″ x 24″, 84″ x 24″, 72″ x 30″, 96″ x 30″, 84″ x 36″, 108″ x 36″ (arranged randomly).

(work in progress)

48. David Gray. *Unit Q.* 1967. Painted aluminum and chrome plated steel, 72″ x 14″ x 96″.

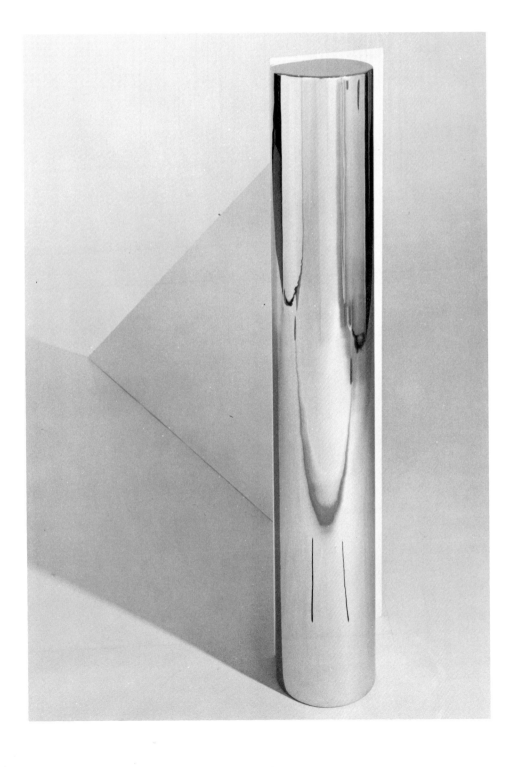

49. Robert Grosvenor. *Still No Title*. 1966.   Fiberglass, steel, plywood, 13′ x 8′ x 24′.

See page 123 for color reproduction

110

50. Lloyd Hamrol. *Five by Nine*. 1966.   Formica on wood, closed dimensions: 6″ x 30″ x 30″.

51. Lloyd Hamrol. *Five by Nine*. 1966.   Formica on wood, closed dimensions: 6 ″ x 30″ x 30″.

52. Lloyd Hamrol. *Five by Nine.* 1966.   Formica on wood, closed dimensions: 6 ″ x 30″ x 30″.

114

116

57. Duayne Hatchett. *Summer Solstice*. 1966. Stainless steel, 58½″ x 112″ x 30″.

117

58. Duayne Hatchett. *Largo*. 1966.   Painted steel, 82″ x 86″ x 29½″.

118

62. Robert Hudson. *Space Window*. 1966.   Painted steel, 69″ x 60″ x 57″.

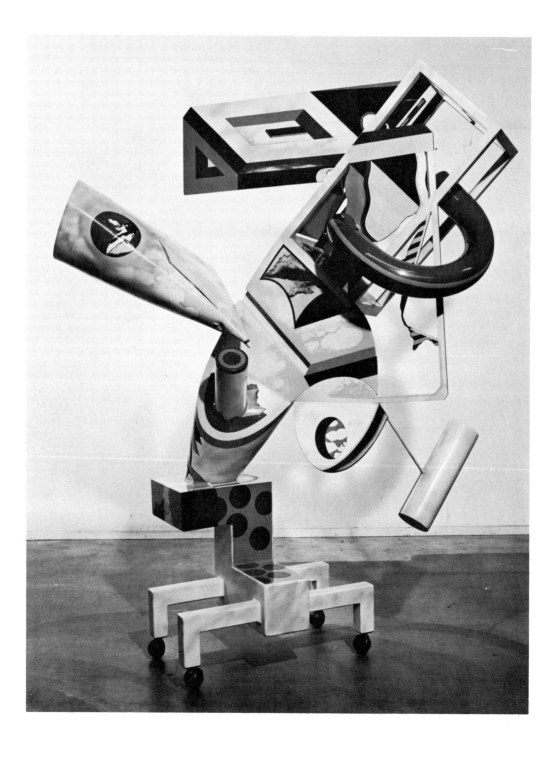

63. Robert Hudson. *Space Wrap With a Western Cut*. 1966.

Painted steel, L. 72″.

64. Donald Judd. *Untitled.* 1965.

Perforated steel, 8″ x 120″ x 66″.

122

49. Robert Grosvenor. *Still No Title*. 1966.   Fiberglass, steel, plywood, 13′ x 8′ x 24′.

56. Paul Harris. *Woman Smelling Her Roses*. 1966.   Acrylic resin, cloth, wood. paint, 6o″ x 24″ x 42″.

124

59. Robert A. Howard. *Landscape XX*. 1965-66. Painted steel, 80″ x 13′ x 30″.

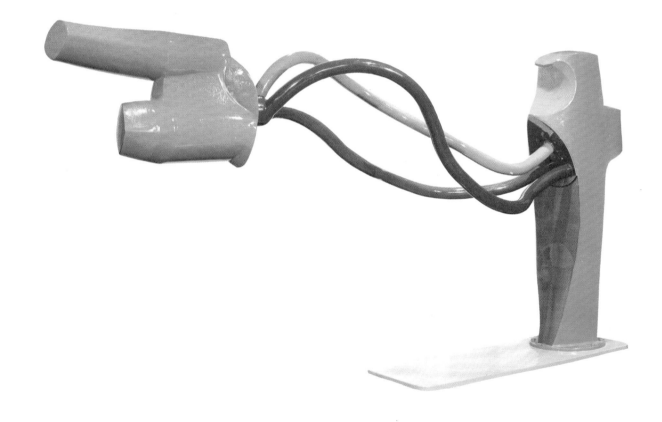

126

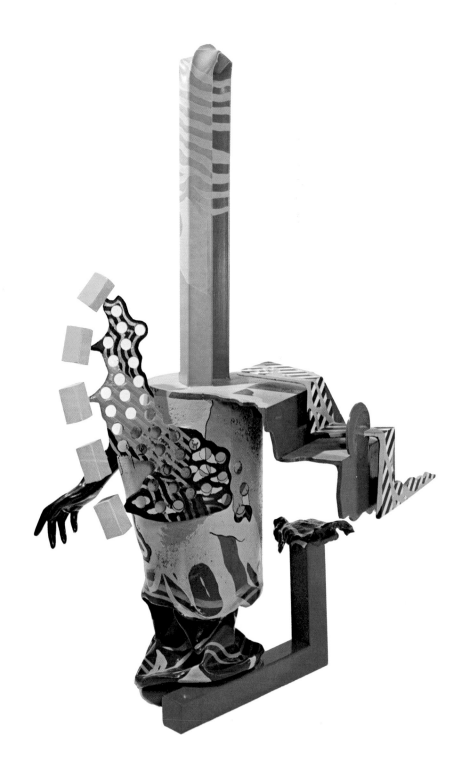

65. Donald Judd. *Untitled*. 1966.   Galvanized iron and painted aluminum, 40″ x 190″ x 40″.

128

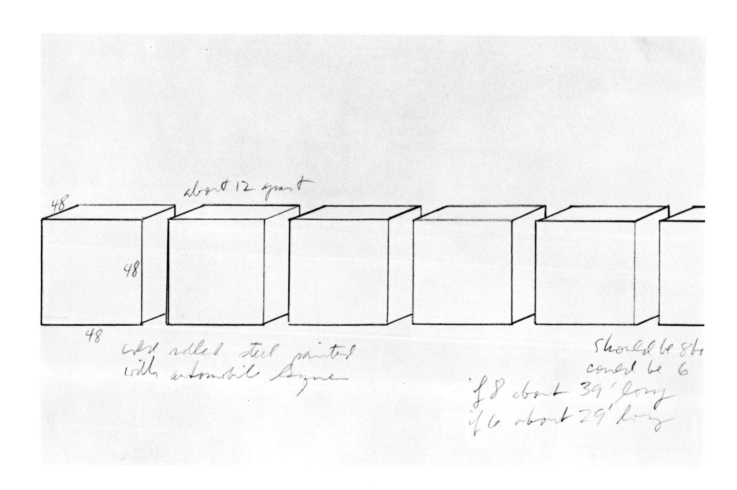

68. Ellsworth Kelly. *Blue Disk.* 1963.   Painted aluminum, 70″ x 72″.

69. Edward Kienholz. *The State Hospital*. 1966. Mixed media, 8′ x 12′ x 10′.

See page 143 for color reproduction

132

71. Lyman Kipp. *Muscoot*. 1967.

See page 144 for color reproduction

Painted steel, 14′ x 6′ x 4′.

133

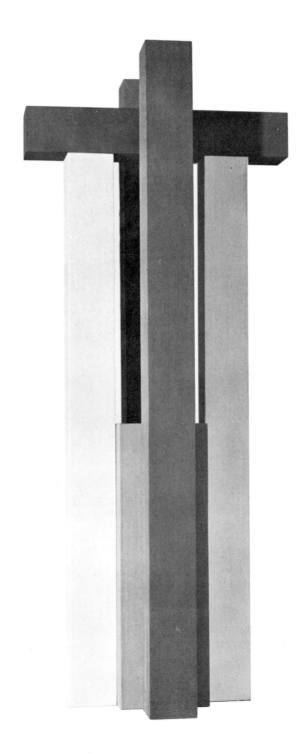

134

73. Gary Kuehn. *Untitled*. 1965.　　　　　　　　　　　　　　Wood, steel, bolts, enamel, tar, 7′ x 2′6″ x 12″.

136

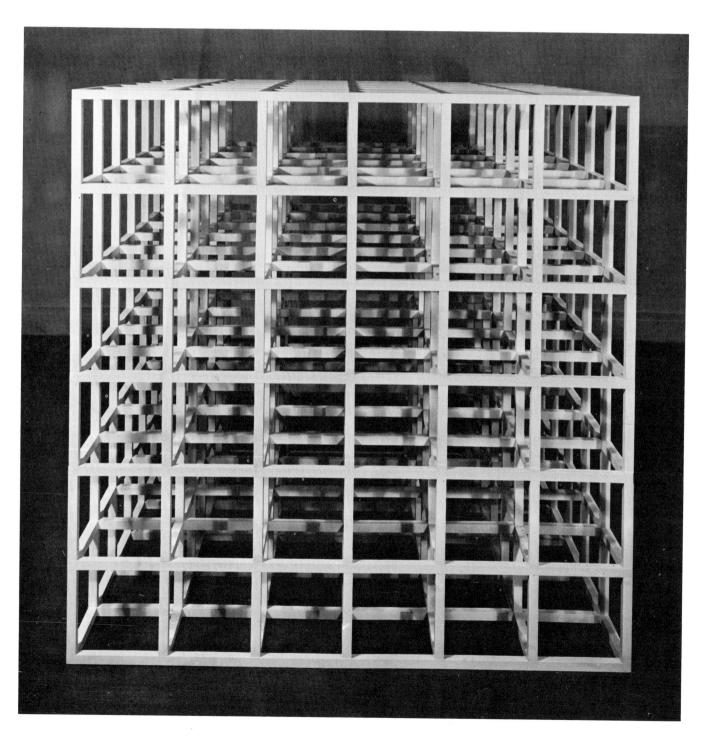

140

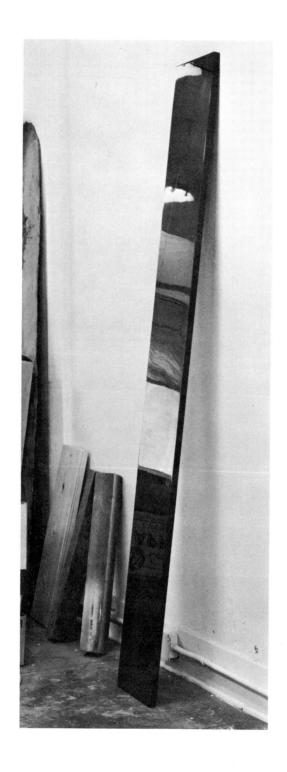

80. John McCracken. *Untitled.* 1966.   Lacquer, fiberglass, plywood, 84″ x 46″ x ½″.

142

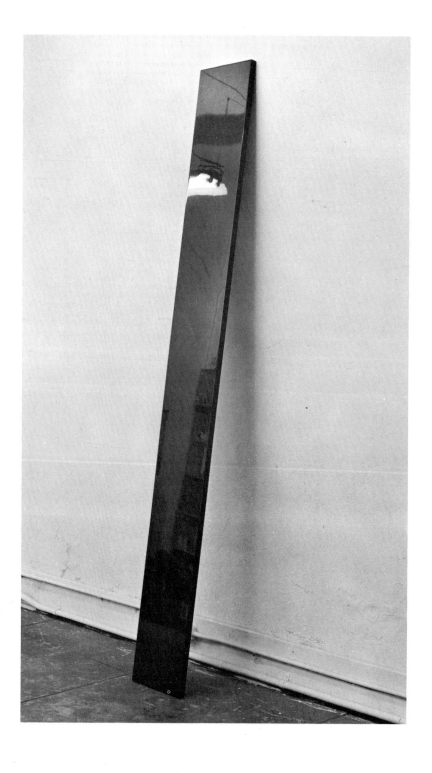

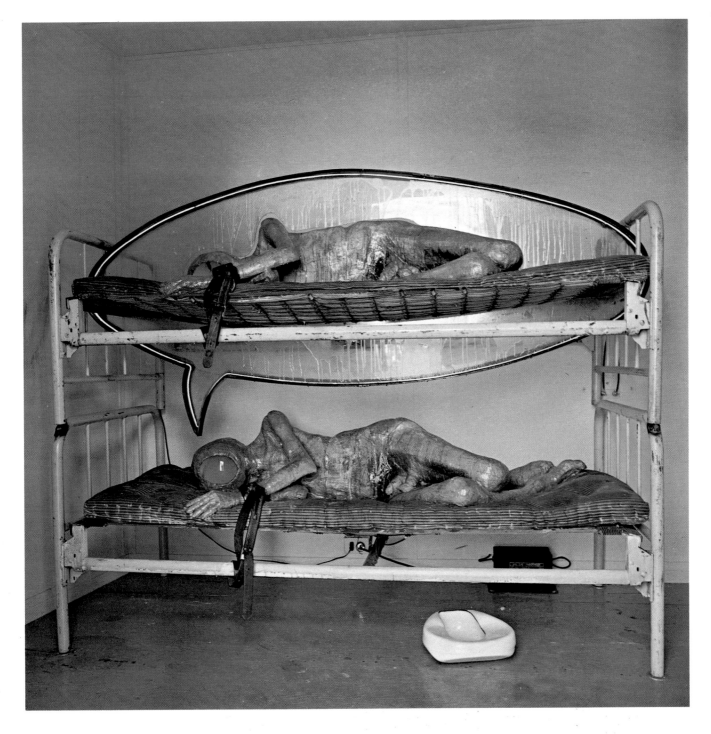

74. Gary Kuehn. *Untitled.* 1965.   Structolite, wood, enamel, 96″ x 96″ x 12″.

146

83. Marisol. *The Dealers*. 1965-66.   Mixed media, 74″ x 74″ x 47″.

148

86. John Mason. *Oval Form.* 1966.   Clay, H. 60"

88. Charles Mattox. *Opposing V's.* 1966.

Painted fiberglass, 6′ x 6′ x 2′.

152

92. Robert Murray. *Track*. 1966.

Steel and painted aluminum, L. 14'.

See page 157 for color reproduction

154

84. John Mason. *Red X*. 1966.

Clay, H. 60″.

89. Charles Mattox. *Green Triangle with Red Cube*. 1966.   Painted fiberglass and metal, 4′ x 4′ x 10″.

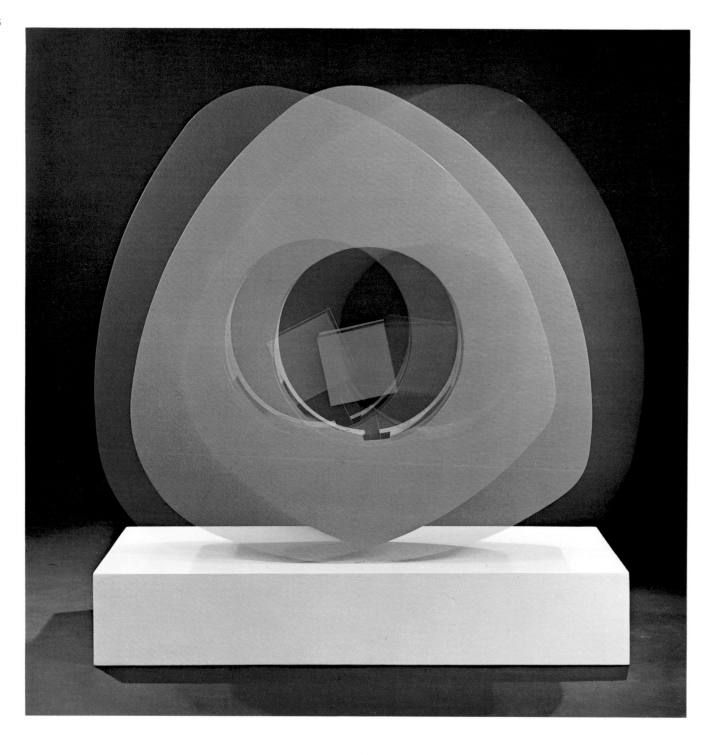

158

94. Reuben Nakian. *Goddess of the Golden Thighs.* 1964-65.   Bronze, 6′ x 12′.

160

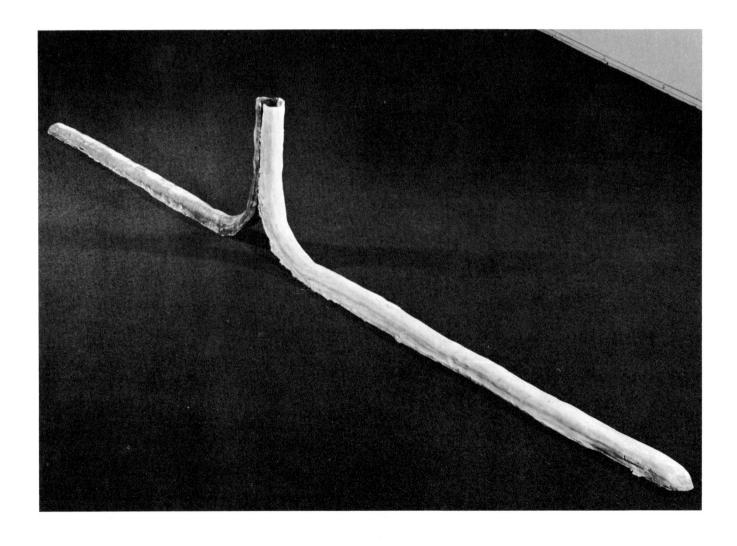

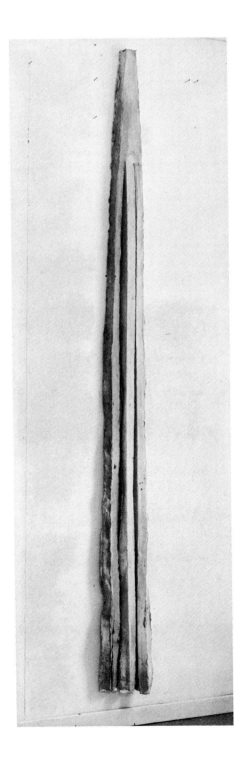

97. Bruce Nauman. *Platform made up of the space between two rectilinear boxes on the floor.* 1966.   Fiberglass, 7″ x 80″ x 36″.

162

164

101. Isamu Noguchi. *Lessons of Muso Kokuchi.* 1962.   Bronze, five units: 17″ x 19″ x 19″, 5″ x 19″ x 20″, 3″ x 25″ x 25″, 12″ x 25″ x 25″, 18″ x 20″ x 24″.

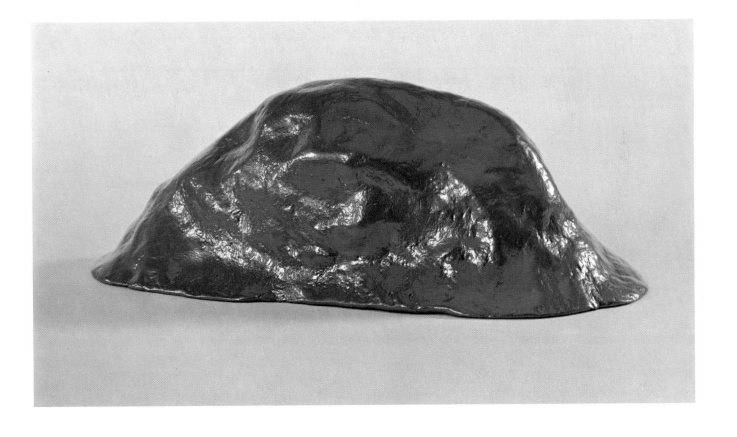

115. Richard Randell. *Blue Klacker*. 1966-67. Enamel on aluminum, 40″ x 13′8″ x 26″.

168

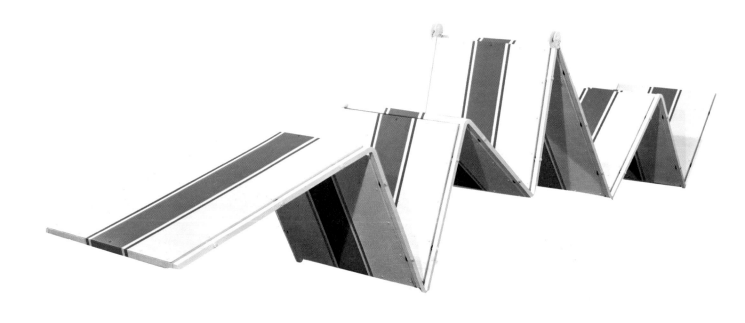

102. Claes Oldenburg. *Giant Ice Cream Cone.* 1962.   Painted canvas and foam rubber, 150″ x 50″ x 50″.

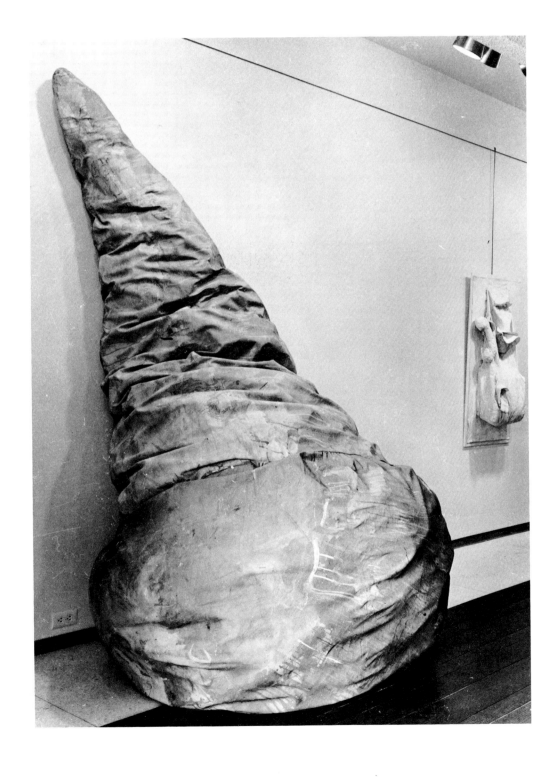

170

104. Claes Oldenburg. *Baked Potato.* 1963.

Plaster and jersey, 14″ x 24″ x 14″.

105. Claes Oldenburg. *Giant Blue Shirt with Brown Tie.* 1963.   Canvas, cloth, kapok, dacron, metal, plexiglass, 54″ x 82″ x 12″.

172

106. Claes Oldenburg. *Light Switch*. 1964.

Formica, wood, metal, 48″ x 48″ x 12½″.

107. Claes Oldenburg. *Falling Shoestring Potatoes.* 1965. Painted canvas and kapok, 9′ x 46″ x 42″.

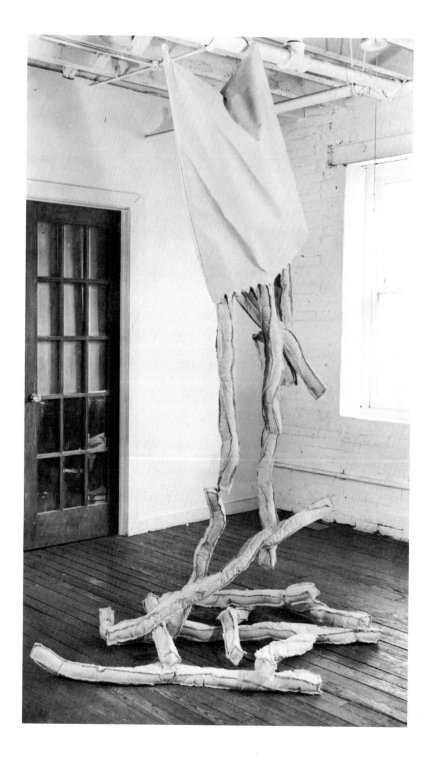

176

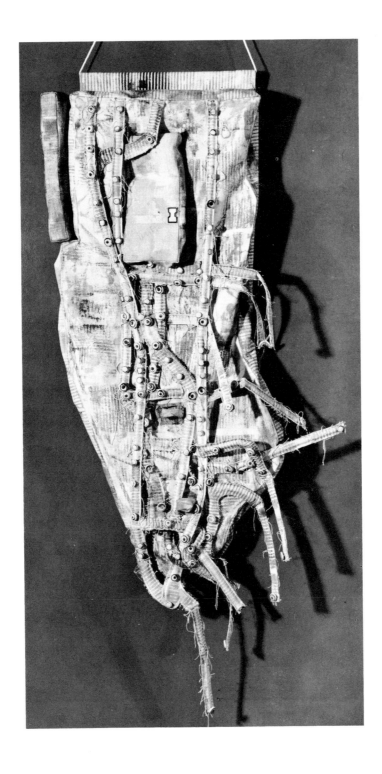

178

112. Harold Persico Paris. *Pantomina Illuma.* 1965-66. Plastic, rubber, stainless steel, 8′ x 8′ x 11′4″.

180

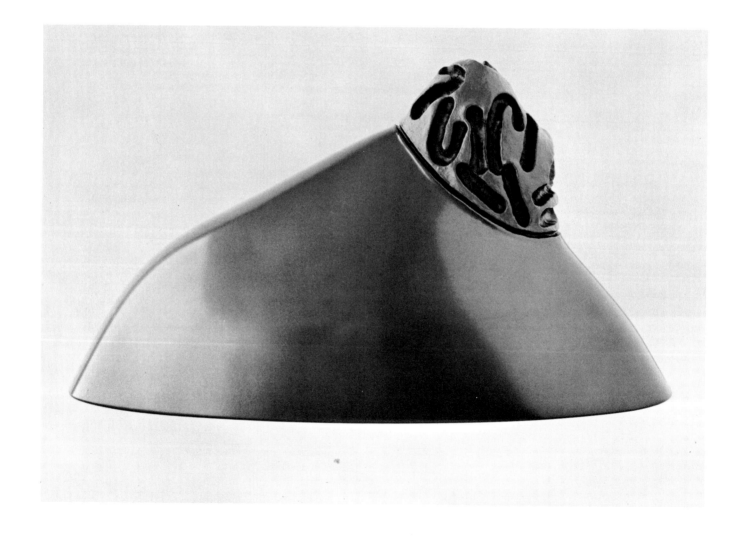

116. Richard Randell. (drawing for) *Five Striped Klacker*. 1967.   Enamel on aluminum, 27″ x 26′ x 27″.

181

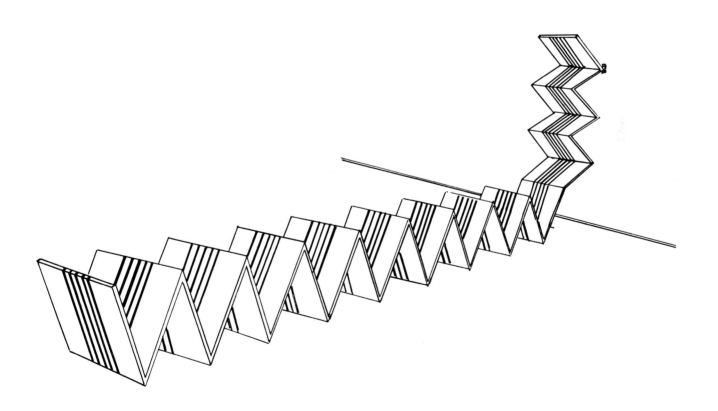

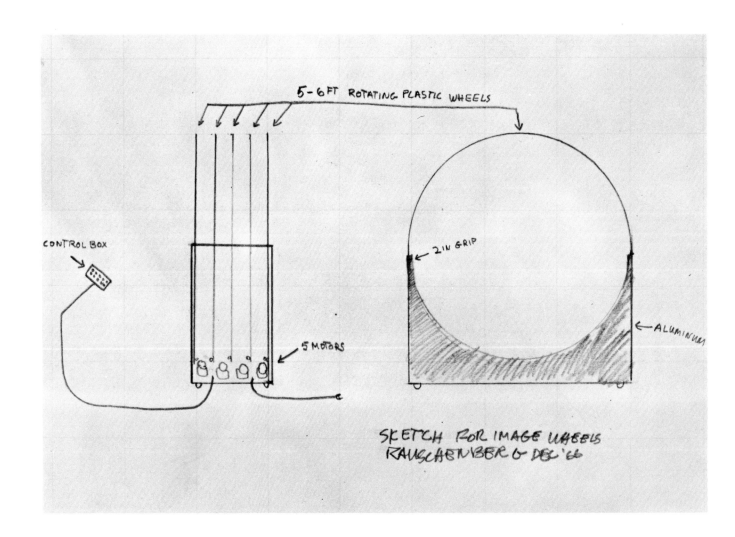

5-6 FT ROTATING PLASTIC WHEELS

CONTROL BOX

2 IN GRIP

ALUMINUM

5 MOTORS

SKETCH FOR IMAGE WHEELS
RAUSCHENBERG DEC '66

119. George Rickey. *Four Planes, Hanging.* 1966.

184

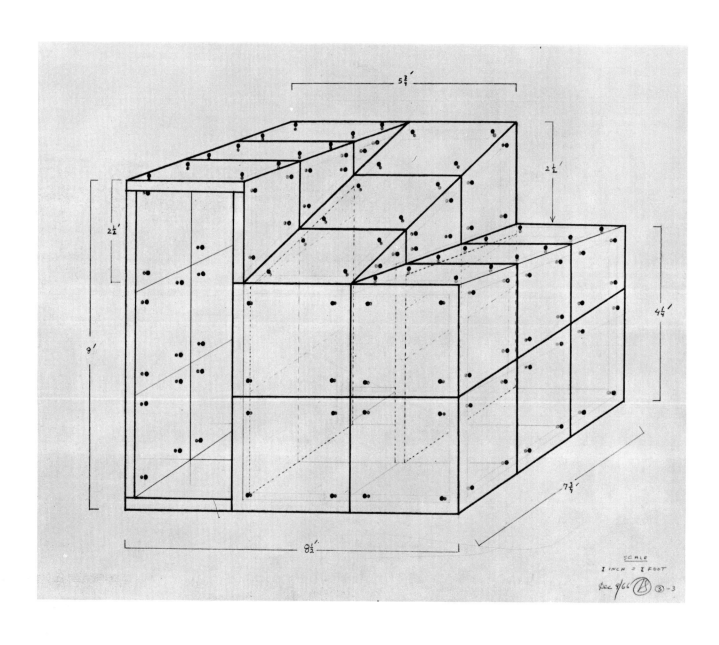

186

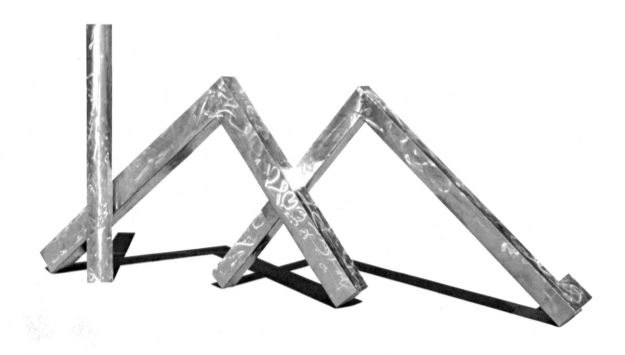

121. George Segal. *The Gas Station*. 1964.

Plaster, metal, glass, stone, rubber, L. 25'.

122. David Smith. *Noland's Blues*, 1961.

Painted steel, 99⅛″ x 44¼″ x 20½″.

188

123. David Smith. *Circle III*. 1962.   Painted steel, 95½″ x 72″ x 18″.

124. David Smith. *Untitled.* 1962-63.   Stainless steel, 97″ x 63″ x 27½″.

192

127. David Smith. *Untitled*. 1964.

Mild steel, 82¾″ x 67″ x 29½″.

129. Tony Smith. *Cigarette*, model: 1961.   Wood mock-up to be made in steel: 1967, wood mock-up: 15′ x 26′ x 18′.

194

132. Robert Smithson. *Alogon #2*. 1966.   Painted steel, ten units; square surfaces: 2½″, 3″, 3½″, 4″, 4½″, 5″, 5½″, 6″, 6½″, 7″.

133. Kenneth Snelson. *Cantilever*. 1967.   Floating compression cantilevered: aluminum and steel, L. 30′.

134. Robert Stevenson. *Untitled.* 1966.   Plexiglass, 8′ x 3′ x 3′.

See page 204 for color reproduction

198

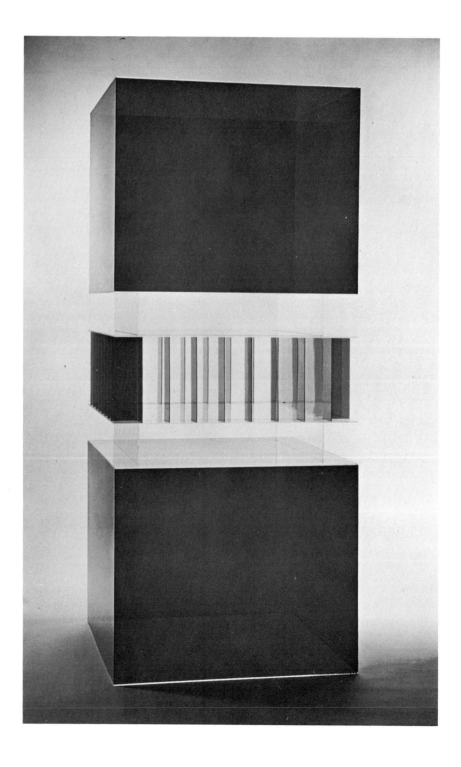

135. George Sugarman. *Two in One*. 1966. Painted wood, 7′x 11′6″.

See page 205 for color reproduction

199

200

138. Ernest Trova. *Study Falling Man: Venice Landscape.* 1965-66.   Silicone bronze, 90″ x 14′ x 72″.

See page 215 for color reproduction

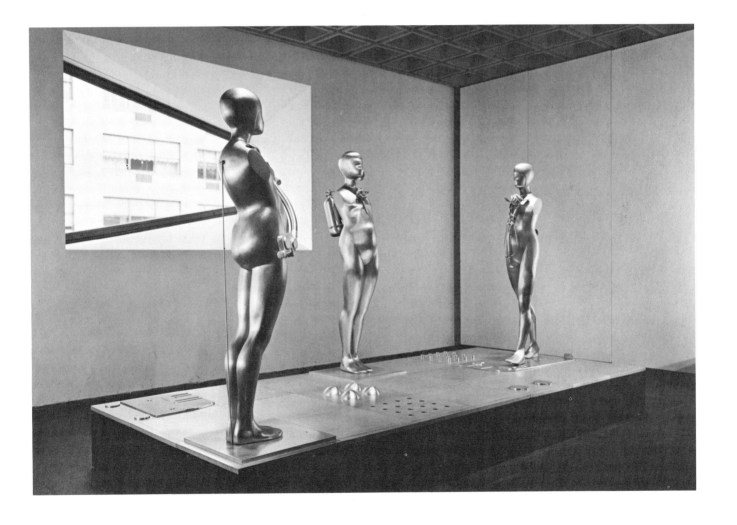

202

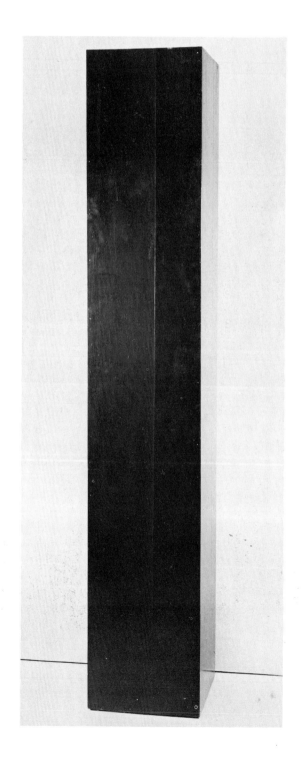

130. Tony Smith. *Willy*. 1962.

Wood mock-up to be made in steel: 1967, wood mock-up: 7′8″ x 12′ x 18′.
Photograph of earlier painted wood mock-up

204

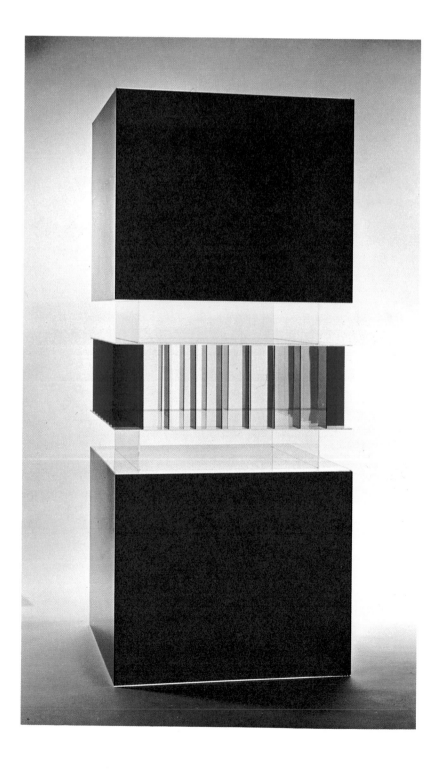

135. George Sugarman. *Two in One*. 1966.

Painted wood, 7′ x 11′6″.

206

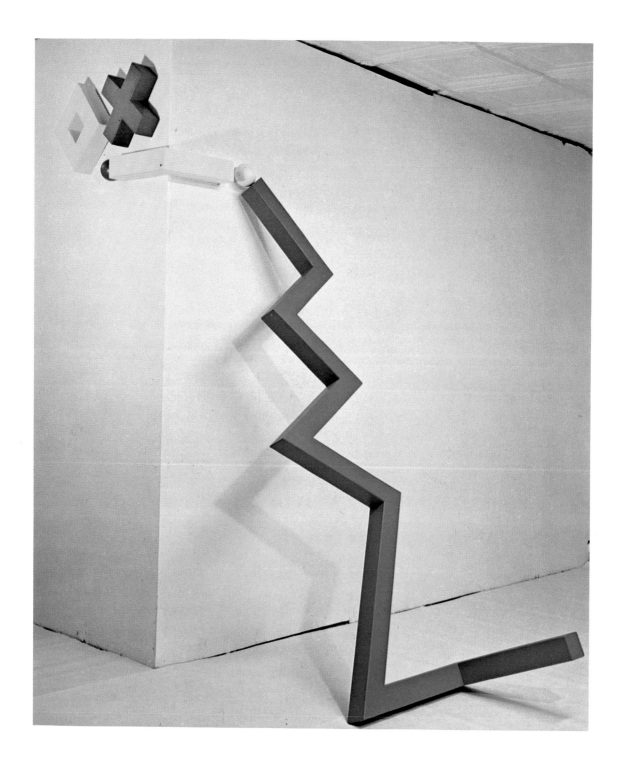

140. Anne Truitt. *Shrove.* 1962.   Painted wood, 60½″ x 10″ x 10″.

208

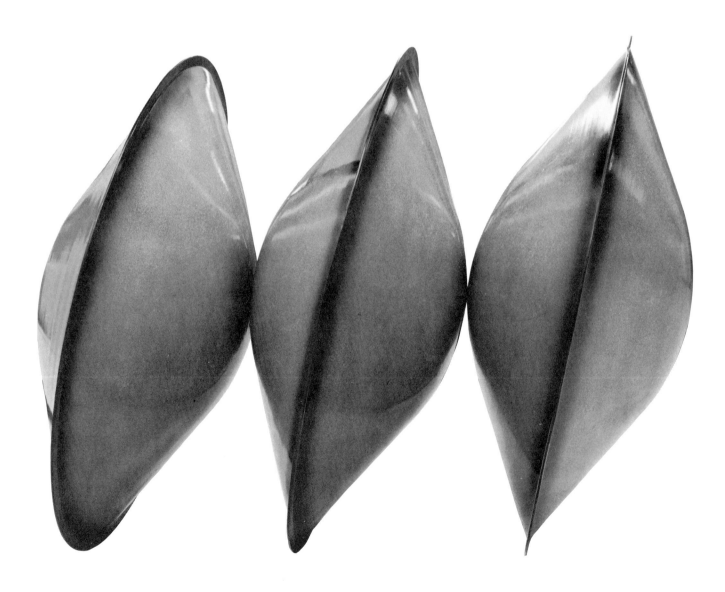

142. DeWain Valentine. (drawing for) *Double Top*. 1967. Fiberglass reinforced plastic, 54″ x 76″ x 54″.

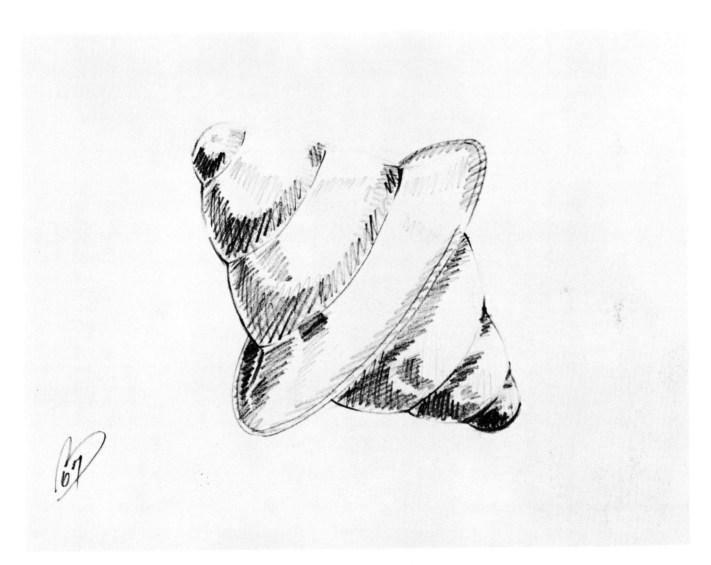

143. Vasa. *Blue in the Middle*. 1966.   Acrylic lacquer on wood, 8′ x 6′ x 22″.

See page 216 for color reproduction

210

144. Stephan Von Huene. *The Hermaphroditic Horseback Rider*, 1966.　　　　　　　　Wood and leather, 78″ x 26″ x 29″.

212

146. David Von Schlegell. *Untitled.* 1966.   Polished aluminum, 88″ x 10′ x 8′.

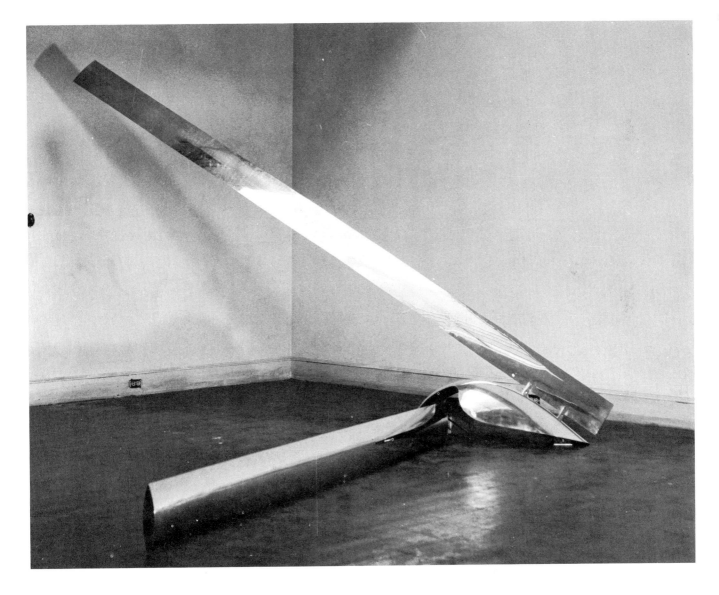

147. David Von Schlegell. *Untitled.* 1967.

Polished aluminum, 78″ x 42′ x 5′.

138. Ernest Trova. *Study Falling Man: Venice Landscape.* 1965-66.   Silicone bronze, 90″ x 14′ x 72″.

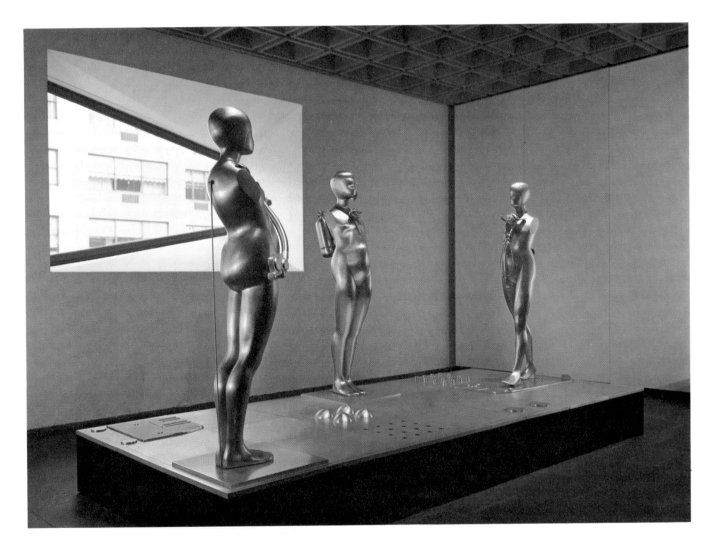

143. Vasa. *Blue in the Middle*. 1966.   Acrylic lacquer on wood, 8′ x 6′ x 22″.

151. David Weinrib. *Spatial Sculpture IV.* 1964.　　　　Enameled steel, plastic, wood, 96″ x 84″ x 60″.

217

218

220

222

153. David Weinrib. (sketch for) *Orange Circle.* 1967. Plastic, 27″ x 73″ x 37″.

154. H. C. Westermann. *The Plush*. 1963-64.　　　Wood, metal pipe, carpeting, 62″ x 29″ x 21″.

224

225

226

161. Norman Zammitt. *Solid Construction-Laminated*. 1966.   Acrylic plastic, 19½" x 29⅝" x 4¼".

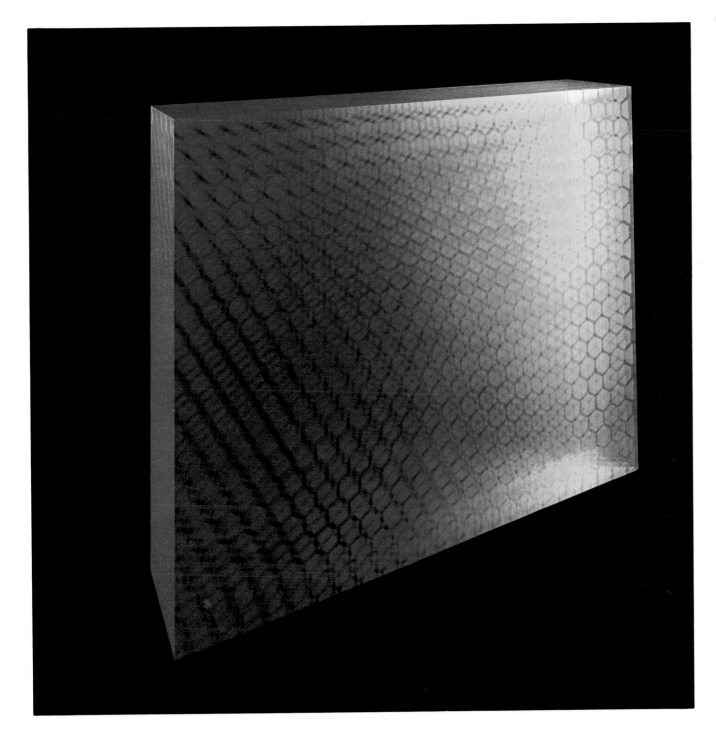

228

158. William T. Wiley. *Enigma Bone*. 1964.   Mixed media, 48″ x 24″ x 54″.

230

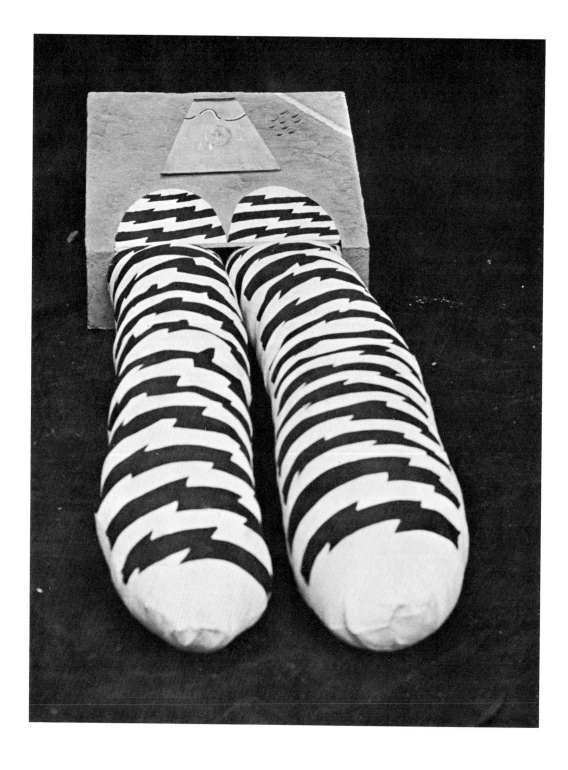

160. William T. Wiley. *Untitled.* 1964.   Mixed media, 24″ x 36″ x 12″.

232

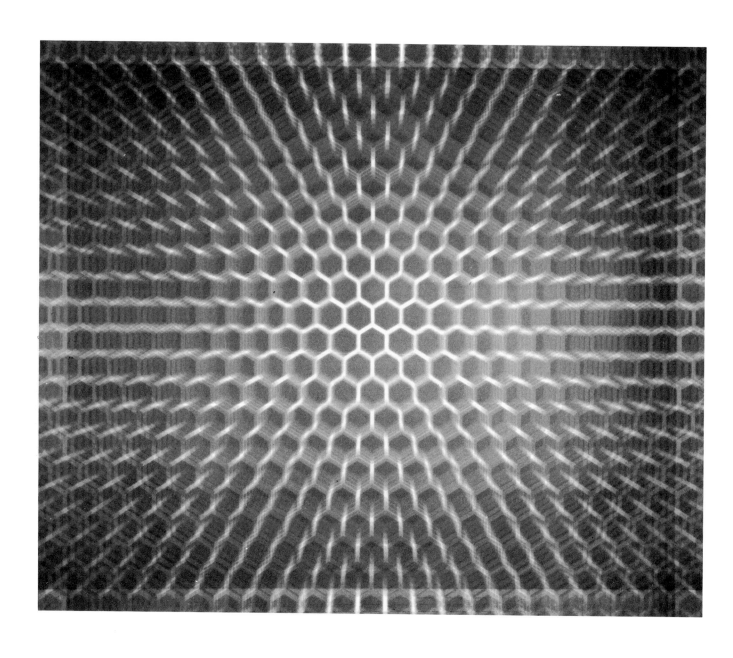

163. Norman Zammitt. *Solid Construction-Laminated*. 1966.

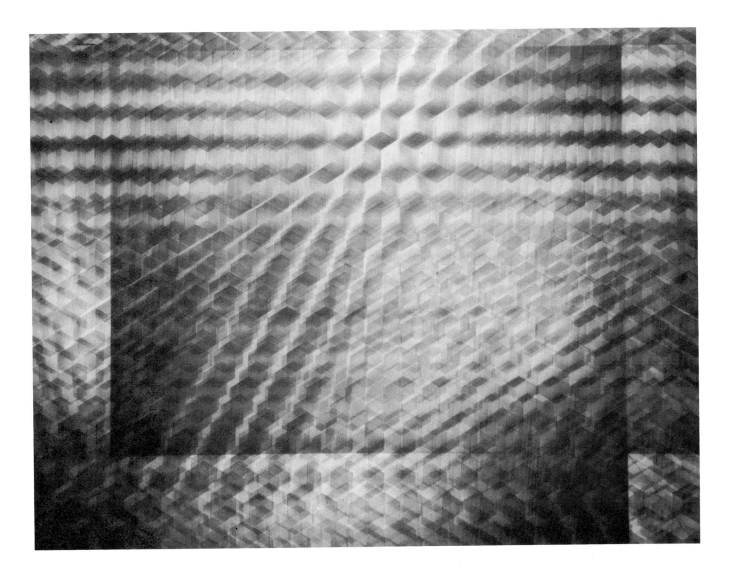

164. Wilfrid Zogbaum. *Islais Creek.* 1961.

Painted steel, H. 85″.

165. Wilfrid Zogbaum. *II*. 1962.

Metal and stone, 69″ x 37″ x 26″.

General Bibliography:
A Selective Listing
(chronologically)

GOOSSEN, E. C. "The End of the Object," *Art International*, vol. 3, no. 8, 1959, pp. 40-42, illus. pp. 40-42.

HESS, THOMAS B. "U. S. Sculpture: Some Recent Directions," *Portfolio*, (including *Art News Annual*), no. 1, 1959, pp. 112-127, 146, 148, 150-152.

ASHTON, DORE. "La Sculpture Américaine," *XXᵉ Siècle*, vol. 22, no. 15, December 1960, pp. 85-91.

SEITZ, WILLIAM C. "Assemblage: Problems and Issues," *Art International*, vol. 6, no. 1, February 1962, pp. 26-34, illus. pp. 26-34.

ROSE, BARBARA. "New York Letter," *Art International*, vol. 7, no. 5, May 25, 1963, pp. 54-57, illus. pp. 54-57.

"California Sculpture Today," *Artforum* (special issue), vol. 2, no. 2, August 1963.

ROSE, BARBARA. "Americans 1963," *Art International*, vol. 7, no. 7, September 25, 1963, pp. 77-79, illus. pp. 77-79.

COPLANS, JOHN. "Notes from San Francisco," *Art International*, vol. 7, no. 8, November 10, 1963, pp. 91-94, illus. pp. 91-93.

LIPPARD, L[UCY] R. "New York," *Artforum*, vol. 2, no. 11, May 1964, pp. 52-54, illus. p. 52.

KOZLOFF, MAX. "American Sculpture in Transition," *Arts*, vol. 28, no. 9, May-June 1964, pp. 19-24, illus. pp. 19-24.

FULLER, MARY. "San Francisco Sculptors," *Art in America*, vol. 52, no. 3, June 1964, pp. 52-59, illus. pp. 52-59.

COPLANS, JOHN. "Circle of Styles on the West Coast," *Art in America*, vol. 52, no. 3, June 1964, pp. 24-41, illus. pp. 24-41.

COPLANS, JOHN. "Formal Art," *Artforum*, vol. 2, no. 12, Summer 1964, pp. 42-43, ill. p. 43.

FACTOR, DONALD. "Assemblage," *Artforum*, vol. 2, no. 12, Summer 1964, pp. 38-39, illus. p. 39.

KOZLOFF, MAX. "Art and the New York Avant-Garde," *Partisan Review*, vol. 31, no. 4, Fall 1964, pp. 535-544, 549-554, illus. pp. 545-548.

MONTE, JAMES. "Polychrome Sculpture," *Artforum*, vol. 3, no. 2, November 1964, pp. 40-43, illus. pp. 40-43.

ROSE, BARBARA. "New York Letter: Recent American Sculpture," *Art International*, vol. 8, no. 10, December 1964, pp. 47-48, ill. p. 47.

ASHTON, DORE. "Unconventional Techniques in Sculpture: New York Commentary," *Studio International*, vol. 169, no. 861, January 1965, pp. 22-25.

HESS, THOMAS B. "The Disrespectful Handmaiden," *Art News*, vol. 63, no. 9, January 1965, pp. 38-39, 57.

KOZLOFF, MAX. "The Further Adventures of American Sculpture," *Arts*, vol. 39, no. 5, February 1965, p. 29.

ROSE, BARBARA. "Looking at American Sculpture," *Artforum*, vol. 3, no. 5, February 1965, pp. 29-36, illus. pp. 29-36.

LIPPARD, LUCY R. "New York Letter," *Art International*, vol. 9, no. 2, March 1965, pp. 46, 48, illus. p. 48.

COPLANS, JOHN. "The New Abstraction on the West Coast U.S.A.," *Studio International*, vol. 169, no. 865, May 1965, pp. 192-199, illus. pp. 192-199.

JURGEN-FISCHER, KLAUS. "New Abstraction," *Kunstwerk* (special issue), April-June 1965, pp. 3-6, 104-105, 114-116, illus. pp. 13, 17-18, 46-47, 51, 82.

MEADMORE, CLEMENT. "New York: Scene I: Sculpture," *Art and Australia*, vol. 3, no. 2, September 1965, pp. 124-129, illus. pp. 124-129.

"Waldorf Panel 2," *It Is*, Autumn 1965, pp. 77-80, 109-113, illus. pp. 17-56, 65-72, 81-108, 117-131.

BELZ, CARL AND KURT VON MEIER. "Funksville: The West Coast Scene," *Art and Australia*, vol. 3, no. 3. December 1965, pp. 198-201, 232, illus. pp. 198-201.

SEITZ, WILLIAM C., ed. *Contemporary Sculpture*, New York, The Art Digest, (Arts Yearbook 8), 1965.

BOURDON, DAVID. "E = mc² a go-go," *Art News*, vol. 64, no. 9, January 1966, pp. 22-25, 57-59, illus. pp. 22-25.

LIPPARD, LUCY R. "New York Letter: Recent Sculpture as Escape," *Art International*, vol. 10, no. 2, February 20, 1966, pp. 48-58, illus. pp. 53-55.

LEIDER, PHILIP. "Kinetic Sculpture at Berkeley," *Artforum*, vol. 4, no. 9, May 1966, pp. 40-44, illus. pp. 40-44.

COATES, ROBERT M. "The Art Galleries: Art and the Machine," *The New Yorker*, vol. 42, no. 13, May 21, 1966, pp. 177-179.

BOURDON, DAVID. "Our Period Style," *Art and Artists*, vol. 1, no. 3, June 1966, pp. 54-57, illus. pp. 54-57.

LIPPARD, LUCY R. "Rejective Art," *Art International*, vol. 10, no. 8, October 20, 1966, pp. 33-36, illus. p. 37.

GRIBLINS, FRANCK TH. "Sculptuur in New York, de nieuwe golf," *Museum Journaal*, ser. 2, no. 3, 1966, pp. 53-63.

LIPPARD, LUCY R. *Pop Art*, Frederick A. Praeger, New York, 1966.

Selected Group Exhibitions
with Reviews

1959 Museum of Modern Art, New York. *Recent American Sculpture*. [Catalog with text by James Thrall Soby. Includes Calder, Chamberlain, Kohn, Nakian, D. Smith, Westermann. Shown at Los Angeles County Museum of Art, 1960.]

1960 Martha Jackson Gallery, New York. *New Forms—New Media I*. [Catalog with essays by Lawrence Alloway and Allan Kaprow. Includes Antonakos, Bladen, Calder, Chamberlain, Chryssa. Conner, Cornell, Doyle, Flavin, Forakis, Nevelson, Oldenburg, Rauschenberg, Zogbaum.]

Whitney Museum of American Art, New York. *Annual Exhibition 1960 Sculpture and Drawings*. [Catalog. Includes Calder, Chryssa, Cornell, De Rivera, Kipp, Kohn, Nevelson, Noguchi, D. Smith, Sugarman, Zogbaum.]

1961 Museum of Modern Art, New York. *The Art of Assemblage*. [Catalog with text by William C. Seitz. Includes Chamberlain, Conner, Cornell, Kienholz, Marisol, Nevelson, Rauschenberg, Samaras, D. Smith, Westermann.]

1962 World's Fair, Seattle. *Art Since 1950*. [Catalog with text by Sam Hunter. Includes Calder, Chamberlain, Chryssa, Cornell, De Rivera, Doyle, Kohn, Nevelson, Noguchi, D. Smith, Sugarman, Zogbaum.]

Whitney Museum of American Art, New York. *Annual Exhibition 1962 Sculpture and Drawings*. [Catalog. Includes Calder, Chamberlain, Chryssa, Cornell, De Rivera, Kipp, Kohn, Liberman, Lye, Marisol, Nevelson, Noguchi, D. Smith, Weinrib, Zogbaum.]

Whitney Museum of American Art, New York. *Fifty California Artists*. [Catalog. Organized by the San Francisco Museum of Art. Includes Acton, Anderson, Conner, Kienholz, Light, Mason, Price, Voulkos, Wiley.]

1963 London City Council, Battersea Park, London. *Sculpture in the Open Air*. [Catalog with text by Sir Herbert Read. Includes Agostini, Calder, Caro, Chamberlain, De Rivera, Nakian, Rickey, D. Smith, Voulkos.]

Museum of Modern Art, New York. *Americans 1963*. [Catalog. Includes Chryssa, Kohn, Marisol, Oldenburg.]

Rose, Barbara. "Americans 1963," *Art International*, vol. 7, no. 7, September 25, 1963, pp. 77-79, illus. pp. 77-79.

Oakland Art Museum, Oakland, California. *Pop Art USA*. [Catalog with text by John Coplans. Includes Berlant, Oldenburg, Rauschenberg, Trova, Westermann.]

San Francisco Art Institute. *82nd Annual Exhibition*. [Included Acton, Anderson, Conner, Geis, Kienholz, Light, Mason, Mattox, Paris, Zogbaum.]

Coplans, John. "Notes from San Francisco," *Art International*, vol. 7, no. 8, November 10, 1963, pp. 91-94, illus. pp. 91-93.

Ventura, Anita. "The Prospect Over the Bay," *Arts*, vol. 37, no. 9, May-June 1963, pp. 19-20.

Museu de Arte Moderna, São Paulo, Brazil. *VII Bienal*. [Catalog. Includes Agostini, Chryssa, Kipp, Segal, Sugarman, Weinrib.]

1964 Dwan Gallery, Los Angeles. *Boxes*. [Catalog. Includes Agostini, Bell, Berlant, Cornell, Kienholz, Marisol, Morris, Nevelson, Oldenburg, Price, Rauschenberg, Samaras, Westermann.]

The Jewish Museum, New York. *Recent American Sculpture*. [Catalog. Includes Agostini, Chamberlain, di Suvero, Segal, Sugarman.]

R[aynor], V[ivien]. "In the Galleries: Recent American Sculpture," *Arts*, vol. 39, no. 3, December 1964, pp. 67-68.

Rose, Barbara. "New York Letter: Recent American Sculpture," *Art International*, vol. 8, no. 10, December 1964, pp. 47-48, ill. p. 47

Pasadena Art Museum. *New American Sculpture*. [Catalog with text by Walter Hopps. Includes Chamberlain, Price, Westermann.]

San Francisco Art Institute. *83rd Annual Exhibition*. [Included Acton, Benton, Geis, Hudson, Mattox.]

Monte, James. "Polychrome Sculpture," *Artforum*, vol. 3, no. 2, November 1964, pp. 40-43, illus. pp. 40-43.

Wadsworth Atheneum, Hartford. *Black, White and Gray*. [Included Flavin, Kelly, Liberman, Morris, Rauschenberg, T. Smith, Truitt.]

Judd, Donald. "Black, White and Gray," *Arts*, vol. 38, no. 6, March 1964, pp. 36-38, illus. pp. 36-38.

Walker Art Center, Minneapolis. *Ten American Sculptors*. [Catalog. This exhibition was for the United States section of the VII Bienal in São Paulo, Brazil, 1963.]

Kozloff, Max. "American Sculpture in Transition," *Arts*, vol. 38, no. 9, May-June 1964, pp. 19-25, illus. pp. 21, 23, 25.

Whitney Museum of American Art, New York. *Annual Exhibition 1964 Contemporary American Sculpture*. [Catalog. Includes Agostini, Anderson, Calder, Chamberlain, Chryssa, Conner, Cornell, De Lap, De Rivera, D. Gray, Hudson, Kienholz, Kipp, Kohn, Lye, Marisol, Mason, Nevelson, Noguchi, Oldenburg, Paris, Rickey, Samaras, Segal, D. Smith, Sugarman, Todd, Von Schlegell, Voulkos, Weinrib, Westermann, Zogbaum.]

Hess, Thomas B. "The Disrespectful Handmaiden," *Art News*, vol. 63, no. 9, January 1965, pp. 38-39, 57-58, illus. pp. 38-39.

Kozloff, Max. "The Further Adventures of American Sculpture," *Arts*, vol. 39, no. 5, February 1965, pp. 24-31, illus. pp. 25-31.

Lippard, Lucy R. "New York Letter," *Art International*, vol. 9, no. 2, March 1965, p. 48, ill. p. 48.

Rose, Barbara. "Looking at American Sculpture," *Artforum*, vol. 3, no. 5, February 1965, pp. 29-36, illus. pp. 29-36.

1965 Buffalo Fine Arts Academy. *Kinetic and Optic Art Today*. [Catalog. Includes Bell, Lye, Rickey.]

Ashton, Dore. "Vision and Sound: Today's Art at Buffalo," *Studio International*, vol. 169, no. 865, May 1965, p. 211, ill. p. 211.

John Daniels Gallery, New York. *Plastics*. [Included Forakis, Judd, Myers, Samaras, Smithson, Weinrib.]

La Jolla Museum of Art. *Some Aspects of California Painting and Sculpture*. [Catalog. Includes Benton, Berlant, DeLap, Gerowitz, D. Gray, Hamrol, Paris.]

New York University. *Concrete Expressionism*. [Catalog with text by Irving Sandler (reprinted in *Art News*, vol. 64, no. 2, April 1965, pp.

65-66, ill. p. 38). Includes Bladen, Sugarman, Weinrib.]

Ashton, Dore. "Art," *Arts and Architecture*, vol. 82, no. 6, June 1965, pp. 10-11, ill. pp. 10-11.

Kozloff, Max. "Art: The Variables of Energy," *The Nation*, vol. 200, no. 19, May 10, 1965, pp. 513-514.

Lippard, Lucy R. "New York Letter," *Art International*, vol. 9, no. 5, June 1965, pp. 51-52, illus. p. 52.

World's Fair, New York, American Express Pavilion. *Art '65: Lesser Known and Unknown Painters: Young American Sculpture—East to West*. [Catalog with text by Wayne V. Andersen. Includes Benton, Geis, Grosvenor, Harris, Hatchett, Howard, Hudson, Randell, Von Schlegell.]

Rhode Island School of Design, Providence. *Contemporary Boxes and Wall Sculpture*. [Catalog with text by Daniel Robbins. Includes Cornell, Morris, Nevelson, Rauschenberg, Samaras, Westermann.]

Museu de Arte Moderna, São Paulo, Brazil. *VIII Bienal: Exhibition of the United States of America*. [Catalog with text by Walter Hopps. Includes Bell, Judd.]

Kozloff, Max. "Art: São Paulo in Washington," *The Nation*, vol. 202, no. 9, February 28, 1966, pp. 250-252.

Tibor de Nagy Gallery, New York. *Shape and Structure*. [Included Andre, Bell, Morris, Murray.]

Lippard, Lucy R. "New York Letter," *Art International*, vol. 9, no. 2, March 1965, pp. 46, 48, ill. p. 48.

Whitney Museum of American Art, New York. *Young America 1965*. [Catalog. Includes Hudson, Morris, Murray, Samaras, Todd.]

World House Galleries, New York. *Sculpture from All Directions*. [Included Bladen, Calder, Caro, di Suvero, Doyle, Forakis, Hudson, Judd, LeWitt, Murray, Myers, Randell, Rickey, D. Smith, Todd, Weinrib.]

Berkson, William. "In the Galleries: Sculpture from All Directions," *Arts*, vol. 40, no. 3, January 1966, p. 53, ill. p. 53.

Lippard, Lucy R. "New York Letter: Recent Sculpture as Escape," *Art International*, vol. 10, no. 2, February 20, 1966, pp. 48-49, illus. pp. 53-54.

1966 University of California, Berkeley. *Directions in Kinetic Sculpture*. [Catalog with text by Peter Selz and George Rickey. Includes Benton, Lye, Mattox, Rickey.]

Leider, Philip. "Kinetic Sculpture at Berkeley," *Artforum*, vol. 4, no. 9, May 1966, pp. 40-44, illus. pp. 40-44.

University of California, Irvine. *Abstract Expressionist Ceramics*. [Catalog with text by John Coplans. Includes Mason, Price, Voulkos.]

University of California, Irvine. *Five Los Angeles Sculptors*. [Catalog with text by John Coplans. Includes Bell, DeLap, D. Gray, McCracken, Price.]

The Art Institute of Chicago. *68th American Exhibition*. [Catalog. Includes Agostini, Bladen, Chryssa, Kelly, Kienholz, Lye, Marisol, Morris, Nevelson, Rauschenberg, Segal.]

Dwan Gallery, New York. *10*. [Catalog. Includes Andre, Flavin, Judd, LeWitt, Morris, Smithson.]

Michelson, Annette. "10 x 10: Concrete Reasonableness," *Artforum*, vol. 5, no. 5, January 1967, pp. 30-31, illus. pp. 30-31.

Finch College Museum of Art, New York. *Art in Process: The Visual Development of a Structure*. [Catalog. Includes Chryssa, Flavin, Judd, Kipp, LeWitt, Morris, Smithson.]

Bochner, M. "Art in Process—Structures," *Arts*, vol. 40, no. 9, September-October 1966, pp. 38-39, illus. pp. 38-39.

Fischbach Gallery, New York. *Eccentric Abstraction*. [Catalog with text by Lucy R. Lippard (reprinted in *Art International*, vol. 10, no. 9, November 1966, pp. 28, 34-40, ill. p. 36.) Includes Kuehn, Nauman.]

Antin, David. "Another Category: 'Eccentric Abstraction,'" *Artforum*, vol. 5, no. 3, November 1966, pp. 56-57, illus. pp. 56-57.

The Jewish Museum, New York. *Primary Structures*. [Catalog with text by Kynaston McShine. Includes Andre, Bell, Bladen, Caro, DeLap, De Maria, Doyle, Flavin, Forakis, Gerowitz, D. Gray, Grosvenor, Judd, Kelly, Kipp, LeWitt, McCracken, Morris, Myers, T. Smith, Smithson, Todd, Von Schlegell.]

Ashton, Dore. "The 'Anti-Compositional Attitude' in Sculpture:

New York Commentary," *Studio International*, vol. 172, no. 879, July 1966, pp. 44-45, illus. pp. 44-45.

Bochner, M. "Primary Structures," *Arts*, vol. 40, no. 8, June 1966, pp. 32-34, illus. pp. 32-35.

Bourdon, David. "Our Period Style," *Art and Artists*, vol. 1, no. 3, June 1966, pp. 54-57, illus. pp. 54-57.

Kozloff, Max. "Art," *The Nation*, vol. 202, no. 23, June 6, 1966, pp. 693-694.

Robins, Corinne. "Object, Structure or Sculpture: Where Are We?," *Arts*, vol. 40, no. 9, September-October 1966, pp. 33-37, illus. pp. 33-35, 37.

La Jolla Museum of Art, La Jolla, California. *New Modes in California Painting and Sculpture*. [Catalog. Includes Bell, DeLap, Gerowitz, D. Gray, McCracken, Vasa, Zammitt.]

Nelson Gallery—Atkins Museum, Kansas City, Missouri. *Sound Light Silence: Art that Performs*. [Catalog with text by Ralph T. Coe. Includes Antonakos, Judd, Lye, McCracken, Oldenburg, Rauschenberg.]

Pincus-Witten, Robert. "Sound, Light and Silence in Kansas City," *Artforum*, vol. 5, no. 5, January 1967, pp. 51-52.

Seattle Art Museum. *Ten from Los Angeles*. [Catalog with text by John Coplans. Includes Bell, DeLap, D. Gray, McCracken, Mattox, Price.]

San Francisco Museum of Art. *Kinetic Currents*. [Included Calder, Mattox, Rickey, Trova.]

University of Pennsylvania, Institute of Contemporary Art, Philadelphia. *7 Sculptors*. [Catalog with essays on each artist. Includes Caro, Chamberlain, Judd, Liberman, D. Smith, Truitt.]

Walker Art Center, Minneapolis. *Eight Sculptors: The Ambiguous Image*. [Catalog with essays by Martin Friedman and Jan van der Marck. Includes Judd, Morris, Oldenburg, Samaras, Segal, Trova, Westermann.]

Whitney Museum of American Art, New York. *Annual Exhibition 1966 Sculpture and Prints*. [Catalog. Includes Agostini, Antonakos, Bell, Benton, Berlant, Bladen, Calder,

238

Chamberlain, Chryssa, Cornell, De-
Lap, De Maria, De Rivera, di Su-
vero, Doyle, D. Gray, Hamrol,
Hatchett, Howard, Hudson, Judd,
Kelly, Kienholz, Kipp, Kohn, Kuehn,
LeWitt, Liberman, McCracken,
Morris, Myers, Murray, Nakian,
Nevelson, Noguchi, Oldenburg,
Paris, Price, Rickey, Samaras, Segal,
T. Smith, Smithson, Snelson, Sugar-
man, Todd, Trova, Valentine, Von
Schlegell, Weinrib, Wiley.]

Kramer, Hilton. "Art: A Wide-
Ranging Whitney Annual," *New
York Times*, December 16, 1966,
p. 57.

Kramer, Hilton. "Plastic Toys and
Ersatz Monuments," *New York
Times*, December 25, 1966, p. 17.

Whitney Museum of American Art
(The Howard and Jean Lipman
Foundation), New York. *Contempo-
rary American Sculpture: Selection
1*. [Catalog with text by John I. H.
Baur. Includes Antonakos, Bell,
Chamberlain, Conner, DeLap, di
Suvero, Judd, Kiesler, Morris, Olden-
burg, Price, Samaras, Trova, Von
Schlegell, Voulkos.]

Biographies and Bibliographies;
By Artist: A Selective Listing

Arlo Acton
Born Knoxville, Iowa, 1933

One-man exhibitions:
1961 Lawrence Drake Gallery, Carmel
1962 Bolles Gallery, San Francisco
1965 Lanyon Gallery, Palo Alto,
    California
    Nicholas Wilder Gallery,
    Los Angeles
1966 Nicholas Wilder Gallery,
    Los Angeles
Resident San Francisco

Articles and reviews
Ventura, Anita. "The Prospect Over the Bay," *Arts*, vol. 37, no. 9, May 1963, p. 20, ill. p. 20.
Magloff, Joanna. "Reviews: San Francisco: Arlo Acton," *Art News*, vol. 63, no. 2, April 1964, p. 20.
Fuller, Mary. "San Francisco Sculptors," *Art in America*, vol. 52, no. 3, June 1964, p. 53, ill. p. 53.
Snyder, Susan R. "Los Angeles: Arlo Acton," *Artforum*, vol. 4, no. 6, February 1966, p. 17, ill. p. 16.

Peter Agostini
Born New York, 1913

One-man exhibitions since 1960:
1960 Stephen Radich Gallery, New York
1962 Stephen Radich Gallery, New York
1963 Stephen Radich Gallery, New York
    Columbia University, New York
1964 Richard Gray Gallery, Chicago
    Stephen Radich Gallery, New York
1965 Richard Gray Gallery, Chicago
1966 Stephen Radich Gallery, New York
Resident New York

Articles and reviews
For a bibliography through July 1964 see:
The Jewish Museum, New York, *Recent American Sculpture*, 1964.
Kozloff, Max. "Peter Agostini," *Recent American Sculpture*, New York, The Jewish Museum, 1964, pp. 9-10, ill. p. 11.
"Plaster Cornucopia," *Time*, vol. 84, no. 20, November 13, 1964, pp. 96, 99, ill. p. 99.
Raynor, Vivien. "In the Galleries: Agostini," *Arts*, vol. 39, no. 3, December 1964, p. 69, ill. p. 69.

Ashton, Dore. "Visual Pleasure from Austerity: New York Commentary," *Studio International*, vol. 169, no. 862, February 1965, p. 95, ill. p. 92.
Edgar, Natalie. "Reviews and Previews: Peter Agostini," *Art News*, vol. 65, no. 1, March 1966, p. 10, ill. p. 14.
Adrian, Dennis. "New York," *Artforum*, vol. 4, no. 7, March 1966, p. 51, ill. p. 50.

Jeremy Anderson
Born Palo Alto, California, 1921

One-man exhibitions since 1960:
1960 Dilexi Gallery, San Francisco
1961 Dilexi Gallery, San Francisco
1962 Dilexi Gallery, San Francisco
1964 Dilexi Gallery, San Francisco
    Metart Galleries, San Francisco
1966 Dilexi Gallery, San Francisco
1967 Pasadena Art Museum
Resident Mill Valley, California

By the artist
Fuller, Mary. "San Francisco Sculptors," *Art in America*, vol. 52, no. 3, June 1964, pp. 52-59, ill. p. 52.

Articles and reviews
Chipp, Herschel B. "Art News From San Francisco: One Man Shows Mostly Constructions," *Art News*, vol. 60, no. 4, Summer 1961, p. 48.
Coplans, John. "Reviews: Jeremy Anderson," *Artforum*, vol. 1, no. 6, November 1962, p. 16, ill. p. 17.
Monte, James. "San Francisco: Jeremy Anderson," *Artforum*, vol. 2, no. 9, March 1964, p. 47, ill. p. 46.

Carl Andre
Born Quincy, Massachusetts, 1935

One-man exhibitions:
1965 Tibor de Nagy Gallery, New York
1966 Tibor de Nagy Gallery, New York
Resident New York

By the artist
Andre, Carl. "Frank Stella," *Sixteen Americans*, New York, Museum of Modern Art, 1959, p. 76.
Rose, Barbara. "ABC Art," *Art in America*,

vol. 53, no. 5, October-November 1965, pp. 57-69, ill. p. 67.

Articles and reviews
Raynor, Vivien. "In the Galleries: Exit Hofmann Left, Enter Albers Right," *Arts*, vol. 39, no. 5, February 1965, p. 54.
Berrigan, Ted. "Reviews and Previews: Carl Andre," *Art News*, vol. 64, no. 4, Summer 1965, p. 21.
Lippard, Lucy R. "New York Letter: April-June 1965," *Art International*, vol. 9, no. 6, September 20, 1965, pp. 58-59, ill. p. 67.
Grossberg, Jacob. "In the Galleries: Carl Andre," *Arts*, vol. 39, no. 10, September-October 1965, p. 72.
Bourdon, David. "The Razed Sites of Carl Andre," *Artforum*, vol. 5, no. 2, October 1966, pp. 14-17, illus. pp. 14-17.
Lippard, Lucy R. "Rejective Art," *Art International*, vol. 10, no. 8, October 20, 1966, pp. 33-36, ill. p. 37.
Bannard, Darby. "Present-Day Art and Ready-Made Styles," *Artforum*, vol. 5, no. 4, December 1966, p. 33, ill. p. 32.

Stephen Antonakos
Born Southern Greece, 1926

One-man exhibitions:
1964 Schramm Galleries, Fort Lauderdale, Florida
    Miami Museum of Modern Art, Miami
    Byron Gallery, New York
Resident New York

By the artist
"New Talent USA: Stephen Antonakos," *Art in America*, vol. 54, no. 4, July-August 1966, p. 29, ill. p. 29.

Larry Bell
Born Chicago, 1939

One-man exhibitions:
1962 Ferus Gallery, Los Angeles
1963 Ferus Gallery, Los Angeles
1965 Ferus Gallery, Los Angeles
    Pace Gallery, New York
1966 Pace Gallery, New York
Resident Venice, California

Articles and reviews

For a bibliography through 1965 see:
John Coplans, *Ten from Los Angeles*, Seattle Art Museum, 1966.

Hopps, Walter. *VIII Bienal do Museu de Arte Moderne, São Paulo, Brazil, 1965: United States of America*, 1965.

Bochner, Mel. "In the Galleries: Larry Bell," *Arts*, vol. 40, no. 3, January 1966, p. 40, ill. p. 40.

Coplans, John. "Los Angeles: Object Lesson," *Art News*, vol. 64, no. 9, January 1966, p. 40, ill. p. 40.

Lippard, Lucy R. "New York Letter: Recent Sculpture as Escape," *Art International*, vol. 10, no. 2, February 20, 1966, p. 52, ill. p. 53.

Fletcher Benton

Born Jackson, Ohio, 1931

One-man exhibitions:

1961 Gump's Gallery, San Francisco
1962 Gump's Gallery, San Francisco
1964 Hansen Galleries, San Francosco
        Gump's Gallery, San Francisco
        California Palace of the
            Legion of Honor, San Francisco
1965 Hansen Galleries, San Francisco
        San Francisco Museum of Art
        Esther Robles Gallery, Los Angeles
Resident San Francisco

By the artist

Selz, Peter. *Directions in Kinetic Sculpture*, Berkeley, University of California, 1966, p. 19, ill. p. 19.

Articles and reviews

Monte, James. "San Francisco: Fletcher Benton," *Artforum*, vol. 2, no. 11, May 1964, p. 45, illus. p. 45.

"Movement Movement: Kinetic Artists," *Time*, vol. 87, no. 4, January 1966, p. 69, ill. pp. 66-67.

Tony Berlant

Born New York, 1941

One-man exhibitions:

1963 David Stuart Galleries, Los Angeles
1964 Hansen Galleries, San Francisco
1965 David Stuart Galleries, Los Angeles
Resident Los Angeles

By the artist

Siple, Molly. "Los Angeles: Anthony Berlant," *Artforum*, vol. 3, no. 6, March 1965, p. 16, ill. p. 17.

Tuchman, Maurice. *Five Younger Los Angeles Artists*, Los Angeles County Museum of Art, 1965.

Articles and reviews

Langsner, Jules. "Art News from Los Angeles," *Art News*, vol. 62, no. 4, Summer 1963, p. 47.

Factor, Don. "Los Angeles: Five Younger Los Angeles Artists," *Artforum*, vol. 4, no. 6, February 1966, p. 14.

Ronald Bladen

Born Vancouver, British Columbia, 1918

One-man exhibitions since 1960:

1962 Green Gallery, New York
1967 Fischbach Gallery, New York
Resident New York

By the artist

Rose, Barbara. "ABC Art," *Art in America*, vol. 53, no. 5, October-November 1965, pp. 57-69, ill. p. 63.

Articles and reviews

Sandler, Irving. "Ronald Bladen," *Art News*, vol. 61, no. 8, December 1962, p. 14, ill. p. 14.

Judd, Donald. "New York Exhibitions: In the Galleries: Ronald Bladen," *Arts*, vol. 37, no. 5, February 1963, p. 53.

Sandler, Irving. "Expressionism with Corners," *Art News*, vol. 64, no. 2, April 1965, pp .65-66, ill. p. 38.

Ashton, Dore. "Art," *Arts and Architecture*, vol. 82, no. 6, June 1965, pp. 10-11, ill. p. 11.

Lippard, Lucy R. "New York Letter," *Art International*, vol. 9, no. 5, June 1965, p. 52, ill. p. 52.

Ashton, Dore. "Three Centuries of American Painting: New York Commentary," *Studio International*, vol. 170, no. 868, August 1965, pp. 87-88, ill. p. 87.

Robins, Corinne. "Six Artists and the New Extended Vision," *Arts*, vol. 39, no. 10, September-October 1965, p. 21, ill. p. 19.

Sandler, Irving. "Ronald Bladen," *Artforum*, vol. 5, no. 2, October 1966, pp. 32-33, 35, illus. pp. 32-35.

Alexander Calder

Born Philadelphia, 1898

One-man exhibitions since 1960:

1960 Kunstgewerbemuseum, Zurich
1961 Museum of Modern Art, Caracas
1962 Tate Gallery, London
        Galleria dell'Ariete, Milan
1963 Frank Perls Gallery, Beverly Hills
        Galerie Maeght, Paris
        Perls Galleries, New York
1964 Perls Galleries, New York
        Solomon R. Guggenheim Museum,
            New York
1965 Laing Galleries, Toronto
1966 Galerie Maeght, Paris
1967 Obelisk Gallery, Boston
Resident Roxbury, Connecticut

For bibliographies through October 1964 see:

James Johnson Sweeney, *Alexander Calder*, New York, Museum of Modern Art, 1951.

Solomon R. Guggenheim Museum, New York, *Alexander Calder*, 1964.

By the artist

Gray, Cleve. "Calder's Circus," *Art in America*, vol. 52, no. 5, October 1964, pp. 22-48, illus. pp. 22-48.

Calder, Alexander and Jean Davidson. *Calder, An Autobiography with Pictures*, New York, Pantheon, 1966.

On the artist

Guppy, Nicholas. "Alexander Calder," *Atlantic Monthly*, vol. 214, no. 6, December 1964, pp. 53-60, illus. pp. 54-60.

H[ess], T[homas] B. "Reviews and Previews: Calder," *Art News*, vol. 63, no. 8, December 1964, p. 12.

Lemon, Richard. "Mobiles: The Soaring Art of Alexander Calder," *Saturday Evening Post*, February 27, 1965, pp. 31-34, illus. pp. 30-35.

Andersen, Wayne V. "Calder at the Guggenheim," *Artforum*, vol. 3, no. 6, March 1965, pp. 37-41, illus. pp. 37-41.

Rose, Barbara. "Joy, Excitement Keynote Calder's Work," *Canadian Art*, vol. 22, no.

3, May-June 1965, pp. 30-33, illus. pp. 31-33.

Derrière le Miroir, no. 156, February 1966. [Entire issue devoted to articles and reviews on Calder.]

Arnason, H. H. *Calder*, New York, Van Nostrand, 1966.

Anthony Caro
Born London, 1924

One-man exhibitions since 1960:

1963 Whitechapel Art Gallery, London
1964 Andre Emmerich Gallery, New York
1965 Gallery of Modern Art, Washington, D.C.
1966 Galerie Bischofberger, Zurich
     Andre Emmerich Gallery, New York
Resident London

By the artist

Alloway, Lawrence. "Interview with Anthony Caro," *Gazette*, no. 1, 1961.

Fried, Michael. "Anthony Caro," *Art International*, vol. 7, no. 7, September 25, 1963, pp. 68-72, illus. pp. 69-72.

"Anthony Caro Interviewed by Andrew Forge," *Studio International*, vol. 171, no. 873, January 1966, pp. 6-9, illus. pp. 6-9.

Articles and reviews

"Metrorama: Notes from London: Painted Sculpture by Anthony Caro," *Metro 6*, 1962, pp. 102-107, illus. pp. 102-107.

Whitechapel Art Gallery, London. *Anthony Caro*, 1963. [Introduction by Michael Fried.]

Baro, Gene. "Britain's New Sculpture," *Art International*, vol. 9, no. 5, June 1965, pp. 26-31, illus. p. 28.

Whittet, G. S. "London Commentary," *Studio International*, vol. 170, no. 872, December 1965, p. 244, ill. p. 245.

Russell, John. "Anthony Caro: New Works," *Art News*, vol. 64, no. 8, December 1965, pp. 36, 54, ill. p. 36.

Greenberg, Clement. "Anthony Caro," *Contemporary Sculpture*, New York, The Art Digest (Arts Yearbook 8), 1965, pp. 106-109, illus. pp. 106-109.

Thompson, David. "Venice Biennale: The British Five," *Studio International*, vol. 171, no. 878, June 1966, pp. 234, 241, illus. pp. 234-235.

Russell, John. "Portrait: Anthony Caro," *Art in America*, vol. 54, no. 5, September-October 1966, pp. 80-87, illus. pp. 80-87.

Kramer, Hilton. "Sculpture: Talent Unfolds on Horizon," *New York Times*, November 26, 1966, p. 31.

Benedikt, Michael. "Anthony Caro," *7 Sculptors*, Philadelphia, Institute of Contemporary Art, University of Pennsylvania, 1966, pp. 1-4, ill. p. 6.

XXXIII Venice Biennale 1966, British Pavilion, 1966. [Introduction by David Thompson.]

John Chamberlain
Born Rochester, Indiana, 1927

One-man exhibitions since 1960:

1960 Martha Jackson Gallery, New York
1962 Dilexi Gallery, Los Angeles
     Dilexi Gallery, San Francisco
1963 Pace Gallery, Boston
1964 Leo Castelli Gallery, New York
     Pasadena Art Museum
     Galerie Ileana Sonnabend, Paris
1965 Leo Castelli Gallery, New York
1966 L'Elefante, Venice, Italy
Resident Santa Fe, New Mexico

Articles and reviews

For a bibliography through July 1964 see: The Jewish Museum, New York, *Recent American Sculpture*, 1964.

Creeley, Robert. "John Chamberlain," *Recent American Sculpture*, New York, The Jewish Museum, 1964, pp. 17-18, ill. p. 19.

Coplans, John. "Higgins, Price, Chamberlain, Bontecou, Westermann," *Artforum*, vol. 2, no. 10, April 1964, pp. 38-40, illus. pp. 38-40.

Judd, Donald. "In the Galleries: John Chamberlain," *Arts*, vol. 38, no. 10, September 1964, p. 71.

Edgar, Natalie. "Reviews and Previews: John Chamberlain," *Art News*, vol. 63, no. 10, February 1965, p. 13, ill. p. 13.

Lippard, Lucy R. "New York Letter," *Art International*, vol. 9, no. 3, April 1965, p. 53, ill. p. 53.

Judd, Donald. "John Chamberlain," *7 Sculptors*, Philadelphia, Institute of Contemporary Art, University of Pennsylvania, 1966, pp. 7-9, ill. p. 11.

Chryssa
Born Athens, Greece, 1933

One-man exhibitions:

1961 Betty Parsons Gallery, New York
     Solomon R. Guggenheim Museum, New York
1962 Cordier & Ekstrom Gallery, New York
1966 Pace Gallery, New York
Resident New York

By the artist

Chryssa. "The Artists Say: Chryssa," *Art Voices*, vol. 4, no. 4, Fall 1965, p. 62, illus. p. 63.

Articles and reviews

Calas, Nicolas. "Chryssa and Time's Magic Square," *Art International*, vol. 6, no. 1, February 1962, pp. 35-37, illus. pp. 35-37.

Tillim, Sidney. "New York Exhibitions: In the Galleries: Chryssa," *Arts*, vol. 37, no. 3, December 1962, p. 48.

Kozloff, Max. "American Sculpture in Transition," *Arts*, vol. 38, no. 9, May 1964, p. 24, ill. p. 25.

B[aker], E[lizabeth] C. "Reviews and Previews: Chryssa," *Art News*, vol. 65, no. 1, March 1966, p. 12, ill. p. 14.

Berkson, William. "In the Galleries: Chryssa," *Arts*, vol. 40, no. 7, May 1966, pp. 60-61, ill. p. 61.

Krauss, Rosalind. "New York," *Artforum*, vol. 4, no. 10, June 1966, p. 52, ill. p. 53.

Benedikt, Michael. "New York Letter," *Art International*, vol. 10, no. 7, September 15, 1966, pp. 45-46, ill. p. 45.

Bruce Conner
Born McPherson, Kansas, 1933

One-man exhibitions:

1960 Alan Gallery, New York
     Spatsa Gallery, San Francisco
1961 Batman Gallery, San Francisco
     Alan Gallery, New York
1962 Glantz Gallery, Mexico City
1963 San Francisco Art Institute
1964 Robert Fraser Gallery, London
     Alan Gallery, New York
1965 Alan Gallery, New York
     Poses Institute of Fine Arts, Brandeis University, Boston

1965 Fine Arts Gallery, The University of British Columbia, Vancouver
Resident San Francisco

Articles and reviews

Ashton, Dore. "Art," *Arts and Architecture*, vol. 77, no. 3, March 1960, p. 35.

Raynor, Vivien. "New York Exhibitions: In the Galleries: Bruce Conner," *Arts*, vol. 36, no. 2, November 1961, pp. 42-43, ill. p. 43.

Leider, Philip. "Bruce Conner: A New Sensibility," *Artforum*, vol. 1, no. 6, November 1962, pp. 30-31, illus. pp. 30-31.

Ventura, Anita. "The Bay Climate," *Arts*, vol. 38, no. 3, December 1963, p. 30, ill. p. 30.

Magloff, Joanna. "Arts News from San Francisco," *Art News*, vol. 62, no. 9, January 1964, p. 52.

Joseph Cornell
Born Nyack, New York, 1903

One-man exhibitions:

1962 Ferus Gallery, Los Angeles
1965 J. L. Hudson Gallery, Detroit
1966 Robert Schoelkopf Gallery, New York
     Pasadena Art Museum
Resident Flushing, New York

By the artist

Cornell, Joseph. "Monsieur Phot," (scenario) in Levy, Julien, *Surrealism*, New York, Black Sun Press, 1936, pp. 77-88.

Articles and reviews

Motherwell, Robert. "Preface to a Joseph Cornell Exhibition." [Unpublished typescript at Walker Art Center, Minneapolis, written for a proposed catalog to the Cornell exhibition held July 12-August 30, 1953; dated June 26, 1953.]

Goossen, E. C. "The Plastic Poetry of Joseph Cornell," *Art International*, vol. 3, no. 10, 1959-60, pp. 37-40, illus. pp. 37-40.

Langsner, Jules. "Los Angeles Letter," *Art International*, vol. 7, no. 1, January 25, 1963, p. 82, ill. p. 82.

Coplans, John. "Notes on the Nature of Joseph Cornell," *Artforum*, vol. 1, no. 8, February 1963, pp. 27-29, illus. pp. 27-28.

Waldman, Diane. "Cornell: The Compass of Boxing," *Art News*, vol. 64, no. 1, March 1965, pp. 42-45, 49-50, illus. pp. 42-45.

Johnson, Ellen H. "Arcadia Enclosed: The Boxes of Joseph Cornell," *Arts*, vol. 39, no. 10, September-October 1965, pp. 35-37, illus. pp. 35-37.

Cortesi, Alexandra. "Joseph Cornell," *Artforum*, vol. 4, no. 8, April 1966, pp. 27-31, illus. pp. 27-31.

Tony DeLap
Born Oakland, California, 1927

One-man exhibitions since 1960:

1960 Oakland Art Museum, Oakland, California
1961 Quill Gallery, San Francisco
1962 Cain Gallery, San Francisco
1963 University of Wisconsin, Madison
     Dilexi Gallery, San Francisco
1964 San Francisco Art Institute
1965 Robert Elkon Gallery, New York
1966 Felix Landau Gallery, Los Angeles
     Robert Elkon Gallery, New York
Resident Corona del Mar, California

Articles and reviews

For a bibliography through 1965 see:
John Coplans, *Ten from Los Angeles*, Seattle Art Museum, 1966.

Ashton, Dore. "New Sculpture Fresh in Old Techniques: New York Commentary," *Studio International*, vol. 169, no. 866, June 1965, p. 263.

Lippard, Lucy R. "New York Letter: April-June 1965," *Art International*, vol. 9, no. 6, September 20, 1965, p. 59, ill. p. 65.

Danieli, Fidel A. "Los Angeles: Tony De-Lap," *Artforum*, vol. 4, no. 10, June 1966, pp. 14-15, illus. p. 14.

Walter de Maria
Born Albany, California, 1935

One-man exhibitions:

1965 Paula Johnson Gallery, New York
1966 Cordier & Ekstrom, Inc., New York
Resident New York

Articles and reviews

J[ohnston], J[ill]. "Reviews and Previews: New Names this Month: Walter de Maria," *Art News*, vol. 61, no. 10, February 1963, p. 19, ill. p. 19.

Lippard, Lucy R. "New York Letter," *Art International*, vol. 9, no. 3, April 1965, pp. 53-54.

Raynor, Vivien. "In the Galleries: Walter de Maria," *Arts*, vol. 39, no. 6, March 1965, p. 63.

Lippard, Lucy R. "The Third Stream: Constructed Paintings and Painted Structures," *Art Voices*, vol. 4, no. 2, Spring 1965, pp. 44-49.

Adrian, Dennis. "Walter de Maria: Word and Thing," *Artforum*, vol. 5, no. 5, January 1967, pp. 28-29, illus. pp. 28-29.

Jose de Rivera
Born West Baton Rouge, Louisiana, 1904

One-man exhibitions since 1960:

1960 Grace Borgenicht Gallery, New York
1965 Grace Borgenicht Gallery, New York
Resident New York

Articles and reviews

Tillim, Sidney. "In the Galleries: Jose de Rivera," *Arts*, vol. 34, no. 4, January 1960, p. 50.

Ashton, Dore. "La sculpture Américaine," *XXe Siècle*, vol. 22, no. 15, December 1960, p. 90, ill. p. 89.

"Frugal Elegance," *Time*, vol. 77, no. 24, June 9, 1961, p. 73, ill. p. 73.

Raynor, Vivien. "New York Exhibitions: Month in Review," *Arts*, vol. 35, no. 10, September 1961, pp. 35-36, ill. p. 35.

Ashton, Dore. "New Sculpture Fresh in Old Techniques: New York Commentary," *Studio International*, vol. 169, no. 866, June 1965, p. 263, ill. p. 262.

Mark di Suvero
Born Shanghai, 1933

One-man exhibitions:

1960 Green Gallery, New York
1965 Dwan Gallery, Los Angeles
1966 Park Place Gallery, New York
Resident New York

Articles and reviews

For a bibliography through July 1964 see:
The Jewish Museum, New York, *Recent American Sculpture*, 1964.

Johnston, Jill. "Mark di Suvero," *Recent American Sculpture*, New York, The Jewish Museum, 1964, pp. 21-22, ill. p. 23.

"New Talent USA," *Art in America*, vol. 52, no. 4, August 1964, p. 70.

Ashton, Dore. "Unconventional Techniques in Sculpture: New York Commentary," *Studio International*, vol. 169, no. 861, January 1965, p. 23.

Marmer, Nancy. "Los Angeles: Mark di Suvero," *Artforum*, vol. 4, no. 4, December 1965, pp. 13-14, ill. p. 17.

Bourdon, David. "E = mc² à go-go," *Art News*, vol. 64, no. 9, January 1966, pp. 25, 57, ill. p. 24.

Coplans, John. "Los Angeles: Object Lesson," *Art News*, vol. 64, no. 9, January 1966, p. 40.

Hoene, Anne. "In the Galleries: Mark di Suvero, David Novros," *Arts*, vol. 40, no. 7, May 6, 1966, p. 62.

Ashton, Dore. "Artist as Dissenter," *Studio International*, vol. 171, no. 876, April 1966, pp. 165, 167, ill. p. 166.

Tom Doyle
Born Jerry City, Ohio, 1928

One-man exhibitions since 1960:

1965 Folkwang Museum, Essen, Germany
     Kunsthalle, Düsseldorf
1966 Dwan Gallery, New York
Resident New York

By the artist

Bayer, Shawn. "An Interview with Tom Doyle," *The Price*, no. 1, February 1966, pp. 5-15.

Articles and reviews

Whiteside, Forbes. "Three Young Americans," *Oberlin College Bulletin*, vol. 19, no. 1, Fall 1961, pp. 52-57, illus. pp. 53-54, 56.

Lippard, L[ucy] R. "New York," *Artforum*, vol. 2, no. 11, May 1964, pp. 53-54.

Lippard, L[ucy] R. *Tom Doyle*, Kunsthalle, Düsseldorf, 1965.

Kramer, Hilton. "Art: There's Nothing Like Thinking Big, Sometimes," *New York Times*, March 12, 1966, p. 23, ill. p. 23.

B[errigan], T[ed]. "Reviews and Previews: Tom Doyle," *Art News*, vol. 65, no. 2, April 1966, p. 15.

Lippard, Lucy R. "Space Embraced: Tom Doyle's Recent Sculpture," *Arts*, vol. 40, no. 6, April 1966, pp. 38-43, illus. pp. 38-43.

Adrian, Dennis. "New York: Tom Doyle," *Artforum*, vol. 4, no. 9, May 1966, pp. 51-52, ill. p. 54.

Dan Flavin
Born Jamaica, New York, 1933

One-man exhibitions:

1961 Judson Gallery, New York
1964 Kaymar Gallery, New York
     Green Gallery, New York
1965 Green Gallery, New York
     Ohio State University, Columbus
1966 Galerie Rudolf Zwirner, Cologne
     Nicholas Wilder Gallery,
       Los Angeles
     Galeria Sperone, Milan
Resident Cold Springs, New York

By the artist

Flavin, Dan. "The Artists Say," *Art Voices*, vol. 4, no. 3, Summer 1965, p. 72, ill. p. 72.

Rose, Barbara. "ABC Art," *Art in America*, vol. 53, no. 5, October-November 1965, pp. 57-69, ill. p. 68.

Flavin, Dan. ". . . In Daylight or Cool White," *Artforum*, vol. 4, no. 4, December 1965, pp. 20-24, illus. pp. 20, 22-24.

Flavin, Dan. "Some Remarks," *Artforum*, vol. 5, no. 4, December 1966, pp. 27-29.

Articles and reviews

Judd, Donald. "Black, White and Gray," *Arts*, vol. 38, no. 6, March 1964, p. 38, ill. p. 36.

Judd, Donald. "New York Exhibitions: In the Galleries, Dan Flavin," *Arts*, vol. 38, no. 7, April 1964, p. 31, ill. p. 31.

Johnston, Jill. "Reviews and Previews: Dan Flavin," *Art News*, vol. 63, no. 9, January 1965, p. 13.

Lippard, Lucy R. "New York Letter," *Art International*, vol. 9, no. 1, February 1965, p. 37, ill. p. 37.

Hoene, Anne. "In the Galleries: Group Show," *Arts*, vol. 40, no. 6, April 1966, p. 55.

Lippard, Lucy R. "New York Letter: Off Color," *Art International*, vol. 10, no. 4, April 20, 1966, pp. 73-75.

Lippard, Lucy R. "Rejective Art," *Art International*, vol. 10, no. 8, October 20, 1966, pp. 33-36.

Bochner, Mel. "Less is Less (for Dan Flavin)," *Art and Artists*, vol. 1, no. 9, December 1966, pp. 24-27.

Peter Forakis
Born Hanna, Wyoming, 1927

One-man exhibitions since 1960:

1962 Tibor de Nagy Gallery, New York
1964 Tibor de Nagy Gallery, New York
Resident New York

Articles and reviews

J[ohnston], J[ill]. "Reviews and Previews: New Names This Month: Peter Forakis," *Art News*, vol. 60, no. 2, April 1961, p. 19, ill. p. 19.

S[wenson], G[ene] [R.] "Reviews and Previews: New Names This Month: Peter Forakis and Robert Indiana," *Art News*, vol. 60, no. 3, May 1961, p. 20.

Bourdon, David. "E = mc² à go-go," *Art News*, vol. 64, no. 9, January 1966, pp. 22, 57, ill. p. 23.

William R. Geis, III
Born Salina, Kansas, 1940
Resident Stinson Beach, California

Articles and reviews

Ventura, Anita. "Field Day for Sculptors," *Arts*, vol. 38, no. 1, October 1963, p. 64, ill. p. 63.

Stiles, Knute. "San Francisco," *Artforum*, vol. 5, no. 4, December 1966, p. 65.

"William Geis and Bruce Nauman: A Two Man Exhibition," San Francisco Art Institute, 1966. [A mimeographed article about the artists by the Gallery at the time of the exhibition, September 26-October 22, 1966.]

Judy Gerowitz
Born Chicago, 1939

One-man exhibition:

1966 Rolf Nelson Gallery, Los Angeles
Resident Los Angeles

Articles and reviews

Wolfe, Clair. "Los Angeles: Painted Sculpture," *Artforum*, vol. 2, no. 11, May 1964, p. 12.

Danieli, Fidel. "Art News From L.A.: Judy Gerowitz," *Art News*, vol. 65, no. 1, March 1966, p. 20.

Plagens, Peter. "Los Angeles: Judith Gerowitz," *Artforum*, vol. 4, no. 7, March 1966. p. 14, ill. p. 14.

Plagens, Peter. "Los Angeles: Judy Gerowitz," *Artforum*, vol. 4, no. 8, April 1966, p. 14, ill. p. 15.

David Gray
Born Waukesha, Wisconsin, 1927

One-man exhibitions:

1964 Milwaukee Art Center, Wisconsin
1965 Feigen/Palmer Gallery, Los Angeles
     Richard Feigen Gallery, New York
1966 Ferus Gallery, Los Angeles
Resident Costa Mesa, California

Articles and reviews

For a bibliography through 1965 see: John Coplans, *Ten from Los Angeles*, Seattle Art Museum, 1966.

Lippard, Lucy R. "New York Letter: April-June 1965," *Art International*, vol. 9, no. 6, September 20, 1965, p. 60.

Snyder, Susan R. "Los Angeles: David Gray," *Artforum*, vol. 4, no. 8, April 1966, p. 15, ill. p. 16.

Robert Grosvenor
Born New York, 1934

One-man exhibition:

1966 Dwan Gallery, Los Angeles
Resident New York

Articles and reviews

Bourdon, David. "Park Place: New Ideas," *The Village Voice*, November 1965, pp. 11, 25.

Bourdon, David. "E = mc² à go-go," *Art News*, vol. 64, no. 9, January 1966, pp. 23-24, ill. p. 25.

Swain, Richard. "In the Galleries: Robert Grosvenor, Leo Valledor," *Arts*, vol. 40, no. 4, February 1966, p. 55, ill. p. 55.

Robins, Corinne. "Four Directions at Park Place," *Arts*, vol. 40, no. 8, June 1966, pp. 20-24, ill. p. 23.

Lloyd Hamrol
Born San Francisco, 1937

One-man exhibition:

1966 Rolf Nelson Gallery, Los Angeles
Resident Pasadena

By the artist

Tuchman, Maurice. *Five Younger Los Angeles Artists*, Los Angeles County Museum of Art, 1965.

Articles and reviews

Factor, Don. "Los Angeles: Five Younger Los Angeles Artists," *Artforum*, vol. 4, no. 6, February 1966, p. 14.

Coplans, John. "Lloyd Hamrol's 'Multiples,'" *Artforum*, vol. 5, no. 4, December 1966, pp. 50-51, illus. pp. 50-51.

Paul Harris
Born Orlando, Florida, 1925

One-man exhibitions:

1960 Poindexter Gallery, New York
1963 Poindexter Gallery, New York
1964 Lanyon Gallery, Palo Alto, California
     Berkeley Gallery, San Francisco
1967 Poindexter Gallery, New York
Resident Bolinas, California

Articles and reviews

deMott, Helen. "In the Galleries: Paul Harris," *Arts*, vol. 35, no. 1, October 1960, p. 64.

"New Talent USA: Sculpture," *Art in America*, vol. 50, no. 1, 1962, pp. 36-37, illus. pp. 36-37.

Tillim, Sidney. "New York Exhibitions: In the Galleries: Paul Harris," *Arts*, vol. 37, no. 7, April 1963, p. 58, ill. p. 58.

Sandler, Irving H. "Reviews and Previews: Paul Harris," *Art News*, vol. 62, no. 2, April 1963, p. 14, ill. p. 14.

Adams, Alice. "Paul Harris, Poindexter Gallery," *Craft Horizons*, vol. 33, no. 8, May 1963, p. 44, ill. p. 44.

Duayne Hatchett
Born Shawnee, Oklahoma, 1925

One-man exhibitions since 1960:

1963-1964 Calhoun Galleries, Dallas
     Oklahoma Museum of Art, University of Oklahoma, Norman
     Oklahoma State University, Stillwater
     Oklahoma Art Center, Tulsa
     Philbrook Art Center, Tulsa
     Bryson Gallery, Columbus, Ohio
1966 Royal Marks Gallery, New York
Resident Columbus, Ohio

Articles and reviews

Adrian, Dennis. "New York: Duayne Hatchett," *Artforum*, vol. 4, no. 4, December 1965, p. 55, ill. p. 55.

G[ollin], J[ane]. "Reviews and Previews: Duayne Hatchett," *Art News*, vol. 65, no. 1, March 1966, p. 15.

Berkson, William. "In the Galleries: Duayne Hatchett," *Arts*, vol. 40, no. 6, April 1966, p. 58.

Lippard, Lucy R. "New York Letter," *Art International*, vol. 10, no. 4, April 20, 1966, pp. 78-79.

Pincus-Witten, Robert. "New York: Duayne Hatchett," *Artforum*, vol. 4, no. 8, April 1966, p. 51, ill. p. 50.

Robert A. Howard
Born Sapulpa, Oklahoma, 1922

One-man exhibition since 1960:

1967 Royal Marks Gallery, New York
Resident Chapel Hill, North Carolina

Articles and reviews

Ashton, Dore. "New York Commentary," *Studio International*, vol. 170, no. 867, July 1965, p. 43, ill. p. 43.

Robins, Corinne. "In the Galleries: Group Show," *Arts*, vol. 39, no. 9, November 1965, p. 61, ill. p. 61.

Adrian, Dennis. "New York: Robert Howard," *Artforum*, vol. 4, no. 4, December 1965, p. 55.

Robert Hudson
Born Salt Lake City, 1938

One-man exhibitions:

1961 Richmond Art Center, Richmond, California

Batman Gallery, San Francisco
1962 Bolles Gallery, San Francisco
1964 Lanyon Gallery, Palo Alto,
        California
1965 Allan Frumkin Gallery, New York
        San Francisco Art Institute,
        San Francisco
Resident Stinson Beach, California

Articles and reviews

Magloff, Joanna. "Art News from San Francisco," *Art News*, vol. 62, no. 9, January 1964, p. 51.
Leider, Philip. "Three San Francisco Sculptors: Robert Hudson," *Artforum*, vol. 3, no. 1, September 1964, pp. 36, 38-39, illus. pp. 38-39.
Ashton, Dore. "Life and Movement Without Recession: New York Commentary," *Studio International*, vol. 170, no. 872, December 1965, p. 252.
Robins, Corinne. "In the Galleries: Robert Hudson," *Arts*, vol. 40, no. 2, December 1965, p. 55, ill. p. 54.

Donald Judd
Born Excelsior Springs, Missouri, 1928

One-man exhibitions:

1964 Green Gallery, New York
1966 Leo Castelli Gallery, New York
Resident New York

By the artist

Rose, Barbara. "ABC Art," *Art in America*, vol. 53, no. 5, October-November 1965, pp. 57-69, ill. p. 63.
Judd, Donald. "Specific Objects," *Contemporary Sculpture*, New York, The Art Digest (Arts Yearbook 8), 1965, pp. 74-82, illus. pp. 74-82, 79-81.
Glaser, Bruce. "Questions to Stella and Judd," *Art News*, vol. 65, no. 5, September 1966, pp. 55-61, ill. p. 56.

Articles and reviews

Tillim, Sidney. "The New Avant-Garde," *Arts*, vol. 38, no. 5, February 1964, pp. 20-21, ill. p. 21.
Fried, Michael. "New York Letter," *Art International*, vol. 8, no. 1, February 15, 1964, p. 26, ill. p. 25.
Rose, Barbara. "Donald Judd," *Artforum*, vol. 3, no. 9, June 1965, pp. 30-32, illus. pp. 30-32.
Hopps, Walter. *VIII Bienal do Museu de Arte Moderna, São Paulo, Brazil, 1965: United States of America*, 1965.
Grossberg, Jacob. "Reviews and Previews: Donald Judd," *Art News*, vol. 65, no. 2, April 1966, p. 17.
Krauss, Rosalind. "Allusion and Illusion in Donald Judd," *Artforum*, vol. 4, no. 9, May 1966, pp. 24-26, illus. pp. 24-26.
Lippard, Lucy R. "Rejective Art," *Art International*, vol. 10, no. 8, October 20, 1966, pp. 35-36, illus. p. 37.
Friedman, Martin. "Donald Judd," *Eight Sculptors: The Ambiguous Image*, Minneapolis, Walker Art Center, 1966, pp. 22, 24-25, illus. pp. 23-25.
Smithson, Robert. "Donald Judd," *7 Sculptors*, Philadelphia, Institute of Contemporary Art, University of Pennsylvania, 1966, pp. 13-16, ill. p. 18.

Ellsworth Kelly
Born Newburgh, New York, 1923

One-man exhibitions since 1960:

1961 Betty Parsons Gallery, New York
1962 Tooths Gallery, London
1963 Gallery of Modern Art,
        Washington, D.C.
        Betty Parsons Gallery, New York
1965 Sidney Janis Gallery, New York
Resident New York

By the artist

Geldzahler, Henry. "Interview with Ellsworth Kelly," *Art International*, vol. 8, no. 1, February 15, 1964, pp. 47-48, illus. pp. 47-48.

Articles and reviews

Alloway, Lawrence. "Heraldry and Sculpture," *Art International*, vol. 6, no. 3, April 1962, pp. 52-53, illus. pp. 52-53.
Rubin, William. "Ellsworth Kelly: The Big Form," *Art News*, vol. 62, no. 7, November 1963, pp. 32-35, 64-65.
Fried, Michael. "New York Letter," *Art International*, vol. 7, no. 9, Christmas-New Year 1963-64, p. 54, ill. p. 55.

Edward Kienholz
Born Fairfield, Washington, 1927

One-man exhibitions since 1960:

1960 Ferus Gallery, Los Angeles
1961 Pasadena Art Museum
1962 Ferus Gallery, Los Angeles
1963 Alexander Iolas Gallery, New York
        Dwan Gallery, Los Angeles
1964 Dwan Gallery, Los Angeles
1965 Barney's Beanery, Los Angeles
        Dwan Gallery, New York
1966 Los Angeles County Museum of Art
1967 Dwan Gallery, New York
Resident Los Angeles

Articles and reviews

For a bibliography through January 1966 see:
Maurice Tuchman, *Edward Kienholz*, Los Angeles County Museum of Art, 1966.
Lippard, Lucy R. "New York Letter: Recent Sculpture as Escape," *Art International*, vol. 10, no. 2, February 20, 1966, p. 52.
Michelson, Annette. "New York Letter," *Art International*, vol. 10, no. 2, February 20, 1966, p. 60.
Ashton, Dore. "Commentary from New York," *Studio International*, vol. 171, no. 874, February 1966, pp. 80-81, ill. p. 80.
Tillim, Sidney. "The Underground Pre-Raphaelitism of Edward Kienholz," *Artforum*, vol. 4, no. 8, April 1966, pp. 38-40, illus. pp. 38-40.

Frederick J. Kiesler
Born Vienna, 1896
Died 1965

One-man exhibitions since 1960:

1961 Leo Castelli Gallery, New York
1964 Solomon R. Guggenheim Museum,
        New York
1966 Martha Jackson Gallery, New York
1967 Martha Jackson Gallery, New York
For a bibliography through March 1964 see:
Solomon R. Guggenheim Museum, New York, *Frederick Kiesler: Environmental Sculpture*, 1964.

By the artist

Kiesler, Frederick. "Second Manifesto of Correalism," *Art International*, vol. 9, no.

2, March 1965, pp. 16-67, illus. pp. 16-69.
Kiesler, Frederick. *Inside the Endless House*, New York, Simon and Schuster, 1966.

Review
Lippard, Lucy R. "New York Letter," *Art International*, vol. 10, no. 8, October 20, 1966, p. 59, ill. p. 59.

Lyman Kipp
Born Dobbs Ferry, New York, 1929

One-man exhibitions since 1960:
1960 Betty Parsons Gallery, New York
1961 Bennington College, Bennington, Vermont
1962 Betty Parsons Gallery, New York
1964 Betty Parsons Gallery, New York
1965 Betty Parsons Gallery, New York
1966 Betty Parsons Gallery, New York
Resident New York

By the artist
Glaser, Bruce, Lyman Kipp, George Sugarman and David Weinrib. "Where Do We Go from Here?," *Contemporary Sculpture*, New York, The Art Digest (Arts Yearbook 8), 1965, pp. 150-155, ill. p. 151.

Articles and reviews
Zimmerman, Sidney. "In the Galleries: Lyman Kipp," *Arts*, vol. 40, no. 3, January 1966, p. 62.
Lippard, Lucy R. "New Yorker Letter: Recent Sculpture as Escape," *Art International*, vol. 10, no. 2, February 20, 1966, pp. 51-52.
Pincus-Witten, Robert. "Lyman Kipp," *Artforum*, vol. 4, no. 6, February 1966, p. 57, ill. p. 57.

Gabriel Kohn
Born Philadelphia, 1910

One-man exhibitions since 1960:
1963 Otto Gerson Gallery, New York
David Stuart Galleries, Los Angeles
The Art Center, La Jolla
1966 David Stuart Galleries, Los Angeles
Resident Los Angeles

Articles and reviews
Ashton, Dore. "La Sculpture Américaine,"

XXe Siècle, vol. 22, no. 15, December 1960, p. 90, ill. p. 90.
Petersen, Valerie. "Gabriel Kohn Makes a Sculpture," *Art News*, vol. 60, no. 6, October 1961, pp. 48-51, 66-67, illus. pp. 48-51.
Ashton, Dore. "Art," *Arts and Architecture*, vol. 70, no. 1, January 1963, pp. 5, 32, ill. p. 5.
Tillim, Sidney. "New York Exhibitions: Month in Review," *Arts*, vol. 37, no. 5, February 1963, pp. 77-78, ill. p. 77.
Rose, Barbara. "New York Notes," *Art International*, vol. 7, no. 2, February 25, 1963, pp. 77-78, ill. p. 77.
"Fifty-six Painters and Sculptors," *Art in America*, vol. 52, no. 4, August 1964, p. 53, ill. p. 53.
Coplans, John. "Art News from Los Angeles: Sculptors Meet at Long Beach," *Art News*, vol. 64, no. 8, December 1965, pp. 52, 61, ill. p. 52.

Gary Kuehn
Born Plainfield, New Jersey, 1939

One-man exhibitions:
1965 Bianchini Gallery, New York
1967 Bianchini Gallery, New York
Resident Somerville, New Jersey

Articles and reviews
Bianchini Gallery, New York. *Ten from Rutgers*, 1965. [Text by Allan Kaprow.]
W[aldman], D[iane]. "Reviews and Previews: Gary Kuehn," *Art News*, vol. 65, no. 2, April 1966, p. 17.
Lippard, Lucy R. *Eccentric Abstraction*, Fischbach Gallery, New York, 1966; reprinted in *Art International*, vol. 10, no. 9, November 20, 1966, pp. 28, 34-40, ill. p. 36.

Sol LeWitt
Born Hartford, Connecticut, 1928

One-man exhibitions:
1965 John Daniels Gallery, New York
1966 Dwan Gallery, New York
Resident New York

By the artist
LeWitt, Sol. "Ziggurats," *Arts*, vol. 41, no. 1, November 1966, pp. 24-25.

Articles and reviews
Lippard, Lucy R. "New York Letter," *Art International*, vol. 9, no. 2, March 1965, p. 46.
Barnitz, Jacqueline. "In the Galleries: The Box Show," *Arts*, vol. 39, no. 7, April 1965, pp. 57-58.
Lippard, Lucy R. "The Third Stream: Constructed Paintings and Painted Structures," *Art Voices*, vol. 4, no. 4, Spring 1965, p. 48.
Lippard, Lucy R. "New York Letter," *Art International*, vol. 9, no. 6, September 20, 1965, p. 58, ill. p. 65.
Lippard, Lucy R. "New York Letter: Recent Sculpture as Escape," *Art International*, vol. 10, no. 2, February 20, 1966, p. 51.
Lippard, Lucy R. "Rejective Art," *Art International*, vol. 10, no. 8, October 20, 1966, pp. 33-36, ill. p. 37.

Alexander Liberman
Born Kiev, Russia, 1912

One-man exhibitions since 1960:
1960 Betty Parsons Gallery, New York
1962 Betty Parsons Gallery, New York
1963 Betty Parsons Gallery, New York
1964 Betty Parsons Gallery, New York
Robert Fraser Gallery, London
Bennington College, Bennington, Vermont
1965 Galleria dell'Ariete, Milan
Galleria d'Arte, Naples
Resident New York

By the artist
Liberman, Alexander. *The Artist in His Studio*, New York, 1959.

Articles and reviews
Johnson, Philip. "Young Artists at the Fair," *Art in America*, vol. 52, no. 4, August 1964, p. 114, ill. p. 114.
Gray, Cleve. "Ceramics by Twelve Artists," *Art in America*, vol. 52, no. 6, December 1964, p. 41, ill. p. 41.
Goldin, Amy. "In the Galleries: Alexander Liberman," *Arts*, vol. 40, no. 7, May 1966, p. 62, ill. p. 63.
W[aldman], D[iane]. "Reviews and Previews: Alexander Liberman," *Art News*,

vol. 65, no. 5, September 1966, pp. 15-16, ill. p. 14.

Fry, Edward. "Liberman at the Jewish Museum," *Artforum*, vol. 5, no. 2, October 1966, pp. 50-51, illus. pp. 50-51.

Alvin Light
Born Concord, New Hampshire, 1931

One-man exhibitions:
1960 Dilexi Gallery, San Francisco
1961 Dilexi Gallery, San Francisco
1963 Dilexi Gallery, Los Angeles
Resident San Francisco

By the artist
"New Talent USA: Sculpture," *Art in America*, vol. 50, no. 1, 1962, p. 39, ill. p. 39.

Articles and reviews
Ventura, Anita. "The Prospect Over the Bay," *Arts*, vol. 37, no. 9, May 1963, p. 20.
Pettibone, Shirley Y. "Reviews: Alvin Light," *Artform*, vol. 2, no. 1, July 1963, pp. 51-52.
Ventura, Anita. "San Francisco: The Aloof Community," *Arts*, vol. 39, no. 7, April 1965, p. 73, ill. p. 70.
Monte, James. "San Francisco," *Artforum*, vol. 3, no. 8, May 1965, p. 43, illus. p. 43.

Len Lye
Born Christchurch, New Zealand, 1901

One-man exhibitions:
1965 Howard Wise Gallery, New York
Albright-Knox Gallery, Buffalo
1965-1966 Contemporary Art Center, Cincinnati
Resident New York

By the artist
Lye, Len. "Tangible Motion Sculpture," *Art Journal*, vol. 20, no. 4, Summer 1961, pp. 226-227, illus. p. 227.
Lye, Len and Lou Adler. "Description of Roundhead I," *Art Journal*, vol. 20, no. 4, Summer 1961, p. 228, ill. p. 228.
Seckler, Dorothy Gees. "Audience is his Medium!," *Art in America*, vol. 51, no. 2, April 1963, p. 64, ill. p. 65.
Selz, Peter. *Directions in Kinetic Sculp-*

ture, Berkeley, University of California, 1966, pp. 43-44, illus. pp. 42, 45-47.

Articles and reviews
Dandignac, Patricia. "Arts in Architecture: The Visionary Art of Len Lye," *Craft Horizons*, vol. 21, no. 3, May 1961, pp. 30-31, ill. p. 31.
Ashton, Dore. "Vision and Sound: Today's Art at Buffalo," *Studio International*, vol. 169, no. 865, May 1965, p. 211, ill. p. 211.

John McCracken
Born Berkeley, 1934

One-man exhibitions:
1965 Nicholas Wilder Gallery, Los Angeles
1966 Robert Elkon Gallery, New York
Resident Venice, California

Articles and reviews
For a bibliography through 1965 see:
John Coplans, *Ten from Los Angeles*, Seattle Art Museum, 1966.
Coplans, John. "Art News from Los Angeles, John McCracken," *Art News*, vol. 64, no. 8, December 1965, pp. 61-62, ill. p. 52.
Rose, Barbara. "Los Angeles: The Second City," *Art in America*, vol. 54, no. 1, January-February 1966, p. 113, illus. p. 113.
Lippard, Lucy R. "Rejective Art," *Art International*, vol. 10, no. 8, October 20, 1966, pp. 33-36.

Marisol
Born Paris, 1930

One-man exhibitions since 1960:
1962 Stable Gallery, New York
1964 Stable Gallery, New York
1966 Sidney Janis Gallery, New York
Arts Club of Chicago
Resident New York

Articles and reviews
Kozloff, Max. "New York Letter: Marisol," *Art International*, vol. 6, no. 7, September 1962, p. 35, ill. p. 35.
"Young Talent, USA," *Art in America*, vol. 51, no. 3, June 1963, pp. 50-51, illus. pp. 50-51.
Oeri, Georgine. "Marisol," *Quadrum 16*,

1964, pp. 148-149, illus. pp. 148-149.
Campbell, Lawrence. "Marisol's Magic Mixtures," *Art News*, vol. 63, no. 1, March 1964, pp. 38-41, 64-65, illus. pp. 38-41.
Tillim, Sidney. "New York Exhibitions: In the Galleries: Marisol," *Arts*, vol. 38, no. 7, April 1964, p. 28, ill. p. 29.
Lippard, L[ucy] R. "New York," *Artforum*, vol. 2, no. 11, May 1964, p. 54, ill. p. 32.
Ashton, Dore. "Acceleration in Discovery and Consumption: New York Commentary," *Studio International*, vol. 167, no. 853, May 1964, p. 214, ill. p. 213.
"Fifty-Six Painters and Sculptors," *Art in America*, vol. 52, no. 4, August 1964, p. 77, ill. p. 77.

John Mason
Born Madrid, Nebraska, 1927

One-man exhibitions since 1960:
1960 Pasadena Art Museum
1963 Ferus Gallery, Los Angeles
1966-1967 Los Angeles County Museum of Art
Resident Los Angeles

Articles and reviews
For a bibliography through August 1966 see:
Los Angeles County Museum of Art, *John Mason*, 1966. [Essay by John Coplans.]
Coplans, John. *Abstract Expressionist Ceramics*, Art Gallery, University of California, Irvine, 1966.
Langsner, Jules. "Los Angeles," *Art News*, vol. 65, no. 9, January 1967, p. 26.

Charles Mattox
Born Bronson, Kansas, 1910

One-man exhibitions since 1960:
1960 University of California, Berkeley
1961 University of California, Berkeley
1962 Lanyon Gallery, Palo Alto, California
1963 San Francisco Museum of Art
1964 Lanyon Gallery, Palo Alto, California
1967 University of California, Irvine
Resident Los Angeles

By the artist

Mattox, Charles. "New Works by Charles Mattox," *Artforum*, vol. 4, no. 6, February 1966, pp. 38-39, illus. pp. 38-39.
Selz, Peter. *Directions in Kinetic Sculpture, Berkeley*, University of California, 1966, p. 50, illus. p. 51.

Articles and reviews

Coplans, John. "Charles Mattox: Three Machines," *Artforum*, vol. 1, no. 7, December 1962, pp. 32-33, illus. pp. 32-33.
Mundt, Ernest. "Reviews: Charles Mattox," *Artforum*, vol. 1, no. 10, April 1963, p. 11, ill. p. 10.
Coplans, John. *Charles Mattox*, Irvine, University of California, 1967.

Robert Morris

Born Kansas City, Missouri, 1931

One-man exhibitions:

1963 Green Gallery, New York
1964 Green Gallery, New York
     Galerie Schmela, Düsseldorf
1965 Green Gallery, New York
1966 Dwan Gallery, Los Angeles
Resident New York

By the artist

Morris, Robert. "Notes on Sculpture," *Artforum*, vol. 4, no. 6, February 1966, pp. 42-44, illus. pp. 42-44.
Morris, Robert. "Dance," *The Village Voice*, February 3, 1966, pp. 8, 24-25. Part II: February 10, 1966, p. 15.
Morris, Robert. "Notes on Sculpture, Part II," *Artforum*, vol. 5, no. 2, October 1966, pp. 20-23, illus. pp. 20-23.

Articles and reviews

Rose, Barbara. "New York Letter," *Art International*, vol. 7, no. 9, December 5, 1963, pp. 63-64, ill. p. 63.
B[errigan], T[ed]. "Reviews and Previews: Robert Morris," *Art News*, vol. 63, no. 10, February 1965, p. 13, ill. p. 13.
Judd, Donald. "In the Galleries: Robert Morris," *Arts*, vol. 39, no. 5, February 1965, p. 54.
Lippard, Lucy R. "New York Letter," *Art International*, vol. 9, no. 2, March 1965, p. 46, ill. p. 48.

Lippard, Lucy R. "New York Letter," *Art International*, vol. 9, no. 4, May 1965, pp. 57-58, ill. p. 58.
Rose, Barbara. "ABC Art," *Art in America*, vol. 53, no. 5, October-November 1965, p. 63, ill. p. 63.
Friedman, Martin. "Robert Morris," *Eight Sculptors: The Ambiguous Image*, Minneapolis, Walker Art Center, 1966, pp. 18, 20-21, illus. pp. 19, 21.
Antin, David. "Art and Information, 1: Grey Paint, Robert Morris," *Art News*, vol. 65, no. 2, April 1966, pp. 22-24, illus. pp. 22-24.
Factor, Don. "Los Angeles: Robert Morris," *Artforum*, vol. 4, no. 9, May 1966, p. 13, ill. p. 13.
Lippard, Lucy R. "Rejective Art," *Art International*, vol. 10, no. 8, October 20, 1966, pp. 33-36.

Robert Murray

Born Vancouver, 1936

One-man exhibitions:

1965 Betty Parsons Gallery, New York
1966 Betty Parsons Gallery, New York
Resident New York

By the artist

Murray, Robert. "Bad Day at Long Beach (Calif.)," *Canadian Art*, vol. 23, no. 3, July 1966, pp. 6-8, illus. p. 8. [Interview with Barbara Rose.]
Rose, Barbara. "An Interview with Robert Murray," *Artforum*, vol. 5, no. 2, October 1966, pp. 45-46, illus. pp. 45-47.

Articles and reviews

Holstein, Jonathan. "Robert Murray," *Canadian Art*, vol. 20, no. 2, March-April 1963, pp. 114-117, illus. pp. 114-117.
B[errigan], T[ed]. "Reviews and Previews: Robert Murray," *Art News*, vol. 64, no. 2, April 1965, p. 14, ill. p. 14.
Grossberg, Jacob. "In the Galleries: Robert Murray," *Arts*, vol. 39, no. 9, May 1965, p. 59.
Lippard, Lucy R. "New York Letter: April-June 1965," *Art International*, vol. 9, no. 6, September 20, 1965, p. 60.
Rose, Barbara. "Letter from New York,"

Canadian Art, vol. 22, no. 4, September-October 1965, pp. 53-54.

Forrest Myers

Born Long Beach, California, 1941
Resident New York

Articles and reviews

Lippard, L[ucy] R. "New York," *Artforum*, vol. 2, no. 11, May 1964, pp. 53-54.
Lippard, Lucy R. "New York Letter," *Art International*, vol. 9, no. 4, May 1965, p. 53.
Bourdon, David. "E = mc² à go-go," *Art News*, vol. 64, no. 9, January 1966, p. 57, ill. p. 22.
Lippard, Lucy R. "New York Letter: Recent Sculpture as Escape," *Art International*, vol. 10, no. 2, February 20, 1966, p. 50.
Piene, Nan. "New York Gallery Notes," *Art in America*, vol. 54, no. 2, March-April 1966, p. 127.
Robins, Corinne. "Four Directions at Park Place," *Arts*, vol. 40, no. 8, June 1966, pp. 20-24, illus. pp. 20-23.
Mellow, James R. "New York Letter," *Art International*, vol. 10, no. 7, September 15, 1966, p. 57, ill. p. 70.
Factor, Donald. "Anthony Magar, Forrest Myers at Dwan," *Artforum*, vol. 5, no. 4, December 1966, pp. 54-55, illus. pp. 54-55.

Reuben Nakian

Born College Point, Long Island, 1897

One-man exhibitions since 1960:

1960 Egan Gallery, New York
1961 VI Bienal, São Paulo, Brazil
1962 Egan Gallery, New York
     Los Angeles County Museum of Art
1963 Gallery of Modern Art, Washington, D.C.
1966 Museum of Modern Art, New York
Resident New York

Articles and reviews

For a bibliography through 1965 see:
Frank O'Hara, *Nakian*, New York, Museum of Modern Art, 1966.

Hess, Thomas B. "In Praise of Reason," *Art News*, vol. 65, no. 4, Summer 1966, pp. 22-25, 60, illus. pp. 22-25.
"I'm on the Satyr's Side," *Newsweek*, vol. 68, no. 1, July 1966, p. 83, ill. p. 83.
Rose, Barbara. "Nakian at the Modern," *Artforum*, vol. 5, no. 2, October 1966, pp. 18-19, illus. pp. 18-19.

Bruce Nauman

Born Fort Wayne, Indiana, 1941

One-man exhibition:

1966 Nicholas Wilder Gallery, Los Angeles
Resident San Francisco

Articles and reviews

"William Geis and Bruce Nauman: A Two Man Exhibition," San Francisco Art Institute, 1966. [A mimeographed article about the artists by the Gallery at the time of the exhibition, September 26-October 22, 1966.]
Lippard, Lucy R. *Eccentric Abstraction*, New York, Fischbach Gallery, 1966; reprinted in *Art International*, vol. 10, no. 9, November 20, 1966, pp. 28, 34-40, ill. p. 37.
Stiles, Knute. "San Francisco," *Artforum*, vol. 5, no. 4, December 1966, p. 65, ill. p. 64.

Louise Nevelson

Born Kiev, Russia, 1900

One-man exhibitions since 1960:

1960 Museum of Modern Art, New York
David Herbert Gallery, New York
Devorah Sherman Gallery, Chicago
Galerie Daniel Cordier, Paris
1961 Martha Jackson Gallery, New York
Pace Gallery, Boston
Staatliche Kunsthalle, Baden-Baden, Germany
1962 Martha Jackson Gallery, New York
1963 Sidney Janis Gallery, New York
Hanover Gallery, London
1964 Pace Gallery, New York
Pace Gallery, Boston
Gimpel-Hanover Gallery, Zurich
Documenta: Kassel, Germany
Pace Gallery, New York
1966 Ferus-Pace Gallery, Los Angeles

1967 Whitney Museum, New York
Resident New York

On the artist

Kramer, Hilton. "The Sculpture of Louise Nevelson," *Arts*, vol. 32, no. 9, June 1938, pp. 26-29, illus. pp. 26, 28-29.
Sawin, Martica. "New York Letter," *Art International*, vol. 3, no. 9, 1959, pp. 9-10, ill. p. 9.
Fried, Michael. "New York Letter," *Art International*, vol. 7, no. 2, February 25, 1963, p. 62, illus. p. 63.
"Louise Nevelson," *Art International*, vol. 7, no. 8, November 10, 1963, pp. 72-73, illus. pp. 72-73.
Roberts, Colette. *Nevelson*, Paris, Editions Georges Fall, 1964.
Coates, Robert M. "The Art Galleries: Louise Nevelson," *The New Yorker*, vol. 40, no. 42, December 5, 1964, pp. 160-162.
Seitz, William C. *Nevelson*, Pace Gallery, New York, 1964, pp. 5, 8.

Isamu Noguchi

Born Los Angeles, 1904

One-man exhibitions since 1960:

1961 Cordier & Warren Gallery, New York
Fort Worth Art Center, Fort Worth, Texas
1963 Cordier & Ekstrom Gallery, New York
1965 Cordier & Ekstrom Gallery, New York
1967 Cordier & Ekstrom, Inc., New York
Resident New York

By the artist

Kuh, Katharine. *The Artist's Voice*, New York and Evanston, Harper & Row, 1962, pp. 171-187.
Ashton, Dore. "Dollo Studio di Isamu Noguchi," *Domus*, no. 415, June 1964, pp. 52-55, illus. pp. 52-55.
Noguchi, Isamu. "New Stone Gardens," *Art in America*, vol. 52, no. 3, June 1964, pp. 84-89, illus. pp. 84-89.

Articles and reviews

"Toward the Timeless," *Time*, vol. 73, no. 22, June 1, 1959, p. 70, ill. p. 70.
Ashton, Dore. "Isamu Noguchi," *Arts and*

Architecture, vol. 76, no. 8, August 1959, pp. 14-15, illus. p. 14-15.
Ashton, Dore. "La Sculpture Américaine," *XXe Siècle*, vol. 22, no. 15, December 1960, pp. 89-90, ill. p. 88.
"Floating," *Newsweek*, vol. 57, no. 21, May 22, 1961, p. 92, ill. p. 92.
Pease, Roland F, Jr. "New York Notes: Isamu Noguchi," *Art International*, vol. 5, nos. 5-6, June-August 1961, p. 95, ill. p. 95.
Raynor, Vivien. "In the Galleries: New York Exhibitions: Noguchi," *Arts*, vol. 37, no. 9, May 1963, pp. 105-106, ill. p. 105.
Ashton, Dore. "Art: Isamu Noguchi," *Arts and Architecture*, vol. 80, no. 6, June 1963, pp. 6-7, illus. p. 6.
Michelson, Annette. "Noguchi: Notes on a Theater of the Real," *Art International*, vol. 8, no. 10, December 1964, pp. 21-25, illus. pp. 21-25.
B[enedikt], M[ichael]. "Reviews and Previews: Isamu Noguchi," *Art News*, vol. 64, no. 3, May 1965, p. 13, ill. p. 13.
Ashton, Dore. "New Sculpture Fresh in Old Techniques: New York Commentary," *Studio International*, vol. 169, no. 866, June 1965, pp. 260-261, ill. p. 260.

Claes Oldenburg

Born Stockholm, 1929

One-man exhibitions since 1960:

1960 Reuben Gallery, New York
1961 The Store, New York
Martha Jackson Gallery, New York
1962 The Store, New York
Green Gallery, New York
1963 Green Gallery, New York
Dwan Gallery, Los Angeles
1964 Dwan Gallery, Los Angeles
Sidney Janis Gallery, New York
1966 Robert Fraser Gallery, London
Moderna Museet, Stockholm
Sidney Janis Gallery, New York
Resident New York

By the artist

Martha Jackson Gallery, New York. *Environments, Situations and Spaces*, 1961.
"New Talent UCA: Sculpture," *Art in America*, vol. 50, no. 1, 1962, pp. 32-33, illus. pp. 32-33.
Oldenburg, Claes. "The Artists Say: Claes

Oldenburg," *Art Voices*, vol. 4, no. 3, Summer 1965, p. 62, illus. p. 63.

McDevitt, Jan. "The Object: Still-life," *Craft Horizons*, vol. 25, no. 5, September-October 1965, pp. 31-32, 55-56, illus. p. 52.

Oldenburg, Claes. "Extracts from the Studio Notes (1962-64)," *Artforum*, vol. 4, no. 5, January 1966, pp. 32-33, illus. p. 32.

Glaser, Bruce, ed. "Oldenburg, Lichtenstein, Warhol: A Discussion," *Artforum*, vol. 4, no. 6, February 1966, pp. 20-24, ill. p. 20.

Baro, Gene. "Oldenburg Monuments," *Art and Artists*, vol. 1, no. 9, December 1966, pp. 28-31, illus. pp. 28-29, 31.

Oldenburg, Claes. *Injun and Other Histories*, New York, Something Else Press (A Great Bear Pamphlet), 1966.

On the artist

Tillim, Sidney. "In the Galleries: Claes Oldenburg," *Arts*, vol. 34, no. 9, June 1960, p. 53.

Johnson, Ellen H. "The Living Object," *Art International*, vol. 7, no. 1, January 25, 1963, pp. 42-45, illus. pp. 42-45.

Johnson, Ellen H. "Is Beauty Dead?," *Oberlin College Bulletin*, vol. 20, no. 2, Winter 1963, pp. 56-66, illus. pp. 58, 61, 64.

Oeri, Georgine. "Object of Art," *Quadrum 16*, 1964, pp. 4-6, illus. p. 5.

Kozloff, Max. "Art: New Works by Oldenburg," *The Nation*, vol. 198, no. 18, April 27, 1964, pp. 445-446.

Rublowsky, John. *Pop Art*, New York, Basic Books, 1965.

Rosenstein, Harris. "Climbing Mt. Oldenburg," *Art News*, vol. 64, no. 10, February 1966, pp. 21-25, 56, illus. pp. 21-25.

Berkson, William. "In the Galleries: Claes Oldenburg," *Arts*, vol. 40, no. 7, May 1966, pp. 57-58, ill. p. 57.

Baro, Gene. "Claes Oldenburg, Or the Things of This World," *Art International*, vol. 10, no. 9, November 20, 1966, pp. 40-43, illus. pp. 40, 45-49.

Linde, Ulf. "Two Viewpoints." [Insert made in Stockholm catalog for London showing at Robert Fraser Gallery, 1966. Also includes article by Gene Baro; see above.]

van der Marck, Jan. "Claes Oldenburg," *Eight Sculptors: The Ambiguous Image*, Minneapolis, Walker Art Center, 1966, pp. 14, 16-17, illus. pp. 15-17.

Harold Persico Paris

Born Edgemire, Long Island, 1925

One-man exhibitions since 1960:

1961 Paul Kantor Gallery, Beverly Hills
    Silvan Simone Gallery, Los Angeles
1962 Paul Kantor Gallery, Beverly Hills
1965 Hansen Galleries, San Francisco
1967 Hansen Galleries, San Francisco
    Mills College Art Gallery, Oakland
Resident Oakland, California

Articles and reviews

Langsner, Jules. "Los Angeles Letter," *Art International*, vol. 5, no. 4, May 1, 1961, p. 48, ill. p. 48.

Chipp, Herschel B. "Art News from San Francisco: One-Man Shows Mostly Constructions," *Art News*, vol. 60, no. 4, Summer 1961, p. 48.

Pugliese, Joseph. "Work in Progress," *Artforum*, vol. 2, no. 7, January 1964, pp. 34-36, illus. pp. 34-36.

Ventura, Anita. "Arts of San Francisco at the San Francisco Museum," *Arts*, vol. 39, no. 1, October 1964, p. 23.

Lippard, Lucy R. *Eccentric Abstraction*, New York, Fischbach Gallery, 1966; reprinted in *Art International*, vol. 10, no. 9, November 20, 1966, pp. 28, 34-40, ill. p. 38.

Kenneth Price

Born Los Angeles, 1935

One-man exhibitions:

1960 Ferus Gallery, Los Angeles
1962 Ferus Gallery, Los Angeles
1964 Ferus Gallery, Los Angeles
1966 Los Angeles County Museum of Art
    (with Robert Irwin)
Resident Los Angeles

Articles and reviews

For a bibliography through 1965 see:
John Coplans, *Ten from Los Angeles*, Seattle Art Museum, 1966.

Lippard, Lucy R. "Kenneth Price," *Robert Irwin, Kenneth Price*, Los Angeles County Museum of Art, 1966.

Von Meier, Kurt. "Los Angeles Letter,"

Art International, vol. 10, no. 8, October 20, 1966, p. 45.

Coplans, John. *Abstract Expressionist Ceramics*, Art Gallery, University of California, Irvine, 1966.

Lippard, Lucy R. *Eccentric Abstraction*, New York, Fischbach Gallery, 1966; reprinted in *Art International*, vol. 10, no. 9, November 20, 1966, pp. 28, 34-40, ill. p. 38.

Richard Randell

Born Minneapolis, 1929

One-man exhibitions:

1964 Walker Art Center, Minneapolis
1966 Royal Marks Gallery, New York
Resident St. Paul, Minnesota

By the artist

"New Talent USA: Richard Randell," *Art in America*, vol. 54, no. 4, July-August 1966, p. 52, ill. p. 52.

Robert Rauschenberg

Born Port Arthur, Texas, 1925

One-man exhibitions since 1960:

1960 Leo Castelli Gallery, New York
1961 Galerie Daniel Cordier, Paris
    Galleria Dell'Ariete, Milan
    Leo Castelli Gallery, New York
1962 Dwan Gallery, Los Angeles
1963 Leo Castelli Gallery, New York
    The Jewish Museum, New York
    Galerie Ileana Sonnabend, Paris
1964 Whitechapel Art Gallery, London
    Gian Enzo Sperone, Turin
    Galerie Ileana Sonnabend, Paris
1965 Dwan Gallery, Los Angeles
    Contemporary Arts Association, Houston
    Walker Art Center, Minneapolis
1966 9 Evenings: Theatre and Engineering, 25th Street, Armory, New York
1967 Leo Castelli Gallery, New York
For a bibliography through 1962 see:
Alan R. Solomon, *Rauschenberg*, New York, The Jewish Museum, 1963.

By the artist

Rauschenberg, Robert and Dorothy Gees

Seckler. "The Artist Speaks: Robert Rauschenberg," *Art in America*, vol. 54, no. 3, May-June 1966, p. 84.

On the artist

Cage, John. "On Robert Rauschenberg, Artist, and his Work," *Metro 2*, 1961, pp. 36-51, illus. pp. 36, 39-40, 42, 45, 47, 48, 51.

Lippard, Lucy R. "New York Letter: April-June 1965," *Art International*, vol. 9, no. 6, September 20, 1965, p. 57, ill. p. 56.

Tompkins, Calvin. *The Bride and the Bachelors*, New York, Viking, 1965.

Kaprow, Allan. "Experimental Art," *Art News*, vol. 65, no. 1, March 1966, p. 63, ill. p. 63.

George Rickey

Born South Bend, Indiana, 1907

One-man exhibitions since 1960:

1960 Orleans Gallery, New Orleans
     Santa Barbara Museum of Art
1961 University of Oklahoma, Norman
     Phoenix Art Museum
     Kraushaar Gallery, New York
1962 Primus/Stuart Gallery, Los Angeles
     Kunstverein, Düsseldorf
     Gallery Springer, Berlin
     Grand Rapids Art Gallery, Grand
       Rapids, Michigan
1963 Hyde Park Art Center, Chicago
     Williams College Museum of Art,
       Williamstown, Massachusetts
     Rush Rhees Fine Arts Center,
       University of Rochester
     Berkshire Arts Center, Pittsfield,
       Massachusetts
     Dartmouth College, Hanover,
       New Hampshire
     Hyde Park Art Center, Chicago
1964 Staempfli, New York
     Institute of Contemporary Art,
       Boston
     David Stuart Galleries, Los Angeles
1966 Corcoran Gallery, Washington, D.C.
Resident East Chatham, New York

By the artist

Rodman, Selden. *Conversations with Artists*, New York, Capricorn, 1961, pp. 143-148.

Rickey, George. "The Kinetic International," *Arts*, vol. 35, September 1961, pp. 16-21.

Institute of Contemporary Art, Boston. *George Rickey/Kinetic Sculpture*, 1964.

Rickey, George. "The Morphology of Movement," *Art Journal*, vol. 22, no. 4, Summer 1964, pp. 220-231, illus. pp. 220-231.

Rickey, George. "The Métier," *Contemporary Sculpture*, New York, The Art Digest (Arts Yearbook 8), 1965, pp. 164-166.

Rickey, George. "Kinesis Continued," *Art in America*, vol. 53, no. 6, December-January, 1965-66, pp. 45-55, illus. pp. 45-55.

Corcoran Gallery of Art, Washington, D.C. *George Rickey: Sixteen Years of Kinetic Sculpture*, 1966. [Introduction by Peter Selz.]

Selz, Peter. *Directions in Kinetic Sculpture*, Berkeley, University of California, 1966, pp. 13-16, 54, illus. pp. 55-57.

Rickey, George. *Heirs of Constructivism*, New York, Braziller, 1967.

Articles and reviews

Coates, Robert M. "The Art Galleries: Innovations," *The New Yorker*, vol. 37, no. 36, October 21, 1961, p. 179.

Secunda, Arthur. "Two Motion Sculptors: Tinguely and Rickey," *Artforum*, vol. 1, no. 1, June 1962, pp. 16-18, illus. pp. 16-18.

Coates, Robert M. "The Art Galleries: Six," *The New Yorker*, vol. 40, no. 38, November 1964, pp. 164-165.

Lippard, Lucy R. "New York Letter," *Art International*, vol. 8, no. 10, December 1964, p. 61.

Lucas Samaras

Born Kastoria, Macedonia, Greece, 1936

One-man exhibitions since 1960:

1961 Green Gallery, New York
1962 Sun Gallery, Provincetown
1964 Green Gallery, New York
     Dawn Gallery, Los Angeles
1966 Pace Gallery, New York
Resident New York
For a bibliography through October 1966 see:
Lawrence Alloway, *Samaras*, New York, Pace Gallery, 1966.

By the artist

Solomon, Alan. "An Interview with Lucas Samaras," *Artforum*, vol. 5, no. 2, October 1966, pp. 39-44, illus. pp. 39-44.

Articles and reviews

Waldman, Diane. "Samaras: Reliquaries for St. Sade," *Art News*, vol. 65, no. 6, October 1966, pp. 45-46, 72-75, illus. pp. 44-46.

Kozloff, Max. "Art," *The Nation*, vol. 203, no. 16, November 14, 1966, pp. 525-526.

George Segal

Born New York, 1924

One-man exhibitions since 1960:

1960 Green Gallery, New York
1962 Green Gallery, New York
1963 Galerie Ileana Sonnabend, Paris
1964 Green Gallery, New York
Resident New York
For a bibliography through July 1964 see:
The Jewish Museum, New York, *Recent American Sculpture*, 1964.

By the artist

Gruen, John. "Art: A Quiet Environment for Frozen Friends," *New York Herald Tribune*, March 22, 1964, p. 32.

Geldzahler, Henry. "An Interview with George Segal," *Artforum*, vol. 3, no. 2, November 1964, pp. 26-29, illus. pp. 26-29.

Geldzahler, Henry. "George Segal," *Quadrum 19*, 1965, pp. 115-126, illus. pp. 117-125.

Articles and reviews

Friedman, Martin. "Mallary, Segal, Agostini: The Exaltation of the Prosaic," *Art International*, vol. 7, no. 8, November 10, 1963, pp. 70-71, ill. p. 71.

Geldzahler, Henry. "George Segal," *Recent American Sculpture*, New York, The Jewish Museum, 1964, pp. 25-26, ill. p. 27.

Kaprow, Allan. "Segal's Vital Mummies," *Art News*, vol. 62, no. 10, February 1964, pp. 30-33, 65, illus. pp. 30-33.

Johnson, Ellen H. "The Sculpture of George Segal," *Art International*, vol. 8, no. 2, March 20, 1964, pp. 46-49, illus. pp. 46-49.

Kozloff, Max. "American Sculpture in

Transition," *Arts*, vol. 38, no. 9, May-June 1964, p. 22, ill. p. 25.

Ashton, Dore. "Unconventional Techniques in Sculpture: New York Commentary," *Studio International*, vol. 169, no. 861, January 1965, p. 23.

van der Marck, Jan. "George Segal," *Eight Sculptors: The Ambiguous Image*, Minneapolis, Walker Art Center, 1966, pp. 26, 28, illus. pp. 27, 29.

"The Casting of Ethel Scull," *Time*, vol. 87, no. 13, April 1, 1966, p. 69, ill. p. 69.

David Smith

Born Decatur, Indiana, 1906
Died 1965

One-man exhibitions since 1960:

1960 Everett Ellin Gallery, Los Angeles
     French and Company, New York
1961 Otto Gerson Gallery, New York
1963 Balin-Traube Gallery, New York
1964 Institute of Contemporary Art,
     University of Pennsylvania,
     Philadelphia
     Marlborough-Gerson Gallery,
     New York
1965 Los Angeles County Museum of Art
1966 Fogg Art Museum, Cambridge,
     Massachusetts
     Museum of Modern Art, New York
     (traveling exhibition in Europe)

Articles and reviews

For bibliographies through 1965 see:
Los Angeles County Museum of Art, *David Smith: A Memorial Exhibition*, 1965 [Text by Hilton Kramer.]
Fogg Art Museum, Cambridge, Massachusetts, *David Smith, 1906-1965*, 1966.
Baro, Gene. "David Smith, 1906-1965," *Contemporary Sculpture*, New York, The Art Digest (Arts Yearbook 8), 1965, pp. 100-105, illus. pp. 100-103, 105.
Marmer, Nancy. "A Memorial Exhibition: David Smith," *Artforum*, vol. 4, no. 5, January 1966, pp. 42-43, illus. pp. 42-45.
Motherwell, Robert. "David Smith: A Major American Sculptor," *Studio International*, vol. 172, no. 880, August 1966, pp. 65-68, illus. pp. 65-68.
Baro, Gene. "David Smith: The Art of

Wholeness," *Studio International*, vol. 172, no. 880, August 1966, pp. 69-75, illus. pp. 69-75.
Berkson, William. "David Smith," *7 Sculptors*, Philadelphia, Institute of Contemporary Art, University of Pennsylvania, 1966, pp. 31-32, ill. p. 35.
Kozloff, Max. "David Smith at the Tate," *Artforum*, vol. 5, no. 3, November 1966, pp. 28-30, illus. pp. 28-30.

Tony Smith

Born Orange, New Jersey, 1912

One-man exhibitions:

1966 Wadsworth Atheneum, Hartford
     Institute of Contemporary Art,
     University of Pennsylvania,
     Philadelphia
Resident South Orange, New Jersey

By the artist

Morris, Robert. "Notes on Sculpture, Part II," *Artforum*, vol. 5, no. 2, October 1966, p. 21.
Glueck, Grace. "Art Notes: No Place to Hide," *New York Times*, November 27, 1966, p. 19.
Wagstaff, Samuel, Jr. "Talking with Tony Smith," *Artforum*, vol. 5, no. 4, December 1966, pp. 14-19, illus. pp. 14-19.
Wadsworth Atheneum, Hartford and the Institute of Contemporary Art, University of Pennsylvania, Philadelphia. *Tony Smith*, 1966.

Articles and reviews

Judd, Donald. "Black, White and Gray," *Arts*, vol. 38, no. 6, March 1964, p. 37, ill. p. 36.
Kroll, Jack. "Art: Two Sculptors," *Newsweek*, vol. 68, no. 20, November 14, 1966, p. 93.

Robert Smithson

Born Passaic, New Jersey, 1938

One-man exhibitions:

1961 Galleria George Lester, Rome
1962 Castellane Gallery, New York
1966 Dwan Gallery, New York
Resident New York

By the artist

Smithson, Robert. "Don Judd," *7 Sculptors*, Philadelphia, Institute of Contemporary Art, University of Pennsylvania, 1965, pp. 13-16.
Smithson, Robert. "The Crystal Land," *Harper's Bazaar*, May 1966.
Smithson, Robert. "Entropy and the New Monuments," *Artforum*, vol. 4, no. 10, June 1966, pp. 26-31, illus. pp. 26, 28-31.
Smithson, Robert. "The Domain of the Great Bear," *Art Voices*, September 1966.
Smithson, Robert. "Quasi-Infinities and the Wanting of Space," *Arts*, vol. 41, no. 1, November 1966, pp. 28-31, illus. pp. 28-31.

Articles

Michelson, Annette. "10 x 10: 'Concrete Reasonableness,'" *Artforum*, vol. 5, no. 5, January 1967, pp. 30-31, ill. p. 30.

Kenneth Snelson

Born Pendleton, Oregon, 1927

One-man exhibitions:

1966 Dwan Gallery, New York
1967 Dwan Gallery, Los Angeles
Resident New York

By the artist

Snelson, Kenneth. "How Primary is Structure?," *Art Voices*, Summer 1966.

Articles and reviews

"Sculptures to Build With," *Fortune*, vol. 66, no. 5, November 1962, pp. 120-123, illus. pp. 120-123.
Berkson, William. "In the Galleries: Kenneth Snelson," *Arts*, vol. 40, no. 8, June 1966, p. 52, ill. p. 52.
Mellow, James R. "New York Letter," *Art International*, vol. 10, no. 7, September 15, 1966, p. 57.

George Sugarman

Born New York, 1912

One-man exhibitions since 1960:

1960 Widdifield Gallery, New York
1961 Stephen Radich Gallery, New York
1964 Stephen Radich Gallery, New York
1965 Philadelphia Art Alliance,
     Philadelphia

1966 Stephen Radich Gallery, New York
      Dayton's Gallery 12, Minneapolis
Resident New York
For a bibliography through July 1964 see:
The Jewish Museum, New York, *Recent American Sculpture*, 1964.

By the artist

Glaser, Bruce, Lyman Kipp, George Sugarman and David Weinrib. "Where Do We Go from Here?," *Contemporary Sculpture*, New York, The Art Digest (Arts Yearbook 8), 1965, pp. 150-155, ill. p. 151.

Articles and reviews

Ashton, Dore. "No Post-Painterly Painting: New York Commentary," *Studio International*, vol. 168, no. 855, July 1964, p. 44, ill. p. 44.
Sandler, Irving. "George Sugarman," *Recent American Sculpture*, New York, The Jewish Museum, 1964, pp. 33-34, ill. p. 35.
Ashton, Dore. "Unconventional Techniques in Sculpture: New York Commentary," *Studio International*, vol. 169, no. 861, January 1965, p. 23.
Ashton, Dore. "Art," *Arts and Architecture*, vol. 82, no. 6, June 1965, pp. 10-11, ill. p. 11.

Robert Stevenson
Born San Diego, 1924

One-man exhibition:

1963 Quay Gallery, San Francisco
Resident Los Angeles

Articles and reviews

M[onte], J[ames]. "San Francisco: Robert Stevenson," *Artforum*, vol. 3, no. 5, February 1965, pp. 10, 12, ill. p. 13.
Seitz, William C. *The Responsive Eye*, New York, Museum of Modern Art, 1965.

Michael Todd
Born Omaha, 1935

One-man exhibitions:

1964 Pace Gallery, New York
      Hanover Gallery, London
1966 Henri Gallery, Alexandria, Virginia
Resident New York

Articles and reviews

Kozloff, Max. "The Further Adventures of American Sculpture," *Arts*, vol. 39, no. 5, February 1963, p. 31.
Lippard, L[ucy] R. "New York," *Artforum*, vol. 2, no. 11, May 1964, p. 53-54, ill. p. 52.
H[arrison], J[ane]. "New York Exhibitions: In the Galleries: Michael Todd," *Arts*, vol. 38, no. 9, May-June 1964, pp. 41-42, ill. p. 41.
Stevens, Elisabeth. "Washington," *Arts*, vol. 40, no. 5, March 1966, p. 48, ill. p. 48.

Ernest Trova
Born St. Louis, 1927

One-man exhibitions:

1963 Pace Gallery, Boston
      Pace Gallery, New York
1964 Hanover Gallery, London
      Famous Barr Exhibition, St. Louis
      Bicentennial
1965 Pace Gallery, New York
1966 Hanover Gallery, London
      Pace Gallery, Columbus, Ohio
1967 Pace Gallery, New York
Resident St. Louis

By the artist

"Sculptors: The Uses of Ingenuity," *Time*, vol. 89, no. 1, January 6, 1967, p. 76, illus. p. 77.

Articles and reviews

Johnston, Jill. "Reviews and Previews: Ernest Trova," *Art News*, vol. 64, no. 1, March 1965, p. 12.
Grossberg, Jacob. "In the Galleries: Ernest Trova," *Arts*, vol. 39, no. 6, March 1965, p. 67.
Friedman, Martin. "Ernest Trova," *Eight Sculptors: The Ambiguous Image*, Minneapolis, Walker Art Center, 1966, pp. 30, 32, illus. pp. 31-33.
Whitford, Frank. "Trova the Toy-Maker," *Studio International*, vol. 171, no. 876, April 1966, p. 160, illus. p. 160.
Amaya, Mario. "Trova: Elegy for Mechanical Man," *Art and Artists*, vol. 1, no. 1, April 1966, pp. 52-53, illus. pp. 52-53.
van der Marck, Jan. "Idols for the Computer Age," *Art in America*, vol. 54, no. 6, November-December 1966, pp. 64-67, illus. pp. 64-67.

Anne Truitt
Born Baltimore, 1921

One-man exhibitions:

1963 Andre Emmerich Gallery, New York
1964 Minami Gallery, Tokyo
1965 Andre Emmerich Gallery, New York
Resident Tokyo

Articles and reviews

Judd, Donald. "New York Exhibitions: In the Galleries: Anne Truitt," *Arts*, vol. 37, no. 7, April 1963, p. 61.
Judd, Donald. "Black, White and Gray," *Arts*, vol. 38, no. 6, March 1964, p. 37.
C[ampbell], L[awrence]. "Reviews and Previews: Anne Truitt," *Art News*, vol. 64, no. 2, April 1965, p. 14, ill. p. 14.

De Wain Valentine
Born Fort Collins, Colorado, 1936
Resident Los Angeles

Articles and reviews

Frank, Joseph. "Denver," *Artforum*, vol. 3, no. 1, September 1964, p. 50, ill. p. 50.
Danieli, Fidel. "Two Showings of Younger Los Angeles Artists," *Artforum*, vol, 5, no. 2, October 1966, pp. 24-26, ill. p. 25.
Von Meier, Kurt. "Los Angeles Letter," *Art International*, vol. 10, no. 10, December 1966, p. 49, ill. p. 54.

Vasa
Born Yugoslavia, 1933

One-man exhibition:

1966 Herbert Palmer Gallery,
      Los Angeles
Resident Los Angeles

By the artist

"New Talent USA: Vasa," *Art in America*, vol. 54, no. 4, July-August 1966, pp. 60-61.
Review
Wilson, William. "Los Angeles: Vasa," *Artforum*, vol. 4, no. 7, March 1966, p. 14, ill. p. 14.

254

Stephan Von Huene

Born Los Angeles, 1932

Resident Los Angeles

Review

Wurdemann, Helen. "A Stroll on La Cienega," *Art in America*, vol. 53, no. 5, October-November 1965, p. 53, ill. p. 53.

David Von Schlegell

Born St. Louis, 1920

One-man exhibitions since 1960:

1964 University of New Hampshire, Durham

Stanhope Gallery, Boston

Museum of Art, Ogunquit, Maine

1965 Ward-Nasse Gallery, Boston

1966 Royal Marks Gallery, New York

Resident Ogunquit, Maine and New York

By the artist

"New Talent USA: David Von Schlegell," *Art in America*, vol. 54, no. 4, July-August 1966, p. 28, illus. pp. 38-39.

Articles and reviews

Krauss, Rosalind. "Boston Letter," *Art International*, vol. 8, no. 1, February 15, 1964, p. 34.

Kozloff, Max. "The Further Adventures of American Sculpture," *Arts*, vol. 39, no. 5, February 1965, p. 27, ill. p. 25.

R[obins], C[orinne]. "In the Galleries: Group Show," *Arts*, vol. 40, no. 1, November 1965, p. 61.

Adrian, Dennis. "New York: David Von Schlegell," *Artforum*, vol. 4, no. 4, December 1965, p. 55.

Peter Voulkos

Born Bozeman, Montana, 1924

One-man exhibitions since 1960:

1960 Museum of Modern Art, New York

1961 Primus-Stuart Gallery, Los Angeles

1963 David Stuart Galleries, Los Angeles

Hack-Light Gallery, Scottsdale, Arizona

Los Angeles City College

1965 Los Angeles County Museum of Art

Resident Berkeley

Articles and reviews

For a bibliography through March 1965 see:

Los Angeles County Museum of Art, *Peter Voulkos*, 1965.

Marmer, Nancy. "Los Angeles: Peter Voulkos," *Artforum*, vol. 3, no. 9, June 1965, pp. 9-10, illus. pp. 9-10.

Secunda, Arthur. "Exhibitions: Peter Voulkos," *Craft Horizons*, vol. 25, no. 4, July-August 1965, pp. 35-36, ill. p. 35.

Coplans, John. "Voulkos: Redemption Thru Ceramics, Retrospective at Los Angeles County Museum of Art," *Art News*, vol. 64, no. 4, Summer 1965, pp. 38-39, illus. pp. 38-39, 64-65.

Coplans, John. "Abstract Expressionist Ceramics," *Artforum*, vol. 5, no. 3, November 1966, pp. 34, 39, 41, illus. pp. 35, 38-39.

David Weinrib

Born Brooklyn, 1924

One-man exhibitions:

1961 Howard Wise Gallery, New York

1962 Howard Wise Gallery, New York

1963 Howard Wise Gallery, New York

1967 Royal Marks Gallery, New York

Resident New York

By the artist

Glaser, Bruce, Lyman Kipp, George Sugarman and David Weinrib. "Where Do We Go from Here?" *Contemporary Sculpture*, New York, The Art Digest (Arts Yearbook 8), 1965, pp. 150-155, ill. p. 151.

Articles and reviews

Tillim, Sidney. "In the Galleries: David Weinrib," *Arts*, vol. 35, no. 6, March 1961, p. 51, ill. p. 51.

Campbell, Lawrence. "Reviews and Previews: David Weinrib," *Art News*, vol. 61, no. 3, May 1962, p. 11, ill. p. 11.

Judd, Donald. "New York Reports: In the Galleries: David Weinrib," *Arts*, vol. 36, no. 10, September 1962, pp. 45-46.

Kozloff, Max. "New York Letter: Weinrib," *Art International*, vol. 6, no. 7, September 1962, p. 33, ill. p. 33.

Kozloff, Max. "American Sculpture in Transition," *Arts*, vol. 38, no. 9, May-June 1964, pp. 22, 24, ill. p. 23.

Sandler, Irving H. "Expressionism with Corners," *Art News*, vol. 64, no. 2, April 1965, p. 65, ill. p. 38.

Ashton, Dore. "Art," *Arts and Architecture*, vol. 82, no. 6, June 1965, pp. 10-11, ill. p. 10.

H. C. Westermann

Born Los Angeles, 1922

One-man exhibitions since 1960:

1961 Allan Frumkin Gallery, New York

1962 Allan Frumkin Gallery, Chicago

Dilexi Gallery, Los Angeles

1963 Dilexi Gallery, San Francisco

Allan Frumkin Gallery, New York

1965 Allan Frumkin Gallery, New York

1966 Kansas City Art Institute, Kansas City, Missouri

Resident Brookfield Center, Connecticut

Articles and reviews

Schulze, Franz. "Chicago: Westermann Monster-Houses," *Art News*, vol. 57, no. 10, February 1959, pp. 49, 56, ill. p. 49.

S[awin], M[artica]. "In the Galleries: H. C. Westermann," *Arts*, vol. 35, nos. 8-9, May-June 1961, p. 86, ill. p. 86.

Adrian, Dennis. "Some Notes on H. C. Westermann," *Art International*, vol. 7, no. 2, February 25, 1963, pp. 52-55, illus. pp. 52-55.

Rose, Barbara. "New York Letter," *Art International*, vol. 7, no. 9, December 5, 1963, p. 63, ill. p. 62.

Coplans, John. "Higgins, Price, Chamberlain, Bontecou, Westermann," *Artforum*, vol. 2 no. 10, April 1964, pp. 38-40, illus. pp. 38-40.

Friedman, Martin. "H. C. Westermann," *Eight Sculptors: The Ambiguous Image*, Minneapolis, Walker Art Center, 1966, pp. 38, 40-41, illus. pp. 39-41.

Hoene, Anne. "In the Galleries: H. C. Westermann," *Arts*, vol. 40, no. 3, January 1966, p. 57.

Lippard, Lucy R. *Eccentric Abstraction*, Fischbach Gallery, New York, 1966; reprinted in *Art International*, vol. 10, no. 9, November 20, 1966, pp. 28, 34-40, ill. p. 34.

Lippard, Lucy R. "New York Letter: Recent Sculpture as Escape," *Art Interna-*

tional, vol. 10, no. 2, February 20, 1966, pp. 57-58.

William T. Wiley
Born Bedford, Indiana, 1937

One-man exhibitions:
1962 Staempfli Gallery, New York
1964 Staempfli Gallery, New York
1965 Lanyon Gallery, Palo Alto, California
Resident Mill Valley, California

Articles and reviews
"New Talent USA: Paintings," *Art in America*, vol. 49, no. 1, 1961, ill. p. 24.

Ashton, Dore. "New York Commentary: Abstract Expressionism Isn't Dead," *Studio International*, vol. 164, no. 833, September 1962, pp. 104-105, ill. p. 105.

Raynor, Vivien. "New York Reports: In the Galleries: Fairly Nonobjective," *Arts*, vol. 36, no. 10, September 1962, pp. 46-47.

Davis, R. G. "William Wiley Designs Sets, Costumes and Props for the Jarry Classic," *Artforum*, vol. 2, no. 8, February 1964, pp. 36-39, illus. pp. 36-39.

Monte, James. "San Francisco," *Artforum*, vol. 3, no. 8, May 1965, pp. 44-45, ill. p. 44.

Polley, E. M. "San Francisco," *Artforum*, vol. 4, no. 4, December 1965, p. 50, ill. p. 49.

Norman Zammitt
Born Toronto, 1931

One-man exhibitions:
1962 Felix Landau Gallery, Los Angeles
1963 Robert Schoelkopf Gallery, New York
1966 Felix Landau Gallery, Los Angeles
1967 Landau-Alan Gallery, New York
Resident Los Angeles

Articles and reviews
Nordland, Gerald. "Los Angeles Overture," *Arts*, vol. 37, no. 1, October 1962, p. 52.

Judd, Donald. "New York Exhibitions: In the Galleries: Norman Zammitt," *Arts*, vol. 37, no. 5, February 1963, p. 52.

Plagens, Peter. "Los Angeles: Norman Zammitt," *Artforum*, vol. 4, no. 7, March 1966, pp. 14-15, ill. p. 15.

Wilfrid Zogbaum
Born Newport, Rhode Island, 1915
Died 1965

One-man exhibitions since 1960:
1960 Staempfli Gallery, New York
     Staempfli Gallery, New York
1961 Obelisk Gallery, Washington, D.C.
1962 Worth Ryder Gallery, San Francisco
     University of California, Berkeley
     Dilexi Gallery, San Francisco
     Obelisk Gallery, Washington, D.C.
1963 Grace Borgenicht Gallery, New York
     Dilexi Gallery, San Francisco
     Everett Ellin Gallery, Los Angeles
1965 Grace Borgenicht Gallery, New York
1966 Dilexi Gallery, San Francisco

By the artist
Coplans, John. "Reviews: Wilfrid Zogbaum," *Artforum*, vol. 1, no. 1, June 1962, p. 36, ill. p. 37.

"Coplans, DuCasse, Gordon, Hedrick, Ippolito, Smith, Zogbaum," *Artforum*, vol. 1, no. 2, July 1962, pp. 29-35, illus. p. 32.

Articles and reviews
Kramer, Hilton. "Month in Review," *Arts*, vol. 35, no. 1, October 1960, pp. 54-55, ill. p. 55.

Coplans, John. "Reviews: Wilfrid Zogbaum," *Artforum*, vol. 1, no. 7, December 1962, p. 45, illus. p. 44.

Rose, Barbara. "New York Letter," *Art International*, vol. 7, no. 4, April 25, 1963, p. 58.

Ventura, Anita. "Field Day for Sculptors," *Arts*, vol. 38, no. 1, October 1963, p. 64, ill. p. 63.

Tabak, May Natalie. "Zogbaum Makes a Sculpture," *Art News*, vol. 63, no. 8, December 1964, pp. 42-45, 50-54, illus. pp. 42, 45.

Grossman, Jacob. "In the Galleries: Wilfrid Zogbaum," *Arts*, vol. 39, no. 5, February 1965, p. 61, ill. p. 61.

Glossary of Terms

This is a listing of critical terms which have been placed in wide currency by forms and concepts particular to contemporary art, especially sculpture of the Sixties. The reader is referred to passages which most fully define these terms in contextual usage.

Photograph Credits

36,500 copies of *American Sculpture of the Sixties,*

Designed by Louis Danziger,

Printed by Anderson, Ritchie & Simon

for the Los Angeles County Museum of Art

on the occasion of the exhibition, April 28–June 25, 1967.